STREET MAGIC

An Illustrated History of Wandering Magicians and Their Conjuring Arts

STREET CONJURER PERFORMING.

STREET MAGIC

An Illustrated History of Wandering Magicians and Their Conjuring Arts

by Edward Claflin
in collaboration with
Jeff Sheridan, Street Magician

Dolphin Books
Doubleday & Company, Inc.
Garden City, New York
1977

A Dolphin Books Original
ISBN: 0-385-12864-9

Copyright © 1977 by Edward Claflin and Jeff Sheridan
All Rights Reserved
Printed in The United States of America
First Edition

Library of Congress Catalog Card Number 76-55679

Frontispiece: street conjurer in London, ca. 1851. Illustration is from Henry Mayhew's *London Labour and the London Poor. (Sheridan Collection)*

Contents

Introduction   ix
Tribal Ways and Ancient Traces   1
Mysteries of the Fakirs   13
Hindu Tricks and Wonders   25
Oriental Fantasies   35
Jugglers, Mountebanks and Necromancers   47
Wandering Magicians and Their Arts   59
Conjuring at the Fair   73
Stage Illusions and Street Diversions   87
The Age of Houdini   101
Street Magic and Kindred Spirits   113
Street Magic Today   125
Vanish   145
Selected Annotated Bibliography   147
Index   151

ILLUSTRATION CREDITS

The publisher would like to thank a number of collections and photographers for permission to reproduce illustrations appearing in this book.

In the text credit lines accompany each illustration, but names of collections have been abbreviated in some cases. Following is a key to credit lines, listed in italics, as they appear in the captions.

Bibliothèque royale	Copyright Bibliothèque royale
Bruxelles	Albert I*er,* Bruxelles (Cabinet des Estampes)
William Biggart	Photographer
Jean Louis Blondeau	Photographer
Edward Claflin	Photographer
Library of Congress	The McManus-Young and Houdini Collections, Rare Book Division, Library of Congress
Mulholland Collection	Courtesy of the John Mulholland Magic Collection in the Walter Hampden Memorial Library at The Players
NY Daily News Photo	Courtesy of the New York Daily News
NYPL	Courtesy of The New York Public Library Astor, Lenox and Tilden Foundations
NYPL Picture Collection	The New York Public Library Picture Collection
NYPL Prints Division	Prints Division The New York Public Library Astor, Lenox and Tilden Foundations
NYPL Research Division	General Research and Humanities Division The New York Public Library Astor, Lenox and Tilden Foundations
NYPL Theatre Collection	Theatre Collection The New York Public Library at Lincoln Center Astor, Lenox and Tilden Foundations
Sheridan Collection	Courtesy of Jeff Sheridan
Wide World	Courtesy of Wide World Photos
WNEW-TV	Courtesy of WNEW-TV, New York

Acknowledgments

Without street magicians there would be no street magic. I am most grateful for the collaboration of Jeff Sheridan, a street magician who both inspired and aided research in his favorite field of action. Many of the illustrations are from his own collection, and he uncovered many sources. But his greatest contribution is to street magic itself—an art he keeps alive and well on the streets of New York.

I am greatly indebted to Jack Walters, whose care, advice, and editing helped to shape this book. In places where major renovations were needed, he did the blasting, but he also provided constant encouragement during reconstruction. Any graces the prose may have are probably his doing, and errors of fact or judgment are strictly my own.

My thanks also to Peter Tobey, dynamo of publishing. He was patient in the face of all delays and constant in his support.

My thanks to Lindy Hess for the support she has given to *Street Magic,* getting it into print and aiding its itinerant authors.

In pursuit of the history of magic, Jeff Sheridan and I made use of several collections, and we would like to thank those who assisted us during this research. Mr. Louis A. Rachow, librarian of the Walter Hampden Memorial Library, was most helpful in providing books, periodicals, and illustrations from the superb John Mulholland Magic Collection at The Players Club. Mrs. John Mulholland kindly gave permission for reproduction of illustrations from the *Sphinx* magazine. Mr. Lawrence Arcuri and the Society of American Magicians gave me access to the Society's collection at the Lincoln Center Library for the Performing Arts. With an unusual appreciation for the subject of magic, Mr. Leonard N. Beck, curator of special collections, introduced me to the McManus-Young and Houdini Collections at the Library of Congress. Dan Nied generously loaned a number of volumes from his extensive private collection.

In my research I am greatly indebted to Milbourne Christopher—author, collector and stage magician—whose extensive writings cover much of the history of stage magic and conjuring arts.

Photographer William Biggart was patient and persevering in efforts to obtain the pictures of Jeff Sheridan which appear in the chapter on "Street Magic Today."

There were many who gave advice and assistance during the months of preparation. In many ways Candy Cohen gave support and encouragement to Jeff Sheridan, and I, too, thank her for her interest in the book and her reading of an early draft of the manuscript. Kate Samuels, Barbara Sturman, and Sarah Foote helped type a draft of *Street Magic,* and many friends suggested illustrations and resources.

With love and equilibrium, Sarah Foote helped to keep the small ark of magic afloat, and this book is dedicated to her.

Introduction

This book is both a history of street magic and a search for that history. The search begins with the shamans who practiced conjuring in tribal society thousands of years ago, and it ends with street magic today, as practiced by a conjurer named Jeff Sheridan in Central Park, New York. Such a journey and exploration leads one inevitably into side streets and back alleys, along busy thoroughfares and quiet country lanes, to fairgrounds and taverns, through rural parks and city squares. It takes one to numerous countries in all parts of the world. En route, there are encounters with the motley practitioners of the conjuring arts—wizards and fakirs, sorcerers and jugglers, priests and witches. And there are tales of many spellbinding events, of objects vanishing into thin air, heads being severed from bodies, ghosts gamboling in streets and byways, and voices coming out of nowhere.

"Street magic" can be construed to mean a variety of things, from simple performances on the street by wandering jugglers of antiquity to the great outdoor spectaculars of a twentieth-century Harry Houdini. In times past, it was common to see street magicians in the boulevards of Paris, on English fairgrounds, in most of the villages of India, and in the exotic gardens of Japan. Street magic was a folk art, and as such it had many forms and was adopted by many cultures. At present, it is rare to see street magicians—at least in Western cities. Yet they do exist, for the art of street magic has managed to survive throughout the ages.

Historians of magic have often referred to street magicians as those itinerant conjurers who made their living by performing sleight-of-hand magic outdoors. In some cases, their magic was no more than a clever piece of deception, or a bit of charlatanry thinly disguised as a magical occurrence. But there were other cases, as we shall see, when street magic seemed to be the most remarkable of all deceptions, requiring artistry and skill and a precise knowledge of human psychology. In both these forms, "street magic" was a kind of popular entertainment in the guise of magic or illusion, performed outside the boundaries of conventional theater. For our purposes, the term "street magic" is used in this broadest sense.

Magic has a primitive and universal appeal, for we are most attracted by those things which seem mysterious or inexplicable. We are fascinated by events that seem unnatural, contradicting what we have come to recognize and accept as "normal," and we are lured by the suggestion of psychic or supernatural events. Street magic carries this suggestion, but at the same time it is also good theater, a solid form of entertainment no matter where played. It is a legitimate part of the performing arts, and it has much in common with dance, mime, and circus entertainments.

For many years, street magicians were

Jeff Sheridan, a contemporary street magician. Scene is Central Park, New York, on a Sunday afternoon. *(William Biggart)*

A nineteenth-century French *prestidigitateur,* near Château d'Eau, Paris. The well-dressed, graceful performer was supported by an aristocratic audience. *(Sheridan Collection)*

regarded as no more than jugglers, manipulating common knives, cups, or balls. In medieval Europe, and as late as the seventeenth century, the performer of street magic was still regarded as a juggler or "jongleur," though he might be recognized as an adept at performing sleight-of-hand tricks, or deceptions in the shifting of objects. (Depending upon his reputation, he might well be called less complimentary names, such as "charlatan" or "mountebank.") But the outstanding feature of such entertainers was that they could make objects appear or disappear as well as throw them into the air and catch them with remarkable dexterity.

In time, the conjurer's craft came to be recognized as separate from that of the simple juggler, and sleight of hand became an art in itself. In Europe, stage magic was performed as early as the seventeenth century and its

popularity increased in the eighteenth and nineteenth centuries. Throughout this period, stage magic was closely allied to street magic, and many stage magicians got their start in the street, wandering from town to town until they found a performing area in a barn or tavern or discovered a theater where they could display their wonders.

Street magic both gains and loses in the transition to its more elaborate form, stage magic. The stage magician can resort to all kinds of props not used in street magic—mirrors, trap doors, special curtains, and lighting effects. Instead of making a pea disappear from underneath a cup—as a street magician would do—the stage illusionist can make a lion disappear from a cage. What is lost on stage is a certain element of surprise, the surprise experienced by a spectator suddenly confronted by illusion. The pedestrian on the street has not bought a ticket and has not been looking forward to what has already been advertised or reviewed in a theater. To the spectator, street magic is impromptu, a happening. One moment, the passerby is enjoying the normal course of daily life, the next, he is tangled in a web of illusion. The best of the street magicians exploited to the fullest this element of surprise and manipulated the spontaneous reactions of their audiences to make the tricks succeed.

Tricks of street magicians are done by natural means, but many audiences have believed that the performers knew magic of another kind—the occult magic practiced by witches, sorcerers, and wizards. In earliest times the English word "magic" probably denoted priestcraft, thus implying a secret or select order of persons empowered to perform certain ritual acts. Over the centuries the word has taken on many connotations referring to the acts of alchemists, fortune-tellers, prophets, charlatans, and other inscrutable characters. As used today, magic can relate to extra-sensory perception, psychic powers, rituals of the so-called diabolical arts (as in the celebration of the Black Mass), as well as the illusions created by sleight of hand and other means. In some of its ramifications, magic is essentially occult, spiritualistic, and to millions of people remains a mystery which presently defies rational, scientific explanation.

Though we are concerned here only with natural magic, the other connotations of magic invade. In India, the street magician was often a fakir or holy man, and his sleight of hand related to a whole set of religious assumptions connected with Hinduism. In medieval Europe, the magic considered to threaten Church and peasant alike was witchcraft. In some cases the street conjurer was mistaken for a witch or a sorcerer—and persecuted, or prosecuted, accordingly.

During the nineteenth century, spiritualism was an extremely popular cult in Western Europe and the United States. Clever magicians who held séances and demonstrated slate-writing and spirit-rapping were thought to possess psychic powers well beyond the range of human understanding. Street magicians would take advantage of this commonly held attitude by pretending to cast spells, mumbling incantations or using objects associated with occult practices or secret societies.

Fire-eaters dressed as devils' helpers. Their stunts were popularly associated with sorcery and black magic. *(Mulholland Collection)*

But usually street magicians maintained a separate identity, dissociating themselves from the more obscure craft of the sorcerer. Unlike the occult magic, where mysteries are suggested by dark hints and imaginative descriptions, the art of the street magician is displayed in broad daylight "before your very eyes." The performing magician of our interest openly demonstrates what the legendary sorcerers were said to possess—powers of second sight, formulas for transforming material objects, and secrets which gave them incredible physical powers. Like the sorcerer, the street magician took great care to conceal the secrets of his art.

In most cases, the methods or techniques used by performing magicians to create their effects are disappointingly simple. The real "magic" of the performer is not physical but psychological. He first considers what will appear magical before the eyes of his audience. Then he must delude the onlookers by manufacturing illusion without giving away the secret of how he does it. In the process he becomes, seemingly, the man of true magic, the worker of small miracles. With a performing style suggestive of wizardry, with a technique that is secretive while seeming open and "above board," and with the psychological advantage of

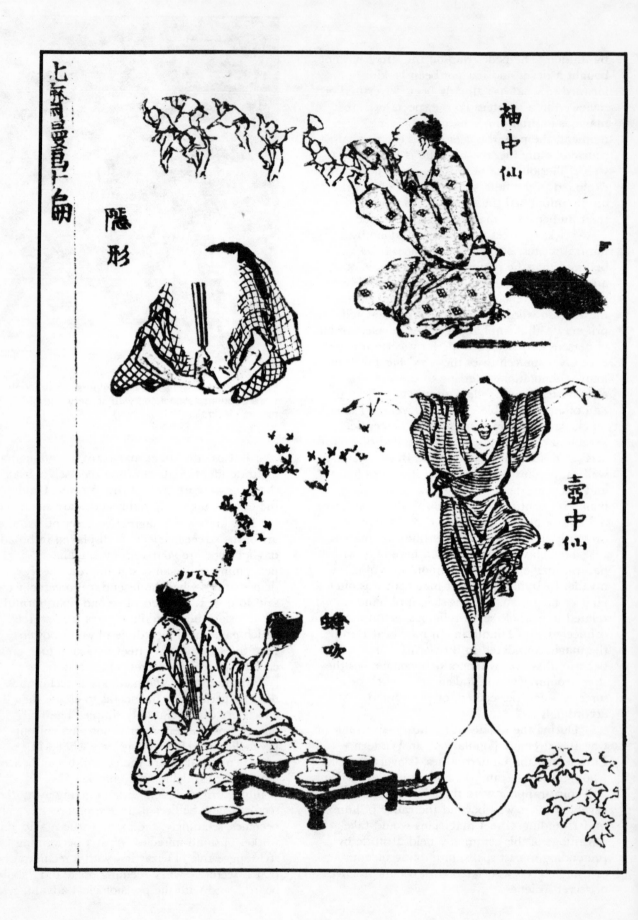

surprise and audacity, the magician *appears* to be a person with great and supernatural powers.

Street magicians in many countries were identified by the kinds of tricks they performed or the costumes they wore. Conjurers in ancient Greece were called *psephopaiktai,* a name referring to the *psephoi,* the little balls they carried with them. The Romans translated this to *calcularius,* after the stones which the conjurer would produce like magic. In Germany the street magician was called *Taschenspieler,* referring to the pocket or bag in which he hid objects. In Italy he was a *giocature di busolotti* or box-player. The inventive French used all the inflections at their command, calling the early conjurers *escamoteurs,* manipulators of little balls of cork; *illusionistes,* for visual illusions; and, in a final burst of Gallic energy, *prestidigitateurs,* a word derived from the Latin *presti* and *digiti* for "nimble fingers." The English called him "juggler" or "conjurer," and said that he practiced the art of "Hocus Pocus."

Many street magicians were anonymous, but there are others known to us by name or reputation—Convinsamy, Sheshal, Carlosbach, Fawkes, and Houdini, to mention a few. For the most part they lived nomadic lives, sometimes changed their names and nationalities, and rarely advertised their performances. The true tales of such magicians—whose personalities were often as elusive as their secrets—are reconstructed from what little we have gleaned from travelers' notes and the obviously biased accounts of other eyewitnesses.

But our tales of street magic have a way of growing and becoming more fanciful with time. Unless the trick be told, where does illusion leave off and reality begin? Who is to question the spectator's vision? Is a strongly felt illusion any less "true" than reality?

In our history, as we pass easily through time and space, we are searching the world for that illusion. It is the illusion of magic and the magic of illusion that we are primarily interested in—not the privy tricks or the key to the secrets themselves. We seek the bafflements, the contradictions, the amusements, and the innumerable emotions that ripple uneasily through the audience. It is not knowledge we are after, but mystery and disguises. We want to gaze at the impossible. We are hungry for surprise, astonishments. In short, we are looking for a true story, but one impossible to explain in all its complexity. When we discover that story, we shall have found—magic.

(Left) In Book X of the *Manga,* published in 1814, the Japanese artist Hokusai portrayed some of the real and imagined tricks of wandering magicians. So-called "sleeve magic" (upper right) and exhaling bees (lower left) suggest tricks which might have been done by sleight of hand. Vanishing magic (upper left) and vase magic (lower right) were probably imaginary. *(NYPL Prints Division)*

(Right) An Italian street magician of the seventeenth century. He wore a large pocket apron and performed cups-and-balls tricks just outside the city walls. *(Mulholland Collection)*

STREET MAGIC

An Illustrated History of Wandering Magicians
and Their Conjuring Arts

Tribal Ways
and Ancient Traces

Magic is a primitive art which has its beginnings in the earliest traditions of tribal conjuring and ceremony. From the very first, magic served a definite purpose in society, and it affected every aspect of daily life. Magic helped make the rain fall and the crops grow. It was invoked to heal the sick, bring good luck to hunters, celebrate the birth of a child, or assure a rich harvest. Magic was also used to banish evil and to assure that the dead were transported safely into eternity. To a non-scientific people, magic both caused and explained daily and seasonal changes, and it was a means of relating inner life to external events in nature.

In most tribal communities or villages there was some kind of magic maker or medicine man trusted by the rest of the community. The magician was entrusted with the spiritual as well as the physical welfare of the people, and they turned to him in times of famine, sickness, or danger. He also kept the spirits favorably inclined toward the villagers, informing them when it was time to show their gratitude and appease the gods and spirits.

Anthropologists have found, too, that the tribal conjurers—shamans, medicine men, witch doctors, or priests—knew sleight-of-hand tricks which have probably been practiced for thousands of years. The form of the tricks may have varied from one tribe to the next, but conjuring acts probably served the same purpose. They proved the shaman had a power beyond the comprehension of the rest of the tribe and hence possessed the right to a greater influence within the society. If his spells and incantations failed to produce the desired results, the shaman could always show some evidence that he still had spiritual strength. He would make an object appear, vanish, or change form, and then declare it was a "sign." If he was dexterous enough, the people would never discover he was playing a trick on them. But there were probably terrible punishments for shamans found to be cheating the gods. So the secrets of the profession were closely guarded.

Occasionally, of course, the medicine man needed a ready excuse when the gods failed to comply with his wishes, and the concept of "black" magic may have been nurtured by wizards who tried to explain their failures. The term "black magic," as used today, refers to the kind of conjuring done for evil or harmful purposes—what one might call "the work of the devil." (White magic, on the other hand, is either completely harmless, or else intended to be helpful or healing.) When the witch doctor was unable to bring about a needed rainfall or heal a sick member of the tribe, he claimed the forces of evil were working their magic against

Part healer, part wizard, the tribal conjurer performed sleight-of-hand tricks proving his supernatural powers. Many techniques first used by medicine men and shamans were later adopted by street magicians. *(Sheridan Collection)*

him. Any success in conjuring was due entirely to the witch doctor's skill, but failures were attributed to causes beyond his control. The concept of a "bad imp" or "evil spirit" may have been the construction of priests, wizards, and soothsayers who needed to explain their shortcomings.

Among the aboriginal tribes of North America, the medicine men were often considered conjurers or magicians as well as high priests, and they were perfectly capable of proving their magical powers. In *The Golden Bough* Sir James George Frazer recorded a number of healing rituals and religious ceremonies in which a shaman would awe the tribespeople with sleight-of-hand tricks.

The earliest tricks are interesting because they were later adopted in similar forms by street magicians and stage magicians in many parts of the world. In modern times the tricks no longer mean what they did to the tribal group, yet they continue to have a common and universal appeal.

Some tribespeople believed that a particular disease might be contained in a bone, pebble, or tuft of fibers which had to be extracted from the patient's body before he or she could recover. A shaman attending the patient might prepare herbs and potions, then begin chanting or shaking his rattle to drive out evil spirits. In some cases the incantations were carried out by the shaman alone, while other traditions called for participation by the whole tribe. At the moment of greatest fervor, the medicine man might raise his empty hand, reach toward the patient, and suddenly snatch a stone out of the victim's body. At the sight of this stone, there was great rejoicing. The source of disease had been discovered. Once it was removed, the patient would heal.

Another kind of magic was involved in an induction ceremony: a dummy or "double" of a young brave would be symbolically destroyed and later resurrected. Among the early tribes living in British Columbia, a warrior had to be initiated into one of four principal clans—the raven, wolf, eagle, or bear clan. A candidate was taken to the center of the village, where he was surrounded by other warriors of the clan. While the rest of the tribespeople looked on, the braves drew their knives, stabbed the candidate, and cut off his head. Or so it seemed. In reality, the conspirators substituted a dummy while the warrior slipped away. The decapitated dummy

was then covered up, given burial rites, and burned on a pyre while the relatives mourned. In fact, for a whole year the novice remained officially "dead" as far as the villagers were concerned, though he was being taught and cared for by the members of the secret society. At the end of that time he returned, riding on the back of a warrior disguised as an animal. In this traditional rite the tribespeople were fully aware the warrior had not been killed, but the effigy represented the death of boyhood so that life in the new clan could begin.

In a society where it was important to prove one's strength and endurance, the shamans had ways to show their powers were almost superhuman. Some knew how to swallow a long stick and bring it up again without gagging. Others used sleight-of-hand techniques to stab themselves without drawing blood. We are not certain what methods they used, but some magic men may have invented trick arrows or spears which could be substituted for the real weapons.

A similar endurance rite was handling red-hot coals with bare hands. To the tribe it may have appeared that the medicine man had divine intervention allowing him to play with fire. Actually he probably protected the palms of his hands by dusting them with a ground-up mineral or some other coating hardly visible to the naked eye. Sometimes the shaman ended the ceremony by scattering the coals among the tribespeople—proving, in case there was any doubt, that the coals really were red-hot.

A number of conjuring tricks, probably thousands of years old, were observed among the Cree, Ojibway, and Menominee Indians of North America. The Cree Indians, who lived in what is now Montana, tied up a medicine man inside an elk skin, and the shaman was forced to make his escape without assistance. The Ojibway had a similar escape trick, but the medicine man was bound hand-and-foot and placed inside a tent. According to tribal lore, the magic man not only escaped from his leather bindings and the tent, but also made the thongs fly invisibly to another tent in the village. Often tricks such as these were performed at the height of a ceremony, when the people had been worked into a state of expectation by preparatory rituals.

Menominee tribes, related to the Ojibway, had several tricks reserved strictly for ceremonial purposes. In one ritual the performer carried a small pouch or bag with white feathers around the opening, and he rolled it up several times to show it was empty. Two dancers—the shaman and a confederate—danced around holding the bag aloft. As the tempo of drumming increased, two snake heads emerged from the top of the bag, wriggled back and forth, and then disappeared again. The nineteenth-century observers who witnessed this demonstration realized immediately the snakes were dummies cleverly concealed in the bag, but they noted that "the trick had made a profound impression on the audience . . . and silence reigned everywhere."

The Menominee also had a clever arrangement to make a doll-like figure come alive and dance in the dust. The medicine man sat on the ground, legs extended, and his assistant covered the master's legs with a long blanket. Then the assistant took two miniature figures made of grass or straw out of a small bag, and placed these dolls on the ground at the feet of the shaman. The assistant seated himself opposite, and the medicine man began chanting. As the chants became shriller, the figures gradually rose from the ground and began dancing up and down between the medicine man and his assistant. After a time, the dancing subsided, the miraculous figures came to rest, and the assistant put them back in his bag. The manipulation was actually carried out by means of a string stretched between the shaman and his confederate. As the assistant placed the dolls on the ground, he attached the string with a piece of sap gum, and throughout the ceremony the shaman operated the dancing dolls with his confederate. To the tribespeople, however, the string was invisible, and the dancing figures seemed to be a clear sign of favor from Ma'nido, the Good Spirit.

In these examples of primitive magic we can find many methods which were later adopted by street magicians and stage magicians in modern times. Producing a bone or pebble from a sick man required the same dexterity needed to produce a card or a billiard ball, as is done today. The decapitation practiced as a rite of entry by the Niska Indians would later be done by street magicians and conjurers in Europe, finally becoming the now-famous trick of sawing a woman in half. The technique used to make the Menominee dolls dance on the ground was, in principle, the same now used to make someone levitate above a stage. In general

the roots of stage magic and street magic reach far into our history as tribal beings, and the fact that magic has universal appeal at least partly results from its primitive character.

But this magic was "primitive" only in the sense that it was very ancient. In fact, the psychological appeal was much more powerful than that of today's magic, produced on a modern stage. In tribal society the medicine man was also a miracle worker, and there was no skepticism or "scientific" testing of the power he claimed to possess. The shaman led the tribe in rituals that began with drumming, chanting, and dancing, and often ended in a state of trance, ecstasy, or possession. No doubt many of the herbs and plants burned during these ceremonies had the power of sedatives or hallucinogens, and the shaman's special potions were probably alcoholic. By the time the miracle worker did his trick, the people were in a state of complete receptivity, ready to witness the most extraordinary examples of magic. Even the most talented magician of today cannot duplicate the perfect conditions created by those earliest conjurers.

With the beginnings of recorded history, we find that priestlike magicians also played a large part in the early civilizations of Egypt and Babylonia. The word "magic" itself probably orginated from the Persian term *mugh*, meaning a fire-worshiper, a word engraved in cuneiform characters on a tablet in Behistan. Another Persian word, *maghdim*, meant wisdom and philosophy. In Babylonia the word *mag* referred to a priest, and from this developed the society of "Magi," high priests or wise men. The Magi, according to extant records, were adept at the spiritual arts, and they probably studied philosophy and science as well. Magic, then, grew out of a combination of humanistic and spiritual studies, mixed with a knowledge of physical science. There is evidence that the Magi had great influence throughout Persia, Chaldea, and Egypt.

The Magis' was a closed society which had its own rituals, observances, and secret writings, and the magicians considered themselves so powerful that they even tried to compel the gods to follow their commands—threatening destruction if the gods refused. Undoubtedly they studied astrology as well as other occult sciences, and they may have actually made astronomical and mathematical discoveries which helped them prophesy natural events or changes. They were occasionally called upon to advise or exhibit their skills, and they may have developed some apparatus to help them perform semi-scientific tricks.

In Exodus we find an account of the magicians who appeared before Pharaoh to match the powers of Moses and Aaron. According to the Old Testament account, Aaron, Moses, and the magicians threw down their rods, and all the rods turned into snakes. The match was concluded when Moses' snake swallowed the other snakes. While this feat was within the range of the other magicians, Moses' other exploits were not. In successive encounters with Pharaoh, Moses turned the waters of the Nile to blood, caused plagues of frogs, gnats, and locusts to sweep over the country, and finally struck down all the first-born in the land of Egypt. Pharaoh's magicians were incapable of preventing these disasters.

The tale of Moses exemplifies the rich, poetic lore surrounding the priestly magic-makers of early civilization. While fact is freely mingled with fiction, we do know that the trick of turning a rod into a snake can be performed with a serpent called *naja haje* commonly found in the Middle East. When the conjurer presses on the back of its neck, the snake becomes as

rigid as a stick. Thrown to the ground, it comes alive and wriggles away. Even today there are street magicians in India who do the trick as adeptly as Moses.

During the many centuries the Magi maintained their semi-mystical, semi-scientific society, they probably influenced the development of religion and philosophy in ancient Greece. The Greek mathematician and philosopher Pythagoras, who lived about the sixth century B.C., was commonly regarded as a magician. In learning the mysteries of the universe, he was also thought to have found out the secrets of nature, giving him a power unknown to common men. Around the city of Athens there were also priests and priestesses who resided in the temples where miraculous things happened. Many of the sanctuaries of the gods and goddesses were rigged with pulleys, levers, trapdoors, speaking tubes, secret passageways, and steam-operated devices. With these mechanisms it was possible to make a statue speak, a door open, or an altar explode with billows of steam. One perfectly inanimate statue of a goddess even yielded milk from its breasts. Being uninformed of the clandestine mechanics, believers were impressed only by the "magic" which took place in the temples. Among the priests and priestesses there must have been the most rigorous laws to make sure their secrets did not become known.

Moses and Aaron, in the presence of Pharaoh, turn a staff into a snake. The trick is still practiced by gali-gali men, itinerant Egyptian magicians. *(Mulholland Collection)*

Mechanical magic, as described in the *Pneumatics* of the Greek scientist Heron in the third century A.D. When the fire was lit, the altar doors opened automatically. *(Sheridan Collection)*

wine and multiplied loaves and fishes until there was enough to feed the crowds. Both tricks might have been carried out by substituting quantities of wine, loaves, and fishes provided by assistants, while changing water to the color of wine is a trick frequently done with chemicals. Other miracles attributed to Jesus—the resurrection of Lazarus and curing the sick by casting out devils—have a close resemblance to initiation rites found in tribal cultures. Certainly many of the early Christians in Rome thought of Jesus as a magician. In the catacombs beneath St. Callisto Chapel are frescoes probably dating from the third century, which show Jesus touching several jars with a magic wand. The artists evidently believed that the wand—also called a "Jacob's rod"—was the instrument of his miraculous powers.

Design from an early Christian sarcophagus, dated third century A.D. Jesus uses a wand to turn water into wine. *(NYPL)*

Ancient sources also tell of a number of thaumaturgists—miracle workers—who washed their hands in burning pitch or walked barefooted over burning coals to show their resistance to fire. Occasionally there were warriors or soldiers who used fire to maintain control. A Syrian, Eunus (or Eunios) breathed fire in order to stop a rebellion in Sicily in 135 B.C. During a slave uprising, Eunus began spouting flames from his mouth. The terrified slaves thought he was blessed by a Syrian goddess, and they turned back and gave up the struggle. Eunus probably accomplished this startling feat by filling a small nut with oil and sulfur. The nut had a hole at each end, and once it was ignited, Eunus could blow into the nut and a steady stream of smoke and fire would emerge from the other end. Though he seemed to "breathe fire," actually the flame never even touched his lips.

Magic, which was important in the Jewish and classical traditions, also played a part in the beginnings of early Christianity. In the Gospel of Matthew, the wise men, or Magi, visited Jesus at his birth, drawn by the astrological sign of the bright star. According to New Testament accounts, the life of Jesus was filled with magical events, and many of the acts he performed were imitated by street magicians in later times. The apostles asserted that Jesus changed water into

The miracle of loaves and fishes. In the sarcophagus of St. Callisto chapel, Jesus was depicted as a magician. *(NYPL)*

The wand is only one of the symbols of magic which have come down to us from ancient times and priestly traditions. The dark robes, peaked hat, and symbols of the occult— which were again seen during the Middle Ages in Europe—may have originated with the Magi, and the symbols of the Zodiac are also from pre-Christian times. Among the secret societies which developed around the Mediterranean, certain methods of conjuring and healing may have been passed on for generations. To people of more recent civilization, the mystery of the pyramids and the rituals of embalming and mummification have a special allure, and even the late-night movie occasionally features walking mummies and cursed treasures of the Nile. Western language and religion, whose roots are in Middle Eastern civilization, carry obvious traces of cultures where people believed in and practiced magic.

Not all of the ancient conjurers were priests, for there were numerous jugglers (e.g., sleight-of-hand performers) who practiced their arts strictly for purposes of entertainment and amusement. In fact, these were the earliest street magicians. They performed freely in streets, markets, and banquet halls, and the tales of their exploits traveled far and wide.

One illustration of the early jugglers is a painting in the burial chamber of Beni Hassan, probably dating from 2500 B.C. or earlier. In the picture two kneeling figures are performing cups-and-balls magic. In the modern form of this trick, the conjurer generally has three cups and three balls. After covering each of the balls with the containers, the juggler would manipulate the objects in such a way that the balls seemed to appear, vanish, and change places mysteriously. In the Egyptian tomb painting, the jugglers have four cups and are about to place one pair on top of the other—or, for all we know, about to make them all disappear.

Another Egyptian source, the Westcar Papyrus inscribed about 1700 B.C., describes a number of talented jugglers who performed about a thousand years earlier. Evidently many of the early wizards of the Nile were kept by the king, and probably performed exclusively for the monarch and his wives. In the court of Snefru a magic worker named Jajamanekh was asked to recover a turquoise hair ornament that one of the ladies had lost while boating. According to the Papyrus, Jajamanekh simply pronounced a magic spell, then picked up half the lake and put it on top of the other half. As he did so, the missing ornament naturally fell out onto the dry sand. Jajamanekh walked across the bottom, picked up the jewel, and returned it to the lady. He said a few more words to the lake, and it dutifully returned to place.

The next ruler, King Khufu (or Cheops) attracted a number of first-rate conjurers to his court. One of the magicians, Weba-aner, presented the king with a small, wax model of a crocodile. According to the Westcar manuscript, the juggler invoked a spirit of transformation, and in a moment the model turned into a full-grown crocodile with snapping jaws.

Tchatcha-em-ankh, another magic worker in the court of Khufu, was an adept at full-scale illusions, and probably had enough knowledge of astrology to impress his audience. The Egyptian source says, "He knoweth how to bind on a head which hath been cut off; he knoweth how to make a lion follow him as if led by a rope; and he knoweth the number of the stars of the house [constellation] of Thoth."

By far the most versatile of Khufu's magicians was Dedi of Dedsnefru. Dedi was said to be over 110 years old, and he maintained his health by eating five hundred loaves of bread and a shoulder of beef every day. Hearing of the extraordinary talents reported of the conjurer (apart from his appetite), Khufu invited Dedi to the court and offered up one of the royal prisoners for a decapitation trick. Not wishing to play the part of executioner, Dedi declined. Instead, he cut off the head of a goose, and placed the head and body at opposite ends of the hall. At Dedi's command the head and body were reunited and the goose began squawking loudly. When the king asked to see the trick again, Dedi used a pelican instead of a goose. Again he succeeded in restoring head to body. When there was a third request, Dedi asked the servants to bring him a full-grown ox. Raising his mighty sword, the magician cut off the head of the ox and, so the story goes, sometime later restored it to its owner.

In ancient Greece and Rome, tumblers, jugglers, and fortune-tellers were respected for their arts. The *Iliad* contains references to a tumbler (*kybisteter*) and to the *thaumatopios* or conjurer. Greeks also had *agyrtae,* strolling vagabonds who combined fortune-telling with juggling. When similar entertainers performed in Rome, they usually presented cups-and-balls tricks. Hence they came to be called *acetabularii* from the Latin *acetabulum,* a cup used to hold vinegar. Evidently these Romans used ordinary household utensils for their tricks.

The Greeks had special schools where the conjuring arts were taught. For a time Xenophon, the most popular conjurer in Athens, had a number of pupils. One was Cratisthenes of Philias, who played with fire so skillfully that, according to a contemporary, he almost made men "discredit the evidence of their own senses." Another student, Diopeithes of Locris, had the ability to spout water or milk from between his lips. In Athens they were amazed at this unusual talent, but a sharp observer in Thebes managed to see how the trick was done. It was the grammarian, Athenaeus, who saw that the conjurer wore bladders filled with wine or milk. When the Locrian squeezed the proper bladder, the liquid spurted up in such a way that it appeared to come from his mouth.

Some of the wandering conjurers of ancient Greece were honored with statues. At the Theatre of Bacchus in Athens, the figure of the juggler Euclides was placed alongside that of the great dramatist Aeschylus. People of Hestiaea and Oreus erected a statue to Theodorus at the Theatre of the Istaians. He was portrayed with a small round object in one hand—the *psephoi* or "little ball" used for cups-and-balls tricks and juggling.

The Romans wrote several accounts of wandering magicians they had seen and appreciated. In a prose satire, the *Metamorphosis* or *Golden Ass,* the traveler-philosopher Apuleius told of a juggler he saw in Athens who swallowed a double-edged sword while riding horseback. Apparently it was a common demonstration, for the juggler performed in front of a colonnade in the heart of the city. Another author, Ludovicus Vives, wrote of *circulatores* who "to the great fear and horror of spectators swallow swords and vomit forth a power of needles, girdles, and coins." Seneca the Younger, in an epistle to Lucilius, summed up his findings with the decision that the tricks were deceptive but intriguing. "It's in the very trickery that it pleases me," he wrote. "But show me how the trick is done, and I have lost my interest therein."

In the days when the street jugglers were treated with honor, people were always pleased to see cups-and-balls tricks. One of the best descriptions of this magic was written by Alciphron of Athens in the second century A.D. The trick, as he describes it, was probably performed outdoors on the street or in the marketplace:

A man came forward and placed on a three-legged table three small dishes, under which he concealed some little white round pebbles. These he placed one by one under the dishes, and then, I do not know how, he made them appear all together under one.

At other times he made them disappear from beneath the dishes and showed them in his mouth. Next, when he had swallowed them, he brought those who stood nearest him into the middle [of the circle], and then pulled one stone from the nose, another from the ear, and another from the head of the man standing near him.

Finally he caused the stones to vanish from the sight of everyone. He . . . rendered me almost speechless and made me gape with surprise.

Cups-and-balls magic. Chinese conjurers used inverted teacups (left) and substituted various objects for the balls. At the end of the trick (right), the magician could produce three balls and three cherries. *(Mulholland Collection/photos by Edward Claflin)*

Since the time of Alciphron, cups-and-balls magic has continued to be the trademark of street magicians everywhere. While the trick is almost universal, it is difficult to tell whether one nationality borrowed it from another, or whether it originated spontaneously in different places. There is certainly nothing symbolic about it, but the trick's appeal might be partially a matter of logic and probability. It is commonly done with three cups and three balls. With two hands, the performer can logically only keep control over two objects at any given moment—or so it would seem. The real trick is to make the ball escape or appear in the cup that has not been disturbed. At the same time the performer is playing with the laws of chance, the probability of finding one, two, or three balls under a given cup. The dexterity of his fingers is matched against the logical minds and the observant eyes of his audience.

Usually the magician finishes a series of cups-and-balls tricks with the transformation of a ball into some larger object. In some cases the conjurer produces from one cup a large, brightly colored ball, a piece of fruit, or even a living animal such as a chick or guinea pig. When performed closeup, the transformation can be as startling to an audience as a fireworks finale or a big-stage illusion. When an object is doubled in size, or comes alive, it is an event which teases the imagination, even if done on a small scale.

The cups-and-balls trick varied according to culture. The late John Mulholland, a modern historian of magic, collected cups from all over the world and observed some of the infinite adaptations possible. In most countries the cups were designed for easy manipulation, but in some cases the jugglers used whatever containers happened to be available. In early Europe—and probably in ancient Greece and Rome—magicians used wooden or pottery cups. When metalworking became more common, the modern Europeans acquired well-made tin or brass cups with wide mouths and narrow bases which could be piled up in a single stack. In the metal cups there was a slight indentation on the sealed, narrow end, so the ball could be placed on top without rolling off.

In China the cups were common ceramic teacups without handles, glazed and painted with colorful designs on the sides. The Japanese, too, used a household implement, the rice bowl, though its flattish, extended shape made it somewhat more difficult to handle. In East India the cups were designed with little knobs, allowing the conjurer to pick them up between two fingers, while Turkish conjurers carved out a long, conical cup of wood.

Performing styles also differed. Western Europeans adopted the standing position of the Romans, and on the street they set up small tables to hold the cups. In later years the tables were equipped with small traps or bags to hold balls and replacement objects. In the East, most Oriental conjurers squatted or sat on the ground with the cups at the same level, and in Turkey the jugglers spread out a carpet on the ground. Some of the conjurers of the East wore long robes which concealed items that were to be substituted for the balls.

A variety of balls came into use, from the crumpled bits of cloth manipulated by Hindus and Japanese to the cork balls or *muscades* of the French. Performers were ingenious in finding objects to substitute. Fruit, vegetables, glass, messages, dolls, or live animals—any of these items might be used if the magician was clever enough to conceal them from the eyes of the audience. John Mulholland described one "finish" carried out by a Chinese performer not long ago. The magician reached up and plucked a coal-black ball from the air, then placed it under the cup. When he lifted the cup, the ball was gone, and a white mouse was in its place. When the mouse tried to run away, the magician trapped it under the cup again. He took another black ball, raised it in the air, and it was instantly transformed to a white ball. When the conjurer lifted the cup the next time, he found a black mouse in place of the white one. He covered the mouse. Moments later, it changed into a frog, and finally a goldfish.

There is something secretive and intimate about cups-and-balls magic, which may account for its particular appeal—and its deceptiveness. Gypsies exploited the trick by asking people to

lay bets on where the ball would be found, "Under this one or that one?" They called it the "shell game" or "thimble-rigging," and though it was presented as a game of chance, the cups were loaded in favor of the gypsy. Few bettors ever won this game, unless they were shills, accomplices, employed by the gypsy himself.

As legitimate entertainment, however, the cups-and-balls has become the practical symbol of the magic profession and has been admired by people throughout the ages. In the sixteenth century A.D., an English author wrote, "Concerning the ball, the plaies and devises thereof are infinite, in so much as if you can by use handle them well, you may showe therewith a hundred feats; but whether you seeme to throw the ball into your left hand, or into your mouth, or into a pot, or up into the aier, it is to be kept still in your hand." The description may not be of much help to a learner, but it conveys the spirit of the trick perfectly, for the plays and devices are certainly infinite. Rabelais described Panurge as an adept with cups-and-balls, and the early mathematicians Ozanam and Guyot went so far as to write treatises relating mathematics and mechanics to the trick. Even today this old street magic sleight retains a special character. In *Modern Magic* the skilled prestidigitator Angelo Lewis wrote, "It is by no means uncommon to find spectators who have received more elaborate feats with comparative indifference become interested, and even enthusiastic, over a brilliant manipulation of the cups-and-balls." This is high praise for a small sleight, but it is after all a sleight which suggests much more than the eye can see.

In India, which has long had the reputation of being a "land of mystery," the cups-and-balls was performed by street conjurers who sat in the dust, deftly manipulating the little wooden cups with rapid movements of their fingers. But these tricks were sometimes combined with illusions that were far more elaborate, and with a mystic philosophy that gave each work of magic a special significance. Street magic of the Hindus has been a part of Indian life for centuries, and from the tales of Indian conjurers came inspiration for magicians everywhere. Our search for street magic leads inevitably to that land of mystery, mango, flute, and fire.

Cups-and-balls magic. The Japanese used shallow saucers and silk balls, producing a geisha doll as a finale. *(Mulholland Collection/photos by Edward Claflin)*

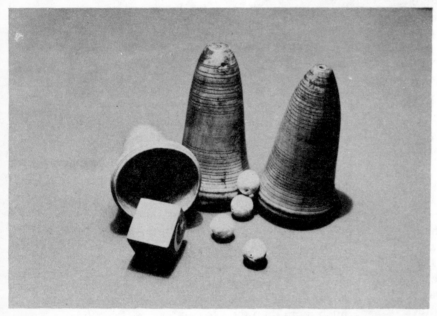

(Left) Turkish conjurers used conical wooden cups and three or four cork balls. Sometimes the star-and-crescent cube was substituted at the end of the trick. (Below) Gypsies played "thimble-rigging" (with sewing thimbles) or "the shell game" (with walnut shells) and gambled on moves of the small pea. *(Mulholland Collection/photos by Edward Claflin)*

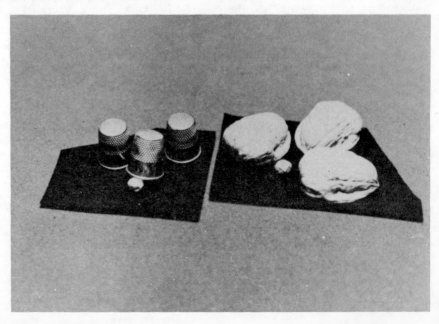

In India street magicians used wooden cups with knobs that could be manipulated between two fingers. Balls were wads of cloth stuffed with cotton.

(Right) European conjurers had large brass cups that could be stacked in a single pile. Cups were roomy enough to hold mice, eggs, or guinea pigs. Balls or "muscades" were made of cork. (Below) Egyptian brass cups were etched with designs and figures. The conjurers used burnt cork balls and a stuffed baby chick. *(Mulholland Collection/photos by Edward Claflin)*

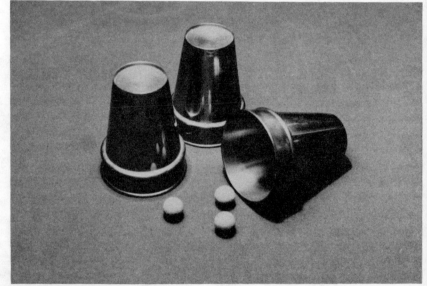

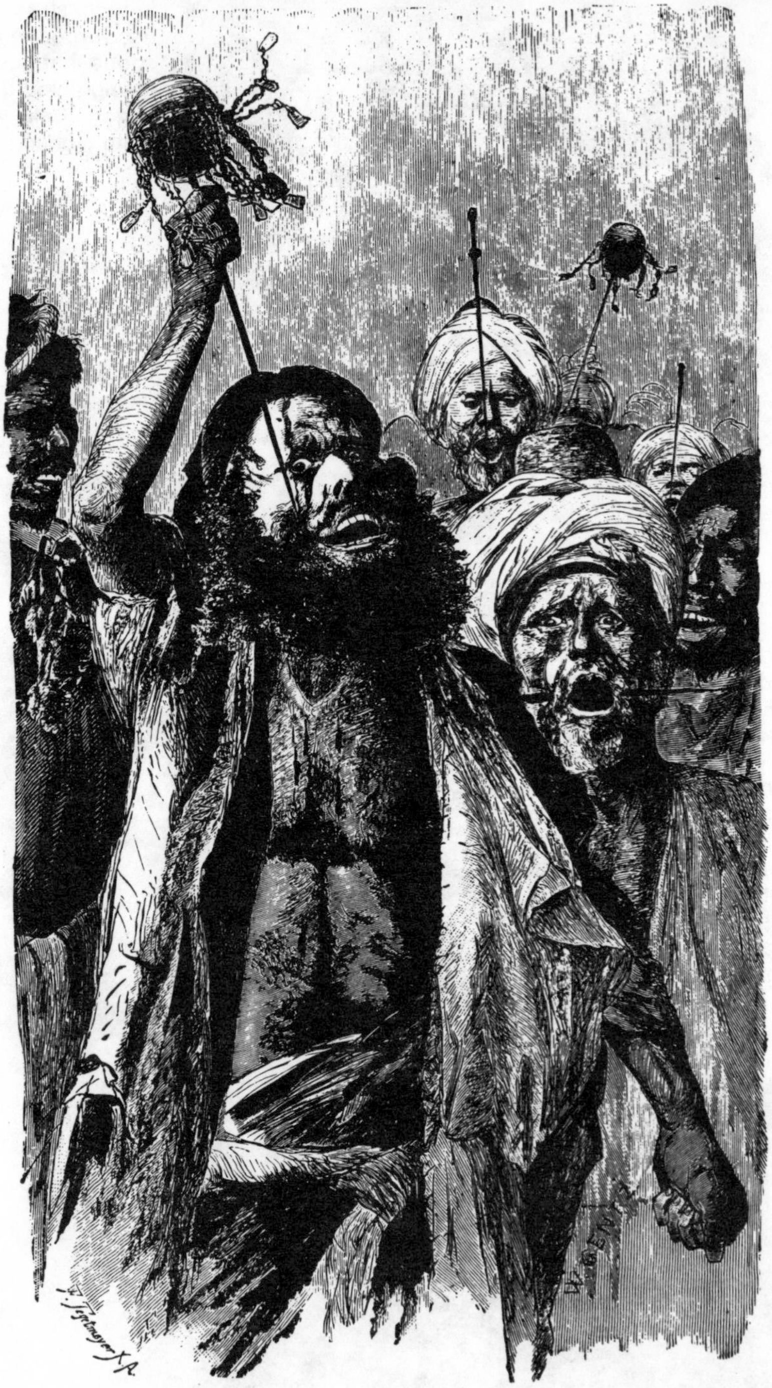

Mysteries
of the Fakirs

Travelers to India have sought and found street magic ever since the days of Marco Polo, for in that mysterious land—at least through the nineteenth century—magic was a culturally important tradition, perpetuated by succeeding generations of conjurers. The early traveler saw a form of magic whose origins were probably as old as Hinduism itself, for the conjuring arts were almost one with the Vedic mysteries. Some of the tricks undoubtedly had their beginnings in Egypt and Mesopotamia, but they acquired distinctive characteristics as they became assimilated with Indian life. Other tricks, originating in India, were passed along through cults and families practicing exclusively the conjuring arts. Eventually the "magic of India" made its way to the West, where many stage magicians imitated the mysteries of the Orient before Occidental footlights.

Indian magicians seemed to be of two classes—the fakirs, or holy men, and the conjurers or jadoo-wallahs. Fakirs very rarely performed, but it was said they could do tricks that were impossible for ordinary men to duplicate, including the now-famous Indian rope trick, the levitation or suspension of a human being in the air, and burial alive.

In addition, fakirs were said to perform acts of abnegation or self-abuse which seemed almost magic. According to stories told by travelers returning from the East, a true fakir could walk across hot coals or broken glass in his bare feet. He could stab himself without drawing blood, walk on water, sleep on a bed of nails, transform material objects to a different form, and make things fly invisibly through the air. The fakir was said to perform publicly only on special occasions, such as public fetes or coronations, the coming of age of a sovereign, grand feasts, or the visits of foreign noblemen. Even on these special occasions it was suspected that the so-called fakirs who performed may have been impostors or renegades, since the true holy men preferred to keep their powers secret.

High-caste fakirs were long regarded as true keepers of the mystical secrets and as leaders in the magic arts in India. Fakirs were found also in a number of Arab countries where the Muslim religion is dominant, but in India they were almost exclusively Hindus. Though this religious order was most active in the nineteenth century, only a few fakirs survive in modern India.

As a religious sect, the fakirs shared some of the characteristics of dervishes, dumbis, sadhus, gosains, and yogis. The word "fakir" itself comes from an Arabic word meaning "needy person," and the true Indian fakir followed strict rules of mendicancy—begging, rather than working, to

Travelers returning from India told of "holy men" who could stab their cheeks without drawing blood. Many Westerners believed that these religious fanatics had magical powers. *(NYPL Picture Collection)*

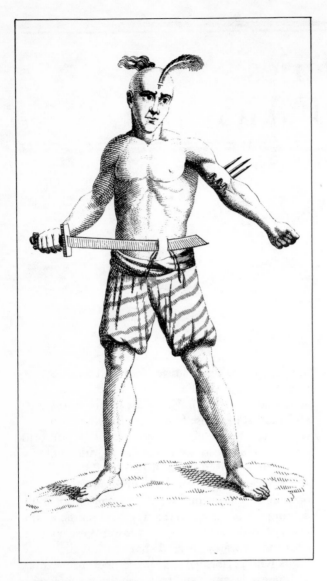

A Dervish passes spikes through his arm, a sword through his stomach and a feather through the skin of his forehead—apparently without feeling the slightest pain. Dervishes belonged to a religious order closely related to the fakirs. *(NYPL Picture Collection)*

keep himself alive. According to the rules of his order, he was supposed to eat no more than absolutely necessary, subsisting on a diet of wheat, rice, milk, butter, and honey. He drank only pure water. Total detachment from the world was his ultimate aspiration. To achieve this goal, the fakir deprived himself of nearly all human possessions, wandered from village to village, and slept only during certain hours. As a result of his ascetic life, the fakir was believed to attain a superior state of being and control over

all bodily functions.

It is extremely difficult for someone raised in the Western tradition to comprehend the spiritual system of devout Hindus and to understand traditions that were part of religious ritual and daily life. A Westerner tends to think of the world as a duality: the "inner life" is mental and emotional, while the world of objective reality is independent of subjective interpretation. But in the Hindu vision the physical world is only an outward manifestation of a oneness, a God, which is inwardly hidden in everything. In a sense, the world itself is an illusion, but it is an illusion that has the significance of being part of a whole creation—which includes man, animal, and the universe. It is not possible to gain religious knowledge solely by studying or exercising the mind. One acquires spiritual power only through strict physical and mental concentration of energies. By harnessing the power to contemplate and see, by concentrating on existence rather than illusion, one can theoretically strip away the masks of the world to reveal pure being. Narrowly interpreted—as it was among some superstitious Hindus—this means that with proper chants, incantations, physical discipline, and spiritual asceticism, the fakirs, sufis, or yogis could gain magical power. There was even a name for that kind of power: *maya,* which meant generally any illusion, trick, artifice, deceit, jugglery, sorcery, or work of witchcraft.

Marco Polo, probably the first real European explorer of India and China, reported in the thirteenth century that the inhabitants of Kashmir "are adept beyond all others in the art of magic, insomuch as they can compel their idols, though by nature deaf and dumb, to speak; they can likewise obscure the day and perform many other miracles." Another early traveler from Arabia, claimed he saw two extraordinary conjurers give a show at the Mogul court in Delhi. One formed himself into a cube, rose in the air, and remained suspended for some time. The other slapped his slipper on the ground, and it, too, rose in the air a short distance from the cube. When the sandal struck the cube, the geometric figure returned to earth and became a man again.

Other legends flourished. There were fakirs who were said to walk on air, and one could move between Calcutta and Delhi at speeds faster than light, or, if you prefer, disappear in the middle of a conversation. There was a priest who could touch the moon with his fingers, and another who could throw the tip of his tongue across the river and propel himself through the water to the other side. One priest even caused a rain of gold to fall on a provincial village.

European and American magicians were intrigued by these and other tales of Indian fakirs reaching the West. During the early years of stage magic, many "tricks of the fakirs" were performed by illusionists in Europe and America, and these helped spark even more curiosity about the mysteries of the East. In the early 1900s, "The Great Nicola," a Western performer, did a version of the Indian rope trick which, according to his playbills, surpassed even the feats of the "ancient Hindoo fakirs." Howard Thurston, a contemporary of Nicola's born in Columbus, Ohio, did another simulation of the rope trick on stage, making a boy vanish from the rope "like a fading cloud." A suspension trick similar to the fakir version was first seen in Paris in a theatre operated by a man recognized as "the father of modern magic," the French magician Jean Eugène Robert-Houdin.

Another borrowed item was the levitation trick—floating a person in air. On the stage, any number of levitations are possible, and it is not known which of the European magicians was the first to borrow this fakir illusion. Servais LeRoy, a Belgian illusionist born in 1865, probably did it with the greatest flair of anyone. He levitated his wife, Talma, to a point high above the stage—and then made her disappear.

A fakir trick that has rarely been imitated by Western magicians is the dangerous act of burial alive. Harry Houdini, who survived so many escapes of his own devising, was once buried without a coffin in a real grave, but the experience was so terrifying he never tried it a second time. He attempted it in three stages. On the first two trials, Houdini was buried under three or four feet of soil and escaped easily. On the third attempt, however, his assistants piled on six feet of dirt, in accordance with Houdini's instructions. Under the tremendous weight, Houdini started to panic and choked on loose dirt that fell into his mouth. He hardly had the presence of mind to keep digging his way free, and he was literally half-dead by the time he reached the surface. His friends had to help drag him from the living grave.

A fanciful illustration of the rope trick, with the fakir in hot pursuit of his assistant. According to most tales, both of them disappeared at the top of the rope. *(Sheridan Collection)*

Houdini never tried it again. But he did match the so-called "Egyptian Miracle Man," Rahman Bey, when that performer visited New York in the twenties. Bey agreed to be "buried" underwater for an hour. Before being sealed in his casket, he made a great show of going into a trance. The first time the casket was lowered in the water, the emergency alarm rang almost immediately, and Bey had to be resurrected after only nineteen minutes. Houdini, in a similar burial, made no attempt to go into a trance—but stayed under water much longer. He was sealed in a metal casket which was lowered into the swimming pool of the Hotel Shelton in New York. Medical authorities had thought it would be impossible for him to survive more than six minutes at the most. Incredibly, he stayed down an hour and a half. He had no secret valves or breathing apparatus. Like the Egyptian, Houdini simply restrained his breathing to a minimum, remained quiet, and survived on the air in the box. His prospective coffin was 6½ feet long, two feet high, and two feet wide.

The Indian rope trick remains an enigma. Reputable travelers have confirmed seeing it—others have flatly denied it can be done. Modern magicians, psychologists, and mystics have investigated the trick to learn the method of presenting the illusion or, given that it might be sheer fantasy, have tried to unearth the sources of the legend. Just when skeptics thought the ghost of the rope trick had at last been laid to rest, there would always be renewed sightings, investigations, or theories. Like an unidentified flying object on the periphery of Indian culture, the rope trick still hovers in the atmosphere—never confirmed but always there.

According to most accounts, the trick was performed by a fakir and his assistant, a small boy. Both were dressed in simple loincloths, like beggars. The trick was preceded by some ceremony, with the boy playing a flageolot or Indian flute and the master beating on a small drum. (In India, the drum was carried by most conjurers and had the same significance as a magic wand.) Near the fakir and his assistant were a coiled rope and a woven basket. The fakir carried a curved dagger at his waist.

The fakir's apprentice laid the coil of rope on the ground in front of his guru. As the fakir

continued beating the drum, the rope rose slowly in the air, apparently drawn upward by some inexorable will. Fully extended, the rope stood upright like a pole planted in the earth.

At a signal from the fakir, the boy clambered hand over hand to the top of the rope. Then he disappeared.

There was silence. Suddenly the boy began giggling and shouting from his invisible perch in the sky. The fakir, obviously displeased, muttered some angry words. The laughter continued. Furious, the fakir leapt to his feet and shouted for the boy to come down. His commands were ignored. The fakir pulled out the curved dagger from his loincloth, clasped it between his teeth, climbed up the rope, and disappeared.

There was the sound of a fierce argument, followed by a shrill scream. A piece of bloody flesh fell from the sky, landing in the basket. It was a human hand.

An illustration published in 1872, showing the Chinese version of the rope trick. From right to left: the conjurer unfurls the rope; magician and assistant climb to the top; the mutilated assistant falls from the sky; and his remains are placed in a basket. (NYPL Picture Collection)

The boy screamed again, pleading for his life, but the fakir apparently intended to be merciless. One by one, pieces of the boy's body fell from the sky into the basket—arms, legs, and, as the cries spluttered away to nothing, the torso and head of what was once a living child.

A short while later, the fakir descended the rope, his body spattered with blood, sanguine dagger between his clenched teeth. He took up his drum and began the beating and chanting again. The rope descended waveringly until it was once again coiled on the ground at the fakir's feet.

Inside the basket, something moved and there was a shout. Out leapt the fakir's apprentice, all in one piece, ready to serve his master again.

In 1355 an Arab who called himself Ibn Batutu ("The Traveler") reported seeing the rope trick while visiting Hangchau, China. The trick seen by Batuta was similar to the Indian version, though the conjurer was a juggler rather than a priest, and he used a single leather thong instead of a piece of rope. It is mentioned in the ancient *Vedanta Sutra* and other writings such as the *Badrayana Vyas,* and the idealist school of Hinduism cited the trick as an example of the difference between illusion and reality. The two forms were as different, it said, "as the magician who in reality remains upon the earth is different from the magician who, with sword and shield, climbs up the string."

During the nineteenth century, a number of witnesses said they had seen the fakir trick, including Maxim Gorki, Maurice Maeterlinck, William Beebe, and Francis de Crosset. In the same period, a number of professional magicians from the West offered large rewards to anyone who would successfully perform the rope trick in the open air. John Nevil Maskelyne, an English magician who ran the Egyptian Hall in London, offered a reward of five-thousand pounds a year to any fakir who could perform the trick according to his conditions. There were no takers.

In 1935, Sir Ralph Pearson, the former lieutenant-governor of the Frontier Province of the Northwest in India wrote to the *Morning Post* of London to say he had actually seen the rope trick in 1900 at Dandachia, in the valley of the Tapti. At the London conference of the East India Association in 1936, another Britisher, Major G.H. Rooke, said he had not witnessed a performance first-hand, but one of his officers had taken a photograph of the trick. The photograph, however, showed neither child nor cord, only a fakir seated on the bare ground. In 1954 a group of native Indian illusionists—all professional stage magicians—investigated every shred of evidence and concluded that the rope trick was no more than a legend.

But a year later, there was a new explanation, and a new set of puzzles. In 1955 the guru Sadhu Vadramakrishna told an investigator, John Keel, that he had performed the rope trick himself when a young man. Keel, an American author and journalist, expressed his skepticism. The guru explained.

He said the trick was usually performed at night with brightly lit torches on the ground to blind the spectators. Sitting near the performers, the audience could not see more than ten feet in the air. Both the fakir and the young boy were experienced acrobats and tightrope walkers.

A horizontal wire or fine horsehair rope was stretched high between two trees, two houses, or in a valley between two steep hills. Then the fakir hung a light string over this "tightwire" and tied the end of the string to the coiled rope. When he pulled on the string, the rope rose in the air, hooked on the tightwire, and remained suspended. As the little boy scrambled up the rope, the fakir might throw incense or hashish into the torches, creating clouds of smoke. Hidden by the vapors, the boy could walk along the tightwire to the tree, roof, or hillside, and scramble to safety.

And the dismemberment of the boy? Vadramakrishna had a simple solution. He cut up pieces of a monkey and hid them in his clothing. Once he had followed the boy up the rope and perched on the wire, he simply dropped down the pieces from the sky.

Though the explanation may seem as far-fetched as the trick itself, the technicalities described by the guru were no more elaborate than what is involved in many stage illusions. This solution would also explain why "fakirs" did not come forward to demonstrate the trick to investigators: even at night, the all-important tightwire would be visible to anyone carrying a flashlight. Finally it also explains why the trick has rarely been done in recent years. India no longer trains expert acrobats like the ones who performed up to a hundred years ago. Climbing the rope was risky enough, but to walk a tightwire at night required extraordinary precision and balance.

While this strictly physical explanation may be the solution, it does not explain the instances when the trick was supposedly seen by daylight. The American magician Kreskin has reviewed some other theories about the rope trick, speculating it was a psychological rather than physical illusion. Kreskin concluded that mass hypnotism was out of the question (most psychologists would concur) though the fakir might have used a kind of mental suggestion technique to present the illusion to a very small audience. Once the legend became known, people would expect to see the rope trick, and they would become vulnerable to autosuggestion. But Kreskin doubted that a mass of people could hallucinate repeatedly, and he concluded that the rope trick must be a "fairy tale"—unless proven otherwise.

To this day the mystery is unsolved. Those who are skeptical must resolve why the legend has so many different sources. Those who believe in the trick have yet to reconcile the differing explanations of method, or to duplicate the trick outdoors. And the few who may hold the key to the mystery will probably never tell.

"Fifteen years spent in India and the Far East have convinced me that the high-caste fakirs, or magicians, of Northern India have probably discovered natural laws of which we in the West are ignorant. That they succeed in overcoming forces of nature which to us seem insurmountable my observation satisifies me beyond doubt."

Harry Kellar, the American magician who wrote these words in 1893, was one not easily deceived by appearances. In his own traveling show—he claimed to have gone around the world a "baker's dozen" times—he specialized in mind-reading, rope-tying, a cabinet séance, and escape tricks. Born in 1849 in Erie, Pennsylvania, Kellar had studied magic with the Fakir of Ava, an Indian role for an American whose real name was Harris Hughes. Through his observation of the Davenport Brothers and other famed "spiritualists" of the time, Kellar had become familiar with the psychic effects which could delude an audience.

It was not, therefore, an innocent traveler who believed the high-caste fakirs knew natural laws "of which we in the West are innocent."

Kellar reached that conclusion after witnessing a levitation trick in Calcutta during the winter of 1875-76. The levitation was performed in the *Maidam* or Great Plaza of Calcutta, and was given for the Prince of Wales, then visiting India. A venerable-looking old man with a long grey beard, the holy fakir was said to have spent his life in study and seclusion. The seat of his brotherhood was either in a monastery of Tibet or in the mountains of northern Hindustan. Kellar described the fakir as "quiet, suave, and secretive," and said he attached "an almost religious significance" to the manifestions of his power. As Kellar described the scene, the audience included not only the Prince of Wales but also native princes and "begums" (princesses) decked out in fine silks. The performance is described vividly:

The old fakir took three swords with straight cross-barred hilts and buried them, hilt downward, about six inches in the ground. The points of these swords were very sharp, as I afterwards informed myself. A young fakir . . ., at a gesture from his master, stretched himself out upon the ground at full length, with his feet together and his hands close to his sides, and, after a pass or two made by the hands of the old man, appeared to become rigid and lifeless. A third fakir now came forward, and, taking hold of the feet of his prostrate companion, whose head was lifted by the master, the two laid the stiffened body upon the points of the swords, which appeared to support it without penetrating the flesh. The point of one of the swords was immediately under the nape of the man's neck, that of the second rested midway between his shoulders, and that of the third was at the base of his spine; there being nothing under his legs. After the body had been placed on the sword points, the second fakir retired, and the old man, who was standing some distance from it, turned and salaamed to the audience.

The body tipped neither to the right nor to the left, but seemed to be balanced with mathematical accuracy. Presently the master took a dagger, with which he removed the soil round the hilt of the first sword, and, releasing [the sword] from the earth, after some exertion, quietly stuck it into his girdle, the body meanwhile retaining its position. The second and third swords were likewise taken from under the body, which, there in broad daylight and under the eyes of all the spectators, preserved its horizontal position, without visible support, about two feet from the ground. A murmur of admiration pervaded the vast throng, and with a low salaam to the Prince, the master summoned his assistant, and, lifting the suspended body from its airy perch, they laid it gently upon the ground. With a few passes of the master's hand, the inanimate youth was himself again.

Though Kellar had a clear view of the entire scene, he was unable to see any kind of brace or mechanism which might have supported the floating body. The magician was thoroughly familiar with every means of concealment used by stage performers, and he himself was perfectly capable of "levitating" a body in a Chicago theatre. But outdoors it was a different thing. Every conventional device was useless in the open plaza, where the fakir was surrounded by spectators. Kellar was skeptic enough to doubt there was "mesmerism" or mass hypnotism involved. But eliminating these possibilities, he was left with only one conclusion, not particularly agreeable to his sense of logic. The fakir's powers, decided Kellar, were simply "unknown."

Another unknown form of levitation was reported by H. J. Burlingame in the biography *Around the World with a Magician and a Juggler*, published in 1891. The magician and juggler was the Baron Hartwig Seeman, a Swedish performer who lived from 1833 to 1886. On June 24, 1872, Baron Seeman and two friends arrived in Calcutta and from there traveled to Benares, the holy city, to become acquainted with the fakirs and to learn some of the secrets of their arts. After making inquiries, Seeman arranged to meet with "the most celebrated of all fakirs," a man named Convinsamy.

Seeman was well informed and equally well practiced in the sleight-of-hand arts and could match the skill of the fakir in most tricks. The fakir was impressed by the skills of his Western visitor and decided to show a member of the brotherhood a few tricks which laymen were never allowed to witness.

One day the fakir said to Seeman, "I feel in me today a power to produce a phenomenon. Have you also felt such a sensation in brain or body?"

Seeman had to admit he had not.

"I do not mean a natural power, which works," Convinsamy continued, "but a supernatural. Then I invoke the souls of my ancestors and they are the ones to show their power; I am only their tool."

To show what his ancestors could do, Convinsamy glanced at a nearby fountain and commanded the water to stop flowing. As the fountain dried up, Seeman heard a rhythmic plucking sound, gradually growing louder. It was now the Westerner's turn. To show the trick could be matched, Seeman placed a music box on the fountain. When Seeman waved his hand, the box began to produce music—keeping perfect tempo with the rhythmic plucking.

Convinsamy nodded his approval, then prepared the most impressive feat of all, a levitation. For this he asked a pretty young girl, one of his followers, to assist him. Some other servants put up a black curtain between two pillars on the veranda. About six feet in front of the curtain, Convinsamy put down a flower stand, and the girl mounted the stand. Then Convinsamy sat down next to Seeman and stretched out his hands toward the girl. For a long time he did not move. Gradually the girl fell into a deep sleep, while the guru held the pose. Seeman watched closely as the girl began to nod off.

Her eyes closed. Convinsamy rose cautiously, crept forward, and removed the flower stand from beneath her feet. She did not fall but remained suspended in mid-air. The Hindu took some rosin from his hair and threw it into the incense burner. When clouds of smoke billowed into the air, the girl slowly began moving her arms and legs. Her body ascended slightly and turned to one side, then the other. Convinsamy went forward again, placed the flower stand beneath her feet, and she descended and awoke.

The trick was over. The curtain was removed, and Convinsamy returned to the seclusion of his temple at Benares. There was a sequel, however, which made an equally profound impression on the traveler. The next morning, Seeman was awakened by a tap on the shoulder and was not at all disappointed to see the young girl who, the day before, had floated so beautifully on air. She had been sent by the fakir.

"Master Seeman," she said, "you come to Convinsamy." He followed the girl and was brought into the presence of the master fakir, who sat with his hands on the ground. Seeman smelled burning flesh and, when the fakir raised his hand, was horrified to see the palm had been scarred by hot coals. Convinsamy, he learned, had inflicted this punishment on himself for disobedience to his order, for the priest had violated the sacred rules in showing his powers to a stranger.

If the fakir thought Seeman had learned the secret of the trick, he was completely mistaken. True, the Westerner paid close attention to the flower stand, where levers or contraptions might have been concealed. And it seemed suspicious that the fakir had to hang up a curtain before performing the levitation. Yet Seeman had watched the girl's movements closely and was baffled by the way she turned back and forth in mid-air. He saw no clues, and even wondered whether he was hallucinating due to the heat and overpowering smell of incense. The memory haunted him, and several years later he found a way to do his own form of levitation on stage. But he never learned for certain the methods of the Indian fakir Convinsamy.

In 1830, a number of European papers carried stories of a Brahmin (a priest of the highest caste) who seemed able to hold himself in the air with only his elbow resting on a pole. Two years later a magician of the same caste, named Sheshal, was said to have duplicated the feat. To Europeans these were the first known cases of human suspension, and many people were certain that a new and greater dimension of the human soul had been discovered.

Sheshal's pieces of equipment for the trick were a four-legged stool, a bamboo pole, and a roll of antelope hide. Unlike most fakirs who wore only loincloths and turbans, Sheshal customarily dressed in a baggy costume from neck to knees, and wore the traditional turban.

To shield the priest from the curious crowd, his assistant held up a piece of cloth. As everyone knew, the fakir had to achieve the proper level of contemplative calm before his soul would raise his body into the air. It took the sage only a few minutes to achieve the proper state of purity. The assistants pulled away the covering, to reveal their master suspended precariously some four feet above the ground.

His eyes were glazed over as in a trance, and his body floated stiffly in the air without the slightest motion. His position was peculiar. One hand hung loosely over the roll of antelope hide,

Sheshal, the "Brahmin of the Air," in a state of prayerful suspension. His right hand rests on a roll of antelope skin while his fingers worry at prayer beads. *(Sheridan Collection)*

idly fondling some prayer beads. The other hand was raised in a magical sign, and his legs were crossed in the lotus position. The buffalo hide on which his right hand was perched had risen to a horizontal position like an armrest, and the opposite end of the leather roll balanced precariously on top of the bamboo pole. The lower end of the pole rested on top of the stool. It appeared the fakir had simply risen to the most comfortable position, without the slightest consideration for the laws of gravity.

It was during the 1840s that Jean Eugène Robert-Houdin presented a replica of the

Two variations of the suspension trick, as depicted in Indian catalogues of the eighteenth century. *(Sheridan Collection)*

suspension trick in his theater in Paris. Like many magicians of his time, Robert-Houdin often added a scientific element to his tricks. In this case, simple chemistry appeared to explain the effect when, in fact, it revealed nothing.

The "mystery" element was ether. Robert-Houdin uncorked a bottle of the potent chemical and held it under the nose of his son, Émile. In the fashionable salon in Paris, where Robert-Houdin conducted this soirée, the fumes wafted quickly to the audience. Émile was soon overcome.

As he fell asleep, Émile leaned with his elbow on a cane resting on a small stool. When his son was lost in dreams, Robert-Houdin lifted the boy's legs from the stage, then gradually raised him until the boy was in a horizontal position. As he rose, the boy seemed to grow miraculously lighter. When at last his father let go of the feet, Émile was stretched out as comfortably as if he were resting on a couch. But his elbow rested on a cane rather than a pillow, and his body was apparently supported by nothing but air. It was as if the boy's dreams,

infused with "ethereal" fumes, could lift him from the earth.

Perhaps the most mystifying of all fakir tricks was the "burial alive."

According to Indian mystical lore, a man prepared for burial alive from earliest childhood. As a boy, the chosen fakir learned to endure hardship and master the skill of contemplative meditation. He was also supposed to attain conscious control over all bodily functions, including his breathing, the beating of his heart, and the process of digestion. The muscles beneath his tongue were severed so that when the time for burial came, his tongue could be pushed back to cover his throat.

When, after many years, the fakir felt prepared for living burial, there were further rigors he had to endure. In the weeks of preparation he was supposed to live on a diet of yoghurt and milk, flush his bowels regularly, and bathe in steaming-hot water. His fast became stricter as the time approached. Then, on the day set aside for his burial the fakir swallowed twenty or thirty yards of linen cloth and pulled it up again to clear his system of any undigested food.

With his assistants and followers gathered around him, the fakir lay down on a plank, folded his arms, and entered a state of trance. His tongue fell back, sealing his esophagus. Eyes, ears, and nostrils were plugged with wax by his assistants. His breathing became imperceptible, and his heartbeat slowed.

The fakir appeared to be dead. Assistants lifted the plank, carried their master to the burial site, and lowered him into the earth. The grave for the living was five or six feet deep, with sheer walls. At the bottom, a narrow crypt had been constructed to hold the body and protect it from worms and decay during its days beneath the ground.

With the fakir safely at rest, the assistants laid another plank over the crypt to protect the body from the crushing weight of the soil. Dirt showered onto the casket. And the grave was packed down.

At a time previously arranged—hours, days, or months later—the attendants returned to the burial site to disinter the fakir. The casket was uncovered, the lid raised. Lying in precisely the same position as when buried, the fakir was emaciated—but otherwise unchanged by the ordeal. Assistants lifted the body out of the grave, placed the fakir on the ground, and removed the wax from his eyes, ears, and nostrils. A moment later the fakir opened his

Burial alive, revealing one method of escape. *(Sheridan Collection)*

eyes and his tongue began to flutter. His chest rose and fell as he took first breaths. He began speaking in a weak voice, first praising God, then reassuring his assistants, and finally expressing his willingness to endure the ordeal once again.

Sometime in the mid-seventeenth century, a group of workmen reported that they uncovered the body of a holy man when digging outside the city of Amritsar, on the fringe of the Himalayas. As they later told investigators, the corpse seemed remarkably well preserved and eventually showed signs of life. Though frightened, the workmen helped the holy man regain consciousness and, as soon as he could speak, asked for details of his experience. He replied that his name was Ramaswamy and he had been buried more than a hundred years. A short time later, he was questioned by the guru scholar and historian, Arjun Singh, who discovered that Ramaswamy did indeed seem to have a remarkable knowledge of events that had occurred a century before.

In the *Calcutta Medical Journal* of 1835, it was reported that the fakir Haridas was buried near the mountain village of Jammu. As with other fakirs, he had taken proper precautions— flushing his bowels, bathing in hot water, and living on only yoghurt and milk before his interment. Before they lowered him into the earth, a physician on the scene gave a physical examination. He reported, "Our examination showed his pulse had stopped. He was physically dead!"

An Oriental scholar and painter, Fyzee Rahamin, told of a yogi who insisted on being buried alive for a year and a day. Again, the account suggests the holy man was on the point of death, in medical terms, at the time of his burial. He was placed in a grave six feet underground. Mr. Rahamin was present when they retrieved the fakir more than a year later, and he reported that the holy man seemed to be in perfectly good health.

Despite these fascinating historical accounts, we now know that burial alive was invariably a deception. In his investigation of this Indian trick, author John Keel discovered several ways of simulating the feat. One method, as one might expect, was to use a passageway leading to a nearby tree or the side of a well. The fakir, or impostor, could stay in his grave for a short time, then make his exit at night when there were no believers in the area. In at least one case, some villagers caught a "buried" fakir just as he was crawling out of the side of a well. The enraged villagers resented the imposture, and viciously attacked the charlatan. But normally the fakir's secret was not discovered, and he could return to the tomb via the passageway a few hours before he was to be unburied.

A second method involved collaboration with the assistants. In this case, the fakir was sealed in a coffin before being lowered into the ground. While the top of the coffin was being nailed down, the fakir slipped out through a trap in the bottom. Dressed in the same clothing as his assistants, he mingled among them and the excited villagers did not notice him in the crowd.

The third method, tried out by John Keel himself, was not even a deception—but it was a burial that could only last a few hours at most. The fakir chose a location where the soil was sandy and porous enough to allow some air to pass, and his grave was rather shallow. It did require some endurance to lie perfectly still, and in this instance the fakir probably commenced meditation—his breathing was slight, his body immobile. The least activity would exhaust the air supply in that shallow crypt, though some air was constantly seeping through the soil.

Keel attempted the feat with the instructions of the guru Govindaswamy. The fakir accepted burial with perfect equanimity— having been through it many times before—but Keel was uncomfortable in the cramped quarters. He pulled the emergency string, a signal arranged between him and friends above ground, but it snagged. Desperately, he fought to maintain his composure and somehow endured the ritual to the end. But like Houdini, Keel never tried it again.

Unfortunately there were many Hindus as well as Westerners who did not realize the deceit involved in burial alive. Even some fakirs were duped, and they attempted long burials with only spiritual preparations. In this case, spiritual strength was not sufficient. Some died in their attempts, and in 1955 the Delhi government passed a statute to outlaw living burials.

Hindu Tricks
and Wonders

ow-caste street conjurers—known as *jadoo-wallahs, djorghis,* or *bhaghats*—often pretended to be holy men, and many Europeans thought they were in fact the same as genuine fakirs. But to the Hindus, the street conjurers were much like other strolling players and performers, and they were considered socially inferior to the priests. In the ancient *Artha Sustra* it was written, "The same rules shall apply to an actor, dancer, singer, player on musical instruments, a rope dancer, a juggler, a bard, pimps, and unchaste women." Conjurers, at that time, were called jugglers, and they were obviously not among high company. In many cases, they looked and acted like beggars, but as they begged for *baksheesh* or alms, they also did cups-and-balls magic or other kinds of tricks.

Because of their magic, some jadoo-wallahs had a reputation for sorcery, and they were occasionally accused of practicing black magic like the *Prayanayoga,* the lowest order of adept in India. According to Hindu law, people were forbidden to practice the black arts, sorcery or witchcraft, and anyone who excited the wrath of the gods should be punished. For this reason, the street conjurers did not pretend to have spiritual powers—unless, of course, they could find a white man in search of that sort of thing.

Often a group of street magicians traveled together to the villages or performed in the market places of the bustling cities. Usually the group had a leader or head magician who styled himself as the guru (religious leader), while the other troupers—who sometimes included his wife and children—contributed to the performance in various ways. They accompanied the head conjurer by playing the drum and flute, and they handed him equipment while he performed. In addition they did some stunts or sleight-of-hand tricks during interludes in the entertainment and collected *baksheesh* when the show was over. Up to the 1900s, the jadoo-wallah and his troupe were a familiar sight throughout India, and whatever their social standing the conjurers were watched and admired for their marvelous sleight of hand.

As early as the seventeenth century, the Emperor Jahangir kept a number of Bengalese conjurers in his court, and he himself kept a record of their exploits. During a typical performance, they made trees of every variety spring up out of the earth—mulberry, apple, fig, almond, walnut, and mango. As they pronounced magical words, beautiful birds appeared on the tree branches. Where a conjurer planted a flower, a geyser of water sprang up, sparkling in the air. In the wink of an eye, the geyser changed to a fountain of roses.

As the people of Jahangir's court watched in amazement, food and animals were transformed to an inconceivable number of

A troupe of Hindu jugglers. Their repertoire included linking rings, trick puzzles, sword swallowing and acrobatic stunts. *(NYPL Picture Collection)*

different forms. A pair of fighting game cocks metamorphosed to partridges, then became battling blacksnakes. With a magical birdcage, the Bengalese conjurers changed singing nightingales to parrots. They turned the cage, and parrots became partridges. The conjurers produced raisins, almonds, figs, and herbs from an empty basket, and citron, pickles, wheat, and tamarind from empty jars. Leaves turned to snakes, rubies to diamonds. A flower behind a mirror faded and blossomed in an ever-changing array of colors, and the pages of a blank Book of Life filled miraculously with images of men and animals.

In later centuries few people reported tricks as varied as these, but European visitors to India certainly returned home with many strange tales. They said there were fakirs who hypnotized the deadly cobra, and the serpents became as docile as children. Other travelers witnessed feats of reincarnation, wherein little children were stabbed to death and came to life again. They saw the miraculous germination of a mango plant—when it grew from a seed to a blossoming tree in a matter of minutes. A fakir, they reported, swallowed grains of sand and blew multitudes of colored crystals from between his lips. An inanimate duck came to life and dove into a pail of water. A magical pitcher changed water from cold to hot, and from hot to cold in an instant. A piece of paper turned into a tiny tent, the tent to a piece of cake. Every visitor, it seemed, had some story to tell of the magic performed by those beggarly-looking jugglers who performed in the street, on a veranda, or anywhere they could earn a few rupees. Rational-minded Europeans were not sure how to accept these wonders, for though they regarded the street folk as simple people, they were faced with mysteries more profound than anything previously seen.

Even in the twentieth century, travelers continued to report the magic of the Indian street magicians. An Englishman saw a Hindu insert a long piece of ribbon into his navel and pull it out through his back. The ribbon was bloody when it emerged. A woman said she saw a juggler place an empty bottle on his arm and concentrate on the bottle as if to hypnotize it. The bottle suddenly shattered and fell from his arm. Before a group of officers, one magician put a gold chain in a piece of paper and threw it across a wide river. He then asked for a piece of bread, and upon breaking it open found the gold chain baked into the center of the loaf. There were also instances where Westerners saw objects, such as a vase or a bunch of bananas, rise into the air without human assistance—a version of the levitation performed with objects rather than human bodies.

Beginning in the 1800s, professional magicians from Europe and America began to investigate techniques used by street magicians in India. They soon learned the sleight of hand involved in the basket trick, mango tree trick, and dozens of similar mysteries. In the process they also discovered a remarkable characteristic of the street conjurers, their willingness to sell tricks. When a sahib (white man) took the jadoo-wallah aside and offered a few rupees for the secrets, the Hindu readily yielded. To modern stage magicians, this practice seemed completely unprofessional. But they did not realize the Indian conjurer had one distinct advantage over the Westerner—he was not worried about the competitive aspects of the performing art. Because of the structure of Hindu society, the conjurer knew the tricks would never be performed by those outside his own caste. And perhaps these street conjurers knew something else about magic. At least unconsciously, they realized that their magic was symbolic rather than secretive. The conjurer was not a sorcerer but a craftsman, and his craft was to show tricks representing an ultimate mystery dealing with human nature itself.

The street conjurers performed with gravity, and this mien helped impress Westerners with the magical quality of their work. Even when doing such common sleights as the cups-and-balls, they evidently did not carry on clever patter or banter with the audience. Some were obviously imitating the fakirs, and they went through the appropriate rituals to simulate trance, meditation, or invocation of the spirits. But they did not want to amuse the audience, for magic itself was a serious matter and they treated it with respect.

One of the strangest traditions in India is the baffling art of snake-charming. The Indian cobra, *naja naja*, has a powerful and deadly venom, is easily irritated, and strikes with lightning quickness. Worst of all, cobras often crawl into Indian houses seeking shelters from

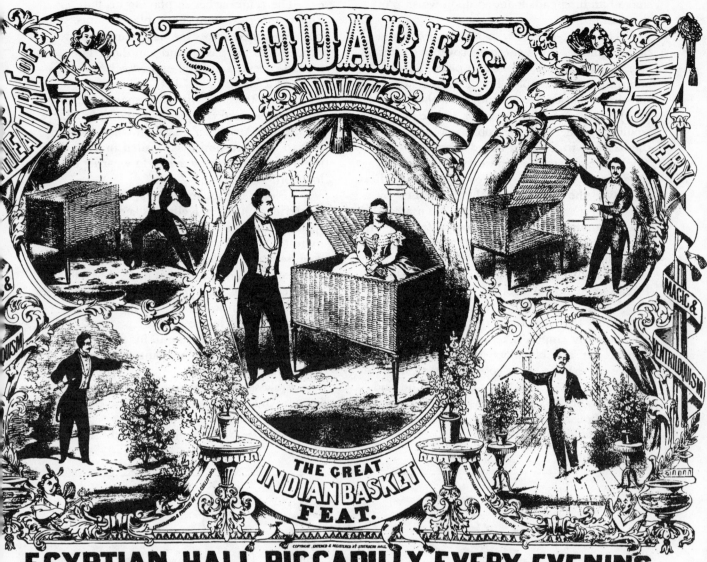

Colonel Stodare's poster, advertising the Indian basket trick. The magician had a long engagement at the Egyptian Hall in London during the 1860s. *(Sheridan Collection)*

the hot sun or monsoon rains, and there they stay, lurking in the darkest corners until aroused.

A full-grown cobra is about five feet long, yellowish or dark brown, and its most distinguishing feature is the spectacled marking on its hood—a black and white pattern that looks almost like a painted skull. When the snake is irritated or prepared to strike, it rises from the ground, rears back, and flares it hood.

Hissing, ready to kill, the creature looks diabolical. Slithering through the sand, gliding into the shade of a veranda, it carries death.

Not surprisingly, the serpent is an object of suspicion, and the subject of much folklore and mythology. Yet Hindu followers consider it a sin to kill cobras, because the creatures are associated with gods. Temples are dedicated to serpents called *Shessha-Nag* and *Basak-Nag,* and there are even rumors of snake-kissing and snake-handling cults founded upon worship of the cobra.

The snake-charmer, or *samp-wallah,* could be recognized by the *pichodi* or covered basket he carried with him from place to place. Snake-charming began simply. The performer would put the basket on the ground, open the cover, and begin playing his flute. For awhile nothing would happen. Then the cobra would rise from the basket with its hood flared, hissing angrily. The snake-charmer, within easy striking distance of the animal, swayed back and forth as he played the flute. Seemingly mesmerised by the conjurer's movement, the snake imitated the swaying motion. The serpent rose to full height, then sank into the basket again, apparently lulled by the sound and motion. The conjurer clapped on the lid. Simple—and only a fellow-Indian knew how dangerous.

Yet there were more risky variations. Sometimes the *samp-wallah's* basket would be unexpectedly empty. Like a prophet of doom he appeared in a public place and warned the people there were many cobras nearby. He would bring the serpents out of hiding, he said, but the people would have to respect the spirit of the cobras and agree not to harm them. His listeners acquiesced.

The conjurer began playing his flute. Snakes emerged from shady places—huts, stones, bushes—glided across the bare, dusty square, slipped into the basket and vanished. The samp-wallah collected his well-earned *baksheesh,* clapped a lid on the basket, and retired.

A few travelers witnessed snake-charming feats that seemed completely impossible. Harry Kellar, the American magician who saw the levitation in Kashmir, was visited in a hotel room in Allahabad by a Hindu wearing only a loincloth and turban.

"Plenty big snake here, sahib," said the mysterious intruder. Kellar looked around the sparsely furnished apartment, but saw nothing more than a rickety cot and a few chairs. The conjurer sat cross-legged in the center of the room and began playing his flute. As Kellar watched, cobras emerged from the corners of the room, glided up to the magician, and surrounded him in the "strike" position. Gradually the Hindu rose to his feet and backed out the door, with the enchanted snakes following close behind.

Professor H.S. Lynn was another well-known American magician who traveled around the world, and he reported his investigations in *The Adventures of the Strange Man,* published 1878.

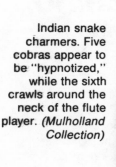

Indian snake charmers. Five cobras appear to be "hypnotized," while the sixth crawls around the neck of the flute player. *(Mulholland Collection)*

Prof. Lynn evidently had a translator, for he recorded every word spoken by the snake charmer.

"Hum jadoogar hai, (I am a conjurer)," said the magician by way of introduction.

After performing a few sleight-of-hand-tricks, the Hindu took up his flute. Then he asked:

"Shall I fetch a snake out of a river, or from the infernal regions, or out of a well, or a mango tree, or out of a snake-hole? Say which."

Before the sahib could make up his mind, the conjurer snatched a young snake out of Professor Lynn's suit pocket. Dropping this snake in a basket, the conjurer then lured another, larger snake by playing his flute. According to Lynn, the large and small snake began to dance together. As the conjurer repeated, "Dekho, dekho, dekho (Look, look, look)," the two snakes turned into one and disappeared.

Stories of this kind were probably accurate. In his recent investigations of Indian tricks, the traveler John Keel learned that the cobra, like most snakes, is stone deaf. The snake is unaffected by the playing of the flute, but it is attentive to any swaying or rhythmic motion. To make the cobra "dance," the snake-charmer swayed back and forth—a motion which of course accompanied the flute-playing. To test his theory, Keel himself tried the trick with permission of a conjurer who loaned both snake and basket for the occasion. Keel found the results were conclusive—the animal responded exactly the same whether or not he played the flute, so long as Keel continued to sway back and forth.

Sometimes the *samp-wallahs* concealed trained snakes near the places where they intended to perform. If undisturbed, the snakes would remain in the shade until they had a signal from the trainer. (In Kellar's story of the incident in Allahabad, the conjurer had probably gone into the hotel room before the magician's arrival.)

Finally, Keel investigated some strange habits attributed to the cobra. He had heard that conjurers sometimes put two snakes in a basket, closed the lid, and then produced a single serpent. Keel learned that it was possible for a large snake to ingest a smaller snake completely. What Professor Lynn witnessed was not so much a miracle as a demonstration of appetite.

When a conjurer was about to perform the mango tree trick, he usually donned the long, plain robe of a holy man and set a small tripod frame on the ground a short distance from the spectators. Casually he picked up the mango seed and, cupping it in his hands, began to murmur some imprecations to *soma*, the god of the plant. Meanwhile an assistant brought forward a long cloth and laid it over the tripod frame. The conjurer prepared a mound of earth, shaped it between his hands, and sprinkled it with water. He made a small depression in the top of the mound, and chanted "Ek, do, tin, char (One, two, three, four)." After which he planted the mango seed and covered it over. The assistant raised the shawl-covered frame and placed this little tent over the mound. Then the conjurer placed both hands inside the shawl—apparently laying his palms on top of the germinating seed—and his eyes clouded over as he went into a trance.

To pass the time, the other troupers did some sleight-of-hand tricks. When their attention returned to the "guru" he removed his hands from the tent, and his assistants lifted the frame away. In a matter of minutes, a plant several inches high had grown up from the seed.

The ritual was repeated in exactly the same way two more times, until the mango tree was about two feet high and sprouting fruit and blossoms. The guru plucked a few of the flowers and one of the small, ripe fruits, and handed them to assistants to distribute among the spectators. As the helpers carried out the holy man's request, they also accepted the alms that he richly deserved.

Many travelers saw the mango tree illusion, and some claimed it was a miracle. Believing the conjurer was a real guru, they thought perhaps he could control the life-force in such a way as to speed up the natural processes. If it were a hoax, they pondered, how could it be done on the ground, in the middle of a circle of spectators? The guru's hands were empty when they entered the tent—and empty when he withdrew them. Furthermore, the onlookers could see he remained perfectly still while the growth took place.

But unfortunately for the mystery, the jadoo-wallah was willing to sell the secret for two or three rupees. To have their curiosity satisfied and to further human enlightenment, a number of magicians paid the bill, including Harry Kellar, H.S. Lynn, Samri Baldwin,

Illustration of the "romance" (left) and "reality" (right) of the mango tree trick, from Samri Baldwin's *The Secrets of Mahatma Land Explained* (1895). *(NYPL Research Division)*

Howard Thurston, and others. As they suspected, the false guru used his long robes to hide mango plants in various stages of growth. Since the young plant is extremely pliable, it could be rolled into a little package and unfurled under cover of the tent. For an added touch, the blossoms and fruit were sometimes made of paper, and assistants could substitute real flora as they passed the flowers among the crowd.

Curiously, one notes a mood of disappointment in reading these magicians' exposés. Of course they had suspected sleight of hand all along. And they wanted to discover the methods. But after all, they had spent their lives dealing with magic and had hoped there might be, in India, some unknown realm to explore. The cloak of mystery fell too easily from the vast sub-continent.

Reverend Hobart Caunter, an Englishman, witnessed a horrifying spectacle which he later described to Thomas Frost, a journalist. The incident—apparently a case of cold-blooded murder—was recorded by Frost in *The Lives of the Conjurers* (1876).

A Hindu, who might have been priest or beggar (Caunter was unable to tell the difference), brought out a lightly woven, wicker basket and held it up for his audience to examine. Then a little girl came forward. She was about eight years old, completely naked, and according to Caunter, "perfect of frame and elastic of limb—a model for a cherub, and scarcely darker than a child of Southern France." The girl stepped into the basket, and the Hindu gently began asking her questions. Evidently he was irritated by her replies, for his voice became increasingly harsh. Finally, in a rage, he seized the tiny child, threw her down in the basket, and began trampling on her. An instant later he leapt out, picked up a sword, and plunged it into the basket. The girl shrieked.

At this point, the Reverend Caunter was almost beside himself. He thought he was watching a maniac, for the Hindu seemed to be in a frenzy. Blood spilled on the ground, the girl sobbed. The good reverend would have rushed forward at once, but the natives all around him watched in stony silence, apparently unmoved by the carnage. Was he hallucinating? Reverend Caunter hesitated a moment.

But it was already too late. The Hindu plunged his sword into the basket again, drawing fresh blood. The shrieks died away. There was silence.

Satisfied, the Indian threw down his sword and peered into the basket. He lifted the basket on its side, then picked it up easily and showed it to the audience. Inside there was nothing.

Some child giggled merrily. From the edge of the crowd, the cherubic little girl—the same girl apparently murdered a moment before—ran forward laughing and shouting. She held out a little cloth bag, pleading for *baksheesh*. And the rupees fell like rain into her hands.

What the good reverend witnessed was neither an hallucination nor a fantasy but one of the standard tricks of the Hindu street conjurers. The secret, of course, was discovered by those relentless magicians of later years who told all. They discovered the wicker basket was complex in its simplicity, for it had a narrow opening and a round-bellied design. Once inside, the child pressed her body against the curved sides where she was totally concealed. As the Hindu plunged his sword through the middle of the basket, he bypassed her body but penetrated little sacks filled with red-dyed liquid.

Reverend Caunter had not noticed, in particular, the loose robe worn by the conjurer. When the Hindu stepped into the basket, the child seized a strap around his waist and hung between his legs where she was concealed under the folds of cloth. While the audience was watching the "murder" take place, the child clung to the magician, screaming piteously. After the screams had died away and the magician had stepped from the basket, the child slipped to the ground and glided unnoticed into the crowd. In other versions of the trick, the child remained concealed in the basket, and it was a twin or a child of the same age who ran in from the audience.

Even professional magicians occasionally saw *jadoo-wallah* tricks that were almost impossible to explain. Samri S. Baldwin, whose stage-name was "The White Mahatma," was familiar with most kinds of stage illusion and sleight of hand when he visited India. But he had trouble explaining "the leaping egg," and finally had to resort to what amounted to brute force in order to learn the method behind the trick.

According to Baldwin, the street magician who called himself a "fakir" carried with him a small, egg-shaped stone he called *Bombay Rawm Sammi*. The mystical stone, he said, was invested with the spirit of a god, and under certain conditions would obey his commands. The fakir then filled a pail with water, sprinkled brick dust on top, and placed *Bombay Rawm Sammi* inside the bucket. He suggested that the spirit would be more cooperative if the rich sahib would give the fakir five rupees. Baldwin did so, and the fakir began chanting. After a couple of minutes, the surface of the water rippled suddenly, and the egg jumped out, landing in the fakir's open hand.

Even when the trick was repeated, Baldwin could not see how it was done. But the next day he accused the fakir of using a thread or horsehair. The juggler was pleased that the

The secret of the basket trick. Lying on his side, the conjurer's assistant could not be seen by the street audience. When the magician plunged his sword through the basket, the blade passed over or under the boy's body. *(NYPL Research Division)*

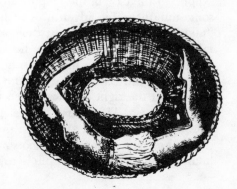

sahib was so far off the mark. In fact he said he would perform the trick again, staying several yards away so there could be no trickery.

This was exactly what Baldwin wanted. When *Bombay Rawm Sammi* had been placed in the water, Baldwin stepped closer to the pail. Before the fakir could stop him, the White Mahatma made his move:

Suddenly, without the slightest warning to the magician, I dashed my hand into the little pail of water and found that I had got hold of something. Just what I could not tell, for the magician himself was naturally very indignant at what was really an unfair action on my part, but my curiosity had got the better part of me. . . .

The magician made a spring for me and for a few seconds it looked as if we might have a life and death tussle. But my interpreter spoke to him rather sharply and said that he was a fool, that I would undoubtedly pay him well as a result of my investigations and he was silly to make a fuss about what, after all, was a very simple matter.

Thus, with my hands still clinched upon the object, so that other onlookers could not see what I was holding, I went into my bedroom accompanied by the fakir himself, and I found that the solution to the marvel was, as in most cases, extraordinarily simple.

In his hands Baldwin found a piece of thin steel curved back to make a spring. It was held in position by a grain of salt. The fakir explained, for a small fee, that the "egg" was placed on top of the spring, and when the salt dissolved *Bombay Rawm Sammi* leapt out of the water. Once again on compatible terms, the Eastern and Western magicians discussed various other aspects of the conjuring arts and parted good friends.

Perhaps it is inevitable that mysterious stories should always emerge from a country like India. Even Baldwin, who proved himself a true skeptic in the case of the leaping stone, records some unfathomable adventures with another "fakir" in Allahabad. On first encounter, the fakir asked Baldwin to remove his shoes, scrutinized them for a moment, and then returned them. Baldwin put on the shoes and found that the right one now fitted the left foot, and vice versa. The fakir took the shoes again, threw them in the air, and when they came down they were several sizes too small. At the fakir's suggestion, Baldwin put a rupee in the toe of each shoe. The shoes fit, and the rupees vanished.

Later Baldwin met the same fakir at the Great Eastern Hotel in Calcutta. The conjurer pointed out that the sahib had put on his waistcoat inside out that morning and had also forgotten to put on his socks. Checking his garb, Baldwin was amazed to see the fakir was right in both observations.

To repair the situation, the magician stretched a handkerchief in front of Baldwin extending from the sahib's chin to his waist, and the waistcoat turned right side out. As for the socks, the fakir said they were now located in a jewel box in the hotel room. When Baldwin queried him, the fakir described the contents of the jewel box in detail. "I was so bewildered," recalled Baldwin, "that for a moment I was fairly staggered. I took my wife and two or three other witnesses into the room and there, stuffed tightly in the box, were the socks which not ten minutes before I could have sworn were upon my feet."

Reverend Hobart Caunter also observed several phenomena which were not explained by later travelers. The minister was approached by a group of conjurers carrying a basket and leading what was described as "a lean, hungry pariah dog." The dog was placed under the basket, the conjurers invoked the spirits, and when the basket was raised, the dog had vanished. In its place was a litter of seven puppies. When covered with the basket again, they all turned into a single goat. The goat changed into a pig. The pig's throat was cut, then it too was dragged under the miraculous basket. The next time the covering was raised, the pig ran out, alive and squealing.

Perhaps Baldwin's and Caunter's stories were both fictional, but judging from their other accounts it is more likely the tales, distorted in the telling, were at least based on true incidents.

Though such magic is rarer in modern times, it seems rash to be totally skeptical. As recently as 1947 the investigator Paul Dare reported the levitation of a vase which occurred "before my very eyes."

The conjurer told Dare to concentrate on a vase that would rise in the air and return to its tray. Dare watched in disbelief as the vase began floating upward.

"I now wish for it to descend," said the

magician, "and to stop for a brief instant."

The vase floated down a few inches, but remained hovering well above the tray. Finally the conjurer asked Dare to cross the room and go near the platter. The sahib complied. The magician said:

"I would like you to put your hand in the center of the empty platter, Sahib."

Dare reached out to the center of the tray. In a place where he saw nothing at all, he felt the side of the pitcher.

The experience has yet to be explained.

Was it a fantasy? Was it hypnotism? An unknown natural law? For centuries people have been asking these questions about the magic of India. In most cases we can say it is only sleight of hand. But the street magic of India is rumor as well as confirmed reality, and the accompanying sense of mystery is something that will never be completely dispelled.

The Indian conjurer Ramo Samee, who made his first appearance on the English stage about 1846. The magician changed the color of sand as it passed between his fingers, cut and restored a thread and performed various juggling feats. He carried a wand resembling a snake, which evidently "came alive" and nipped his assistant on the nose. (Mulholland Collection)

Oriental Fantasies

The magical effects of the Chinese and Japanese conjurers had a poetic beauty quite unlike the style of the East Indian magicians. In both China and Japan there is considerable folklore concerning the first itinerant magicians. In early sketches, they are portrayed in teahouses and private gardens, and they may have gone door-to-door offering their magic, just as other strolling entertainers offered juggling, music, or dance. But as life-styles changed in these Oriental countries during the nineteenth century, the conjurers faded into legend, and their tricks were eclipsed by illusions imported from Europe and America.

Little has been written about street magic in China, but we can find some tricks—later adapted by stage magicians—which may have figured in the early history of that country. Possibly the conjurers in China were never really popular figures, but rather private performers who only appeared before the Khan or in the courts of certain rulers. In visiting one such imperial court, the Chinese author Pu Sing Ling reported he saw a version of the rope trick where the boy climbed the rope and threw down a peach "as large as a basin." When Marco Polo visited the court of Kublai Khan, he reported that all the pitchers moved about as if they were alive, pouring wine, milk, and other beverages for the Khan's guests. A priest, Friar

Odoric, told of similar wonders after his visit to China in 1320. In one court, he said, golden cups flew about in the air and "applied themselves unto men's mouths." The friar also saw "feats ascribed in ancient legends to Simon Magus," such as statues suddenly walking and doors opening apparently of their own volition.

But several tricks that probably originated with Chinese street conjurers have survived to this day. "The linking rings" was a sleight which began with the conjurer displaying a number of unconnected, closed brass rings. After reciting his spell, the magician brought the rings together, linking them in various ways. The illusion was that the rings penetrated each other and then sealed again immediately.

For the "goldfish production," the conjurer began the trick empty-handed, but produced a bowl filled with live goldfish from beneath an empty basket or some other covering. "Freezing water" was a curious sleight that contradicted the senses completely. The magician poured water over his bare hands—or dipped them in a bowl—and the water turned to ice between his fingers. Also, there were various tricks with rice. Some conjurers could serve several helpings of rice from a single bowl, while other Chinese magicians made rice appear to come alive and jump from one hand to the other.

The indefatigable traveler and magician,

Chinese conjurers performing in a village. The troupe included a conjurer who performed the basket trick, and an acrobat who balanced on a pole. Illustration is from a report of the Mission of the East India Company of the United Netherlands to the Tartar and Chinese Kings, published in 1669. *(Library of Congress)*

Chinese beggars performing miraculous feats. From left to right: an escape trick, a fire production and a weight-lifting demonstration. *(NYPL Picture Collection)*

Mendicant priests in China, ca. 1669. As in India, the beggars sometimes pierced their cheeks with needles or performed sleight-of-hand tricks seen as miracles. *(NYPL Picture Collection)*

Animal trainers accompanied troupes of Chinese magicians. Illustration shows giant rats dancing on a stage while the trainer's assistant beats time with a tambourine. *(Library of Congress)*

Oriental version of knife-throwing stunt. Western magicians preferred to use a trick board: a knife popped up from a concealed slot just as the performer pretended to throw a dagger. Inset shows the mechanism. *(Mulholland Collection)*

Dr. Lynn, saw Chinese jugglers cut a man in half with a sword and then restore him to such good health that he danced around the stage. This observation was made, however, toward the end of the nineteenth century, and the division of the corpus may actually have been learned from Western magicians.

Knife-throwing was an act which the Chinese or Japanese probably gave to Western performers. It was more a stunt than a trick. The Oriental knife-thrower hurled a number of daggers at an assistant who stood in front of a board. The performer continued tossing the knives until the assistant's body was completely outlined by the sharp daggers. When imitated in the West, however, the trick was usually done with a "rigged" board equipped with pop-up knives.

In Europe, stage magicians began imitating Chinese tricks almost as soon as they became known. A French magician with the stage name "Phillippe" learned the goldfish production trick from a Chinese juggler who performed in Dublin in 1837, and M. Phillippe made that theatrical item popular in France. Shortly after 1850, the ventriloquist Jacobs improved the fantastical illusion by producing successively three or four glass bowls of water, all containing goldfish. But it was a Chinese conjurer, Tuck Quy, a "chief performer at the Court of Pekin," who drew packed houses at the Drury Lane Theatre in London by performing the knife-throwing feat.

Magic was probably introduced into Japan from China over a thousand years ago, with the first magicians in Japan performing at the roadsides or in the compounds of temples. But the first record of an expert Japanese magician dates from much later, 1670, when Uhon Miyako appeared before the Fourth Shogun. According to a scribe in the Emperor's court, Uhon Miyako gave a varied program of magic, producing three ducks out of an empty basket, changing a yam into an eel, and transforming a picture of a sparrow into a live sparrow.

The twentieth-century magician Ishii Black attempted to trace the origins of some traditional Japanese tricks, and his findings were published in "The Magician" Monthly magazine in 1914. Many of the tricks described by Black were probably performed by wandering magicians in earlier times, though some techniques may have been borrowed from Western performers. The magical effects of the Japanese seem to have required a calm, contemplative style analogous to that of the ancient tea ceremony, in which each gesture and motion was given considered attention. The conjurer often used delicate objects such as fans, eggs, or butterflies—items well-suited for an intimate setting such as a tea garden. Judging from old prints, such magicians appeared frequently at private gatherings when asked to exhibit magic for the benefit of a wealthy man's guests or family.

Black suggests a number of tricks that might have been shown. In one illusion a conjurer placed several eggs one by one on top of a sake bottle, passed a fan over the bottle, and the eggs fell inside. When he broke open the bottle, out flew three or four canaries. Another magician dipped pieces of tissue into a bowl of water, transforming them instantly to the fragile "plum blossoms scattered by the wind." A living Buddha in the Temple of Fujisawa was said to write his name on a single sheet of paper, and it was instantly inscribed on thousands of pages. In the same way a conjurer took dyes of red, blue, green, black, and yellow, and instantly printed thirty pictures of various kinds. A bowl of rice was covered by a second bowl, and the rice doubled in quantity. Covered again, the rice became flowers. With the words, "Go! Vanish!", the magician made rice disappear from a box, and afterward all the guests found a few grains in their clothing.

These tricks could be duplicated by Ishii Black, but there were many other conjuring sleights—once portrayed by Japanese artists— that have never been repeated, and perhaps never will be. The imaginative Japanese artist Katsushika Hokusai made dozens of sketches of the early magicians, illustrations published as woodcuts in Volume X of the *Manga* (1814). According to Japanese folklore, the conjurers were supposed to be able to create extraordinary illusions, and Hokusai shows some conjurers producing little men from a coat sleeve and making sea waves with their hands. If we are to believe the artist, one ancient magician could make his head disappear completely, while another caused his own face to swell by thrusting it into a cloud of smoke. Hokusai also portrayed tricks which may have been common even in his own day, such as sword swallowing, exhaling bees, or changing a piece of paper into

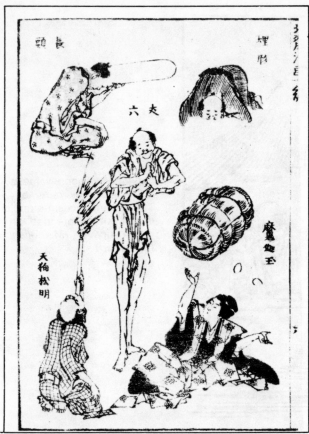

In the *Manga* sketchbooks the Japanese artist Hokusai freely mingled mysterious tricks with impossible illusions. Pages from Book X portray a number of conjurers at work.

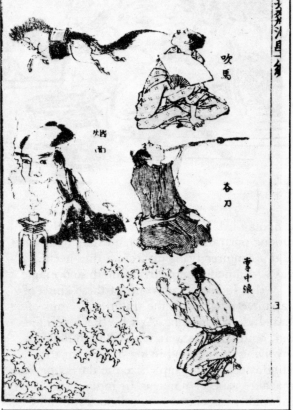

(Above) Exhaling an "energetic horse," creating a "smoke face," swallowing a sword, and making waves with the palms. *(NYPL Prints Division)*

Pages from the *Manga.* Turning a man into a frog, arranging flowers in burning coals and turning paper into a heron. The figure at left is evidently multiplying his own image. *(NYPL Prints Division)*

Japanese villagers witness a Shinto miracle ceremony. The warrior slices the apple in half but his intended victim survives. *(Mulholland Collection)*

a flying bird. But these were mixed freely among portraits of a magician exhaling a horse and a conjurer rising up from a thin-necked vase—a fanciful potpourri of myth and magic.

It is interesting to contrast these kinds of Japanese magic with the traditional forms of East Indian conjuring. As Ishii Black pointed out, both cultures were familiar with illusions involving growth and living things, but the Hindus tended to emphasize the darker or even macabre aspects of magic. In India, magic was invariably associated with religious rites and holy persons, and often attended with fear and superstition. Japanese magic, on the other hand, seems to have been much closer to a theatrical art—closely allied with the symbolic gestures and the traditional patterns of Oriental folk drama. It always held a suggestion of the "Garden of Fantasy," a kind of mystical garden full of delicate creatures, blooming flowers, and sparkling fountains. Many of the tricks expressed extreme subtlety in their form and design.

The exceptions were tricks performed as part of the Shinto miracle ceremonies. As the ancient religion of Japan, Shinto combined the worship of nature with respect for dead heroes and an almost fervent loyalty to the emperor.

Followers of Shintoism were expected to show their courage and loyalty by enduring extreme hardship and danger. One example of the Shinto feats was a decapitation trick done with a genuine *samurai* sword, the deadly weapon used by ancient warriors of Japan. According to the ritual endurance trial, the young warrior knelt on an open platform with hands tied behind his back and neck exposed. The executioner placed a small apple on the warrior's neck—the idea being that a miracle might occur in which the apple protected him from the sword. The blow fell, the apple split in half, but the young warrior survived. It was done by means of a small iron bar inserted in the apple. The iron stopped the blade, then fell to the ground unnoticed as the apple split in two. Nonetheless it was a dangerous trick requiring skill on the part of the executioner and coldblooded courage on the part of the warrior.

But it was not a trick for sleight-of-hand magicians. Through the years, some elements of Shinto rites may have affected the repertoires of Japanese conjurers, but most of them preferred to do harmless sleights with familiar or natural objects. As with other nationalities, the Japanese

In a Japanese house, a magician and his assistant produce a live monkey from one basket and a rice bowl from another. Illustration dates from the eighteenth century. *(Mulholland Collection)*

had their own version of the cups-and-balls. Manipulating little pieces of wadded cloth, they used flattish rice bowls or saucers rather than the usual cups. Instead of the "hocus pocus" pronounced by Western magicians, the Japanese would accompany a transformation with the words, "Na myoho rege kyo." The words are similar to those pronounced in a modern Buddhist temple when one asks to have some wish fulfilled: "Na myo hoo renge kyo."

When performing, the Japanese conjurer would sit on a bamboo mat with his knees tucked underneath, standing only when necessary to perform a particular trick. He kept his paraphernalia in small, lacquered boxes. To one side of the magician sat the *kooken'nin* or assistant, who rarely moved from his station throughout the performance. He was there primarily to amuse the audience, and carried on a continual, humorous conversation with his master. When an aura of ceremony was needed rather than the sound of banter, he would turn to the drum—supported on a stand by his side—and beat it at the appropriate tempo to stir the feelings of his audience.

Sometimes these performances had quite a profound effect on the audience. Some feats of

A female conjurer performs the butterfly trick. The butterfly was made of tissue paper but it fluttered around the fan with lifelike movements. *(Mulholland Collection)*

magic were considered so extraordinary that the Japanese believed there was some kind of deity interfering to help the magician. That deity was called *Inari*, the invisible fox-god, a spirit capable of doing both good and evil. The magician himself was sometimes called *Kitsuri-tsukai*, one who can call upon foxes to do his bidding.

In a visit to Japan in the 1870s, the magician Dr. Lynn met with a number of street magicians in Nagasaki. "I held a reception every morning in my room," he recalled, "at which native jugglers came and taught me many interesting tricks, amongst the others the top-spinning on a single thread and the butterfly trick." The top-spinning was essentially a children's game, but the butterfly trick was an intriguing illusion which was later described in detail by Ishii Black. According to Black, the conjurer usually introduced the trick with a short speech:

"Perhaps of all the creatures of the insect world, there are none so beautiful as butterflies. To see them flying about is a charming spectacle. Unfortunately, we cannot always have them with us, but I will endeavor to create a pair of these delightful creatures for your entertainment this evening.

"I have here a piece of tissue paper which I tear into shape and twist into the form of a butterfly. It quickly comes to life and flies and dances about in the sun."

At St. Martin's Hall, London, a troupe of Japanese jugglers demonstrated the butterfly trick and top-spinning for English audiences. *(NYPL Picture Collection)*

The conjurer fanned the butterfly so that it flew about naturally. Indicating the colorful design on the open fan, he said, "See! The butterfly is attracted by the painted flowers. Being imitation itself, it fancies that the flowers are real. Now, let us procure for him a wife, who shall be his darling."

Beneath the butterfly, the fan stirred lazily, and the fabricated insect rose (apparently of its own volition), fluttered about the magician's head, swooped and turned, and perched on the back of his hand.

Taking up a second piece of tissue, the magician folded it to create a double of the first insect. The "lady" butterfly then joined her mate on the edge of the fan. A moment later, they flew upward, and as the fan followed their movements, they fluttered and dallied with each other as if the flowers and sunlight had actually given them life.

But the lovers were doomed. Despite the breeze from the magician's fan, they wandered away and, tiring, came to rest in a bowl of water. Their fragile wings became wet and heavy, and they sank.

The conjurer waved his fan again. The butterflies rose to the surface. They struggled a moment, fluttered their wings, and took to the air. Again they circled each other. An instant later, they burst into fragments.

Pieces of tissue, like shreds of colored confetti, drifted through the air and lay twinkling, adrift in the bowl of clear water.

In the past, many Japanese conjurers carried with them a pair of wooden ducks that were said to be animated by the spirit of *Inari.* When the magician began his show, he asked an assistant to fill a large bowl with water and bring it to him. This done, he added some fine dust to make the water cloudy. Then he placed the miraculous wooden ducks in the bowl, where they drifted back and forth. From time to time, the magician glanced at the fowl to see whether they had come to life yet, and seeing they were still inert, he stirred the cloudy water so the wooden birds turned about in the current. Finally, when he had finished all other tricks, the conjurer gently lifted the ducks from the water and held them cupped in his hands.

"Behold," said the magician, "these ducks are carved from wood, yet they are endowed with the spirit of life."

He gave the pair to the nearest spectator, and the fragile carved animals were passed from hand to hand among the guests. But even with the closest scrutiny, no one could find anything unusual about the little models. They were returned to the magician.

With great care he placed the two ducks on the water. They floated away from his fingertips, bobbing slightly in the cloudy ripples.

But their lifeless motion was misleading. The magician backed away, his magic fan outstretched. Without changing his attitude, the magician spoke to his honored host, asking him to come forward and lay his hand on the magical birds. The master of the house rose to his feet, bowed, and silently moved forward to carry out the conjurer's wish. He reached for one of the ducks. The shadow of his hand crossed the water. The next instant, a look of bafflement came into his face, and his guests began talking excitedly. The ducks had disappeared—vanished into the cloudy water.

The host pulled back his hand. An instant later, the ducks bobbed to the surface.

With the permission of the conjurer, the host invited his guests forward to touch, if they could, the mystery. With each one it was the same. The ducks dived as soon as any hand approached them and came to the surface only when the threat had passed.

When each guest had tried his luck, the magician himself plunged his hands into the water and seized the magical birds as they dived. Under the water there was a moment's struggle, as though he had to wrest them forcefully from the hands of the spirit, but seconds later he brought them up, dripping wet and glistening. He handed the ducks to his host, who hesitantly accepted the precious birds. Then the magician signaled his *kooken'nin* to empty the water bowl. The assistant lifted the porcelain container, bowed to the guests, and carried the bowl to a nearby stream.

But he did not empty the bowl immediately. First he examined the edge until he found the place where two horsehair threads were attached firmly with pieces of gum. The *kooken'nin* glanced over his shoulder. Certain no one was watching, the magician's apprentice pulled the strings, bringing up two lively, wriggling fish tied by their tails. The *kooken'nin* dropped them into a small container filled with clear water. He watched them a moment, teased them by passing his hand back and forth over the water. Every time the shadow of his hand passed over the fish, they dove in fear—exactly as they had done when the strings were attached to the necks of the model ducks. The assistant sealed the container and slipped it into a hidden pocket in his robe. Then, carrying the empty bowl, he returned to the magician's side.

As is already apparent, water was an important element in many of the tricks of Japanese magicians. In the butterfly mystery, the creatures were evidently attracted to the water, but it was their grave in the end. For the model ducks water was simply the most natural element, the place where one would expect to find the birds paddling and diving. But a completely foreign quality of water was suggested by another trick, "the feast of lanterns." In this instance water had the

Surrounded by wares of his trade, a Japanese magician produces a ribbon from the palm of his hand. Toy animals, parasols and live goldfish were standard props. (Mulholland Collection)

opposite and apparently antagonistic quality of being able to produce fire.

A plain porcelain bowl was passed from hand to hand for inspection, then returned to the conjurer, who filled the bowl with water. The magician waved his fan twice over the bowl, then laid the fan aside and pulled up his sleeves. He plunged his hands in the water. When he withdrew them, there was a small, fragile object cupped between his palms.

He spread his fingers to reveal a small Japanese lantern, a delicate ornament made of thin paper and split bamboo. As the guests watched, a tiny flame began to flicker inside the lantern. It glowed steadily with an ever-increasing fire. With still dripping hands, the magician handed the burning lantern to the *kooken'nin,* who hooked it on a string.

The feat was repeated until there were eleven lanterns, each glowing brightly, strung on a single line. The conjurer declared the next lantern would be the last, for the water had been depleted of its fire. But as he raised the final lantern from the bowl, he saw there was no flame inside. He turned to the guests.

"I have succeeded in producing from this bowl of water eleven lighted lanterns," he explained, "but the twelfth is not burning. The water has robbed me of the last spark which I had intended for this lantern. Now I will see if it is still possible to regain the light."

Handing the lantern to his assistant, the magician searched in one of his lacquered boxes until he found a long piece of tissue. He folded the paper several times until it was stiff and thin as a stick. Then he dipped one end until it just touched the surface of the water.

The tissue burst into flame.

"The water has restored that which it had stolen," said the conjurer. He placed the burning tissue in a dry bowl and let it burn away to ashes. Gathering the ashes in his hand, he lifted them above the lantern. When he spread his fingers, the black ash drifted down over the paper ornament.

"Burn," he commanded.

The wick inside the lantern instantly caught fire.

The fan too was an important agent in Japanese magic, taking the place of the wand used in Western countries. Painted with elaborate designs, gilding, and symbols, it was an object the magician always carried in his hand. And for him it could apparently perform miracles. With only a fan, the conjurer could transform a mere scrap of paper into a genuine egg, the source of life itself.

The magician spread the fan. He unwrapped a plain sheet of tissue and tore out a small circle of paper which he crumpled between his fingers.

An assistant brought forward a finger bowl filled with water. The magician dipped the crumpled ball of tissue into the finger bowl, then quickly raised it again. He tossed the damp wad onto the fan, rolled it backwards, forwards, and sideways along the gilded horizon of the fan's border.

He tossed the wad upward. Already it was growing larger.

Briskly, the paper bounced back and forth on the side of the fan, ever-moving and slowly expanding. As it became larger, it seemed also to become lighter. Now it hovered for an instant before floating down. The creases vanished. The object took on shape and recognizable form—the form of a hen's egg.

The motion of the fan ceased. The egg rested lightly on the rice paper, trembling as though about to vanish.

The magician took the egg in hand and passed it to the honored guests. What they handled was not a scrap of paper, nor even a hollow shell. As they could see, and feel, it was a genuine egg—a mystery created before their very eyes.

The magician turned from his audience and opened one of his precious lacquer boxes. As he did so, a small crumpled object slipped from the palm of his hand and fell into the box. It was a thin, creased membrane—the kind of membrane that lined the inside of an egg. When dry, the membrane filled easily with air, the creases vanished, and it resembled exactly a hen's egg. Moistened, it could be formed into a little wad, indistinguishable from a piece of crumpled, wet tissue.

Jugglers, Mountebanks
and Necromancers

The search for street magic takes us once again into the distant past, to the Middle Ages when sturdy jugglers and footloose conjurers roamed the continent of Europe and the British Isles. Many of their tricks resembled those of Oriental magicians, though it is unlikely that there was any direct interaction between conjurers of those two distant cultures until the seventeenth or eighteenth centuries. But it is interesting that similar tricks were developed by street magicians of both East and West—an indication that the fascination with their form of conjuring was universal. The early European street conjurer was an immensely popular entertainer who tried to amuse and please people with his juggling and sleight of hand. In early references these showmen were always called "jugglers" rather than "conjurers," since the latter term was reserved for those who supposedly practiced occult magic or had the help of the devil. Even as late as 1721, a dictionary still defined a conjurer as "one who is supposed to practice the vile arts of raising spirits and conferring with the devil." Because of the influence of the Church's teachings and the importance of the "devil" in the minds of many superstitious believers, the harmless sleight-of-hand performer sometimes was suspected of being a sorcerer, wizard, alchemist, or witch.

Apparently people of the Middle Ages had ambivalent feelings about the jugglers who strolled the countryside. Their performances were usually welcomed as entertainment, but their methods and supposed practices were, on occasion, condemned. Streets were named after them, statues were erected in their honor, yet they were at times forbidden by churchmen or magistrates to perform in certain cities.

Many jugglers were part of troupes that included contortionists, acrobats, musicians, jesters, and mimes. Undoubtedly the jugglers formed a sort of informal guild for keeping the secrets of their arts to themselves. To be on the safe side, they told their secrets occasionally to a magistrate or priest, in order to escape charges of witchcraft, but they usually protected themselves by playing the roles of buffoons and jesters.

For the juggler the street was a lively stage, where he could set up his props and offer spectators numerous surprises and wonders. In medieval towns and cities, the streets were a center of social and commercial life, the scene of bustling activity. Certain streets would be reserved for tradespeople, merchants, and artisans who set up their stalls and cried out their offers. In Paris there were streets named "Rue des Jouglers" and "Rue de St. Julien des Ménétriers," reserved for the sleight-of-hand

An Italian mountebank selling quack medicines. Typically, the charlatan was accompanied by clowns and jugglers who amused the crowd and encouraged people to buy his potions. Oratory was mixed with sleight-of-hand tricks. *(NYPL Picture Collection)*

48 • Street Magic

performer and other showmen. And a street in
Liverpool, England, still bears the name of the
Juggler.

At the same time, Catholic clergy
denounced the illusionists' profession. In a
sermon delivered in 1150, St. Bernard said, "A
man fond of jugglers will soon enough possess a
wife whose name is Poverty. If it happens that
the tricks of jugglers are forced upon your
notice, endeavour to avoid them, and think of
other things. The tricks of jugglers never please
God." During the twelfth century jugglers were
forbidden to reside in certain French cities, and
by 1250 Louis IX had attempted to drive out of
the country all of the "tumblers and players of
sleight of hand . . . through whom many evil
habits and tastes have become engendered in
the people." Two centuries later, the edicts of
Pope Innocent still enjoined the jugglers to "do
their spiriting gently."

But sleight of hand continued to be a
highly popular entertainment, and jugglers were
not discouraged by official edicts. Many of them
accompanied troubadours or minstrels as they
traveled from place to place.

Jongleurs or *joglars* were the French jugglers
who often traveled with troubadours in Provence
and northern Italy. In addition to their skill
with legerdemain, the jongleurs could walk on
their hands, juggle knives, and imitate bird
songs. By the thirteenth century there were
French *trasgeters* or *tregetours,* who performed
juggling feats and also demonstrated
automata—such as talking heads, singing birds,
and mechanical fish.

Without a fixed patronage, troupes of
players would travel from one castle to the next,
offering their entertainment to the lords and
ladies within. Such amusements must have been
a welcome distraction. At night, while there was
feasting and revelry, the jongleur added to the
entertainment with his feats of sleight of hand
and other extraordinary illusions. By day, the
jongleurs and troubadours played their
instruments and sang at the request of the
knights and ladies.

Then, with the permission of the liege, or
lord, the troupe was free to perform for the
peasants and townspeople nearby. A stage might
be set up on the village green, and a herald or
crier would announce the coming attractions.
Undoubtedly, it was a festive occasion when the
peasants could take a few hours from their

labors to enjoy the fare of the entertainers.

In northern France and the Anglo-Saxon
countries, the minstrels or gleemen had
performing troupes similar to those of the
troubadours. The minstrels also performed
legerdemain, and one advertised, "Well know I
the cork ball, and to make the beetle come alive
and dancing on the table; and so I know many
a fair table game the result of dexterity and
magic—I know how to play with the cutlasses
and with the card and rope." From this account,
we can surmise that he knew cups-and-balls
tricks and probably used the beetle for the final
"production." If he was also familiar with card
tricks and rope tricks, as he claimed, the
minstrel had a repertoire almost as complete as
a modern magician's.

In addition, the tregetours and minstrels
may have understood some principles of
acoustics, optics, and chemistry—principles
which they applied effectively in creating
illusions. One fanciful description of a tregetour's
"scientific" illusion is included by Chaucer in
"The Franklin's Tale," written in the late
fourteenth century. In the tale a man recalls
that "there are sciences by which men create
diverse appearances such as the tregetours
play." He then recalls that tregetours made
water come into a large hall and produced a
barge which rowed up and down on the "lake."
Other visions resembled a fierce lion, flowers in
a meadow, vines with white and red grapes, and
a castle made of limestone. At the bidding of the
tregetour, all these scenes would supposedly
disappear in an instant.

It is possible that the description is based
upon fact—that the illusions were created by
some ingenious tregetours using optical devices
known at the time. And their secrets may have
passed on through generations of jugglers and
conjurers down to magicians of the present day.

By the early fifteenth century, jugglers of
another class could be found on the street
corners of most European cities. These were the
charlatans or mountebanks, who tried to sell
healing drugs and quack remedies to pedestrians
who stopped to watch their show. Often, their
sleight of hand was only an advertisement to
suggest the magical qualities and the amazing
benefits of the secret potions they sold.

Today the words "mountebank" and
"charlatan" have connotations of deceit and
chicanery. But the words themselves have

131

A troupe of wandering entertainers, including tightrope performers, contortionists and a cups-and-balls conjurer. Illustration is from the *Orbis Sensualium Pietus*, published in 1657. (Mulholland Collection)

innocent origins. Mountebank, derived from the Italian, means literally "to mount a bench." And the Latin root of "charlatans" means "to draw a group together." Originally, then, these street performers were simply jugglers who mounted a platform or gathered together an audience.

The words came to be used in a disparaging sense because many of the jugglers claimed to be physicians or healers. Often their medicines were harmless mixtures or compounds, but it is likely that some of their potions contained alchohol, opium, or cannabis, which would produce a narcotic effect on any takers.

Usually the charlatan would offer the elixirs at a cut-rate price—as a special favor to his audience. For a few pennies, he claimed, you could buy an elixir that would assure you of living to a ripe old age. A second nostrum, he swore, would give you unparalleled sexual powers to enliven the endless years to come.

Many spectators would purchase these goods. But by the time the aspiring Don Juans had paid for their bottles, downed the contents,

and gone to bed with spouse or lover, the charlatan had left town. Any complaints could be referred straight to the devil.

In 1608 an English traveler and raconteur, Thomas Coryat, saw some typical Italian mountebanks performing in the streets of Venice. Coryat was impressed by the loquaciousness and dexterity of these performers, and he later described his encounter in a chapter of a travelogue entitled *Coryat's Crudities*.

The mountebanks had set up five or six stages in the Piazza della San Marco—the main square in the heart of Venice. Evidently, their shows were only given at specified times, for Coryat mentions that their platforms were set up once in the morning and again in the afternoon. In addition to the stage performers, there were mountebanks "of the poorer sort," who always performed at street level.

Each of the on-stage mountebanks had a trunk filled with various scientific-looking devices and odd bottles of potions. Some wore masks or vizards and were dressed up as character actors, and Coryat noted that some of the mountebanks were women. Then he

''The Juggler,'' a painting by Hieronymus Bosch (1450-1516). While the magician performs cups-and-balls, a pickpocket lifts the purse of a spectator and a ''familiar'' peers out of the magician's basket. *(Mulholland Collection)*

described their show:

After they are all upon the stage, the musicke begins. Sometimes vocall, sometimes instrumentall, and sometimes both together. This musicke is a preamble and introduction to the ensuing matter: in the meane time while the musick playes, the principall mountebank which is the Capitaine and ringleader of all the rest, opens his truncke and sets abroach his wares; after the musicke hath ceased, he maketh an oration to the audience of halfe an houre long, or almost an houre. Wherein he doth most hyperbolically extoll the vertue of his drugs and confections . . . though many of them are very counterfeit and false.

Coryat was amazed by the "elegant jests and witty conceits" spoken by these mountebanks, and he noticed that many in the audience were lured into buying their wares—which were "oyles, soveraigne waters, amorous songs printed, apothecary drugs, and a Commonweale of other trifles." The chief mountebank began to distribute the commodities, while others in his company continued to mime and play music. Every time the "ringleader" handed out another potion, he would give a short speech—and he must have been an excellent orator, for Coryat estimated there were more than a thousand people in the audience. But the best of the show was yet to come. Coryat continues:

I have observed marveilous strange matters done by some of these Mountebanks. For I saw one of them holde a viper in his hand, and play with his sting a quarter of an houre together, and yet receive no hurt; though another man should have beene presently stung to death with it . . . .

Also I have seene a Mountebank hackle and gash his naked arme with a knife most pitifully to beholde, so that the blood hath streamed out in great abundance, and by and by after he hath applied a certaine oyle unto it, wherewith he hath incontinent both stanched the blood and so thoroughly healed the woundes and gashes, that when he hath afterward shewed us his arme againe, we could not possibly perceive the least token of a gash.

Healing a hackled arm was obviously a powerful advertisement for the mountebank's "oyles and soveraigne waters." But by the early 1600s, when Coryat witnessed this performance, there were probably mountebanks throughout Europe who could perform similar feats.

Coryat's description is also interesting in that it points to the connection between primitive magic and the theater arts. Essentially, the mountebank reverted to a role of physician or healer analagous to the witch doctor of primitive times. To some of the more superstitious watchers, it must have seemed like genuine sorcery when that Venetian miracle worker stabbed his arm fiercely enough to draw blood, and then healed it again.

But we also see in this act the beginnings of genuine theater arts. As noted by Coryat, many in the mountebank's group wore masks and acted out certain roles, while the mountebank's performance included songs, music, and orations. From this kind of play-acting was derived the Commedia dell'Arte or Comedy of Masks, a form of theater-in-the-street which was immensely popular in Renaissance Italy. Jugglers and conjurers often played important parts in these comedies, acting as stock characters or helping to create illusions.

In any mime performance, there are elements of magical illusion, for the mimist tries to create the impression that he or she is dealing with invisible objects. Sometimes this impression—or suggestion—can be so strong that it seems to the audience as though the object actually exists. A magician is doing much the same thing when he pretends to hold an object in his hand but transfers it secretly to his pocket. As long as he pretends to hold the object, the audience will still believe it is there. Only when the magician opens his hand—that is, stops miming—does the audience realize that the object is gone. In effect, it has vanished.

Most street magicians in medieval Europe were regarded as sleight-of-hand performers and nothing more. But there were cases when their nimble tricks were confused with genuine sorcery, and the performers were called literally "magicians"—that is, necromancers, sorcerers, or wizards. In fact, long after the fifteenth century, generally regarded as the end of the "Dark Ages," there were still many people who believed that sleight-of-hand artists had the power of sorcerers.

Magic itself was more than a scattering of irrational beliefs or superstitions. Rather, it was a complete system of concepts which were recognized by many but understood only by a few. Magic was a part of religion, nature, society, and the mysteries of the universe. As in primitive times, magic was a part of daily life, and spirits or demons often were said to lend their will to natural occurrences. When these occurrences were disasters—causing injury, sickness, or death—the people tried to find the witch or sorcerer who had caused the evil. Naturally, sleight-of-hand performers sometimes fell under suspicion.

On the other hand, a performer with some knowledge of the art of illusion could sometimes convince a spectator that he had magical powers—and could profit from the deception.

One example of such a deception was recounted by a sixteenth-century goldsmith, Benvenuto Cellini, in his *Autobiography*. In this case the conjurer was a Sicilian priest who claimed to be a necromancer, one who reveals the future by communicating with the spirits of the dead.

To carry out his spirit-raising, the priest led Cellini to the Roman Colosseum where the ghosts and demons were said to congregate. Cellini was asked to bring along drugs, perfumes, and fire, while the necromancer decked himself in long, flowing robes. After pronouncing some incantations, the necromancer drew a circle on the ground and led Cellini into this magical area. For awhile, the priest continued his exhortations and the goldsmith tended the fire, tossing on herbs and perfumes until clouds of fragrant smoke rose in the air. According to Cellini, "This lasted more than an hour and a half; when several legions appeared, and the Colosseum was all full of devils." Cellini, at the behest of the priest, called out to the devils, but they did not respond.

Some time later there was a second rendezvous which again took place in the Colosseum. At this séance Cellini was accompanied by two friends and a young boy from his shop. Once again, the fire was started, and the pungent smoke billowed up into the night. Then, "the necromancer began to utter those awful invocations, calling by name on multitudes of demons who are captains of their legions, and these he summoned by the virtue

Frivolity, wizardry and profit-making share the scene in this unusual portrait of an *escamoteur* published in 1861. Props included everything from a black kettle to a jack-in-the-box, and an assistant collected money in a tambourine. *(NYPL Picture Collection)*

and potency of God, the Uncreated, Living, and Eternal, in phrases of the Hebrew, and also of the Greek and Latin tongues; insomuch that in a short space of time the whole Colosseum was full of a hundredfold as many [devils] as had appeared upon the first occasion." While his friends tended the fire, Cellini conversed with the devils—successfully this time—and then the necromancer tried "with mild and soft persuasions to dismiss them." However, it was nearly dawn before the devils dispersed—and not until then did Cellini and his friends dare leave the powerful circle. Cellini describes their departure:

When the necromancer had concluded his ceremonies, he put off his wizard's robe, and packed up a great bundle of books which he had brought with him; then, all together, we issued with him from the circle, huddling as close as we could to one another, especially the boy, who had got into the middle, and taken the necromancer by the gown and me by the cloak. All the while that we were going toward our houses in the Banchi, [the boy] kept saying that two of the devils he had seen in the Colosseum were gambolling in front of us, skipping now along the roofs and now upon the ground. The necromancer assured me that, often as he had entered magic circles, he had never met with such a serious affair as this.

It is obvious throughout Cellini's description that the priest played his role according to what was expected of a necromancer of that age. He donned the robes of a wizard, chanted magical incantations, and used smoke and fire to bring out the devils. We do not know for sure how the priest managed to produce the illusion of devils dancing in the Colosseum and gambolling through the streets, but it is quite possible that he employed an early form of the magic lantern or some such optical device. Or it may have been the power of suggestion which influenced the imaginations of the goldsmith and his friends. Whatever the secret, it is clear that Benvenuto Cellini was thoroughly taken in by the necromancer's deceptions.

In such ways many charlatans took advantage of people's beliefs and superstitions. There were probably numerous charlatans who posed as alchemists and claimed to hold the secret to the Philosopher's Stone, which would turn lead into gold. The typical alchemist was a kind of pseudo-scientist who worked with scales, measures, beakers, and crucibles, and derived his inspiration from dusty books filled with magical formulae. It was believed that he could do wonderful things simply because he knew the secret workings of nature.

As the common mountebank became more sophisticated, he may have learned tricks which resembled the arts of the alchemist. For example, he could make water change color by adding a few drops of clear liquid, or he could change a small piece of lead into gold, merely with a pass of his hand. Some sleight-of-hand performers even dressed in bizarre clothing associated with the alchemists—such as black robes and peaked caps—and carried with them large tomes which presumably held the secrets to their "scientific" magic.

Eventually, these alchemist-magicians hit upon the idea of selling the books or pamphlets which were supposed to contain all their secrets. In their final "pitch" for a sale, they could claim that their books revealed profound mysteries, including the key to the ancient arcana. Many spectators, after seeing the amazing performance of the wizard, must have paid high prices, believing that the alchemist's knowledge of the universe was contained in such volumes.

Witchcraft was a field of "black magic" which preoccupied people of the Middle Ages even more than necromancy and alchemy. Black magic, as in tribal society, was considered to be evil carried out in concert with the devil and his helpmates. "White magic," the working of miracles or good deeds, was supposedly the exclusive domain of the Church and her saints. As mentioned previously, the Church often accused sleight-of-hand performers of practicing witchcraft. Also persecuted were the healers and fortune-tellers called "cunning men" who were found in most towns and villages.

The leaders of the Church may have had a special interest in persecuting the jugglers who roamed the street selling natural wonders, for the power of the Church relied upon the submission of every person to the all-knowing and all-seeing God, whose greatest enemy was the Devil. According to this dogmatic concept of the supernatural, the only true miracles were those performed by the blessed or sainted. Whatever was inexplicable could be attributed to God or the Devil, and should be left to the Holy Church to praise or condemn. Yet the clever jugglers seemed to flaunt their skills in defiance of this dogma. They went among the public pretending that magic was only for entertainment, and they peddled their wonders without the direct assistance of God.

It is easy to see how the superstitious could confuse the works of the jugglers with genuine witchcraft. Witches, according to medieval lore, were said to be accompanied by little spirits with mousy bodies and semi-human faces called "imps" or "familiars," and these spirits were supposed to do their bidding. The familiars were actually assistants of the devil, and they could cause blight, injury, sickness, or death. Also,

Visited by a wealthy patron, an alchemist shows proof of his success in turning lead into gold. Many charlatans, pretending to have such powers, used sleight-of-hand methods of substitution. *(NYPL Picture Collection)*

witches were believed to have the secrets to magic potions which were made by stirring together noxious substances on moonless nights.

Obviously, the collections of potions carried by the mountebank could be just as impressive as those supposed to belong to witches. And baffling sleight-of-hand vanishes were easily

explained if one only assumed that there were unseen imps or familiars who helped make things appear or vanish. Or so it would seem to a superstitious observer.

It is impossible to surmise how many sleight-of-hand artists were unjustly accused of being witches or how many were punished, but there must have been frequent confusion in the minds of judges, clerics, and peasants. In the late fifteenth century, for example, a girl in Cologne was charged with witchcraft for having "in the presence of a great company of noble spectators" torn a handkerchief into pieces and then restored it again. Whether she was sentenced to death is not known. But her conjuring was obviously done by sleight of hand. To this day the trick can be performed without any assistance from imps.

Such accusations of witchcraft must have been distressing to rational-minded individuals who understood how such conjuring was actually done. One of the more sane observers was Roger Bacon, a thirteenth-century friar and philosopher with an unquenchable curiosity about magic. In his studies of science and religion, he arrived at the conclusion that "whatever is beyond the ordinary course of nature or art is either superhuman or a pretense, and (if a pretense) full of fraud, for there are men who create illusions by rapidity of the movements of their hands, or by the assumption of various voices, or by ingenious apparatus, or by performing in the dark, or by means of confederacy, thus showing to men many wonderful things which do not exist." Bacon was referring to nimble jugglers when he wrote of "men who create illusion," but unfortunately many of his contemporaries did not share the philosopher's rational views on conjuring.

The persecution of accused witches may have reached its peak during the latter sixteenth and early seventeenth centuries, but the witch hunts were only the culmination of centuries of prejudice and superstition. Throughout Europe and the British Isles, especially during the plague years, witches were hunted down and tried. If found guilty, they were hanged, drowned, or burned at the stake.

One English observer, Reginald Scot, attended some of the trials, and was horrified to see many women accused of witchcraft for

"Saint Jacques and the Magician Hermogenes" by Pieter Bruegel the Elder. Dated 1565, this work is an extraordinary catalogue of the tricks performed by medieval jugglers and attributed to their diabolical "familiars." While the mild-looking juggler practices cups-and-balls, imps and fiends do madcap tricks with knives, fire, swords, eggs, plates and brooms. Many of these acts, including the decapitation (lower left) were described by Reginald Scot in *The Discoverie of Witchcraft*. *(Bibliothèque royale, Bruxelles)*

performing sleight of hand. Scot was a country gentleman and justice of the peace, and he was present at the Assize in Rochester, England, when Margaret Simons was convicted on a charge of witchcraft. Believing that the woman had been unjustly accused, Scot tried to clear up misunderstandings about witches by writing a treatise on the subject. Published in 1584, this treatise was called *The Discoverie of Witchcraft*.

The *Discoverie* was one of the first books to provide a complete and serious description of the sleights then practiced by street conjurers.

As far as we know, Scot had no first-hand experience with conjuring, but he consulted as his authority John Cautares, a Frenchman then living in London. Cautares was described as "a matchless fellow for legerdemain," having "the best hand for conveyance, I think, of any man that liveth this day."

In his chapter on "The Art of Juggling Discovered," Scot provided illustrations as well as details of dozens of tricks. These were legitimate, claimed Scot, as long as they "were not used to harm thy neighbor or to prophane the name of God . . . " He continued:

Many virtues have been abused as much by untrue reports as by illusions and practices of legerdemain, etc. . . .

Such are the miracles wrought by jugglers, consisting in fine and nimble conveyance, called legerdemain: as when they seem to cast away or to deliver to another that which they retain in their own hands; or convey otherwise; or seem to eat a knife; or some such other thing, when indeed they bestow the same secretly into their bosoms or laps. Another point of juggling is when they thrust a knife through the brain and head of a chicken or pullet and seem to cure the same with words—which bird would live and do well if never a word were spoken. Some of these toys also consist in arithmetical devices, partly in experiments in natural magic, and partly in private as also in public confederacies.

Scot argued there were many extraordinary events that could not be explained by the man in the street, but it was not wise to assume that these events were magical or miraculous. "For," he wrote,"if we shall yield that to be divine, supernatural and miraculous which we cannot comprehend, then a witch, papist, conjurer, cozener, and juggler can all make us believe they are gods; or else with more impiety we shall ascribe such power and omnipotency unto them, or unto the devil, as only and properly appertaine to God."

King James I, the same King who authorized a new version of the Bible, could not tolerate the open skepticism expressed in the *Discoverie.* Even as witchcraft trials continued, James I ordered all copies of the book to be seized and burned by the common executioner. And the texts that escaped the conflagration were sometimes misused to prove rather than disprove the guilt of witches.

The Discoverie of Witchcraft was important in clarifying the distinction between the work of the juggler and the work of the devil, and may have saved some innocent conjurers from persecution. It did not, of course, put an end to superstition—for that has survived in everchanging forms to the present day. But it did suggest how one might perform many kinds of conjuring tricks, and the techniques described by Scot were used by many jugglers who wandered Europe and visited the great fairs during later years.

Wandering Magicians and Their Arts

he tricks first described by Reginald Scot in *The Discoverie of Witchcraft* soon became a part of nearly every conjurer's repertoire. During the two hundred years following its publication, conjurers also began to invent new illusions which would eventually have their hour upon the stage. And as people became more familiar with the methods as well as the habits of the conjurer, his status in society gradually improved.

Yet still there were risks for those who openly practiced magic. Sometime after 1560, when Charles IX was king of France, a juggler named Triscalinus appeared in the royal court to give a command performance. In the course of one trick, Triscalinus caused some rings to fly from the fingers of a courtier to the juggler's own hand. According to a member of the court, the entire company rose up against the unlucky (but talented) conjurer and made him confess that he had enlisted the aid of Satan.

In other instances, jugglers were persecuted because they were simply considered undesirables. In 1571 a juggler in Paris was imprisoned for nothing worse than doing a few card tricks in the street. The following year in England, Parliament decreed that "fencers, bear-leaders, common players, minstrels, and jugglers that wandered abroad without license from two justices of the peace at least should be taken, adjudged, and deemed Rogues, Vagabonds, and Sturdy Beggars." Judging from the language of the law, the complaint against "minstrels and jugglers" at that period was an objection to their living habits rather than their witchcraft.

In a popular jingle published about the same time, the acts of the minstrels were depicted as being so offensive that Jesus, as well as Parliament, disapproved. The rhyme contained some curious anachronisms and went like this:

> *When Jesus went to Jairus' house*
> *(Whose daughter was about to die),*
> *He turned the minstrels out of doors,*
> *Among the rascal company:*
> *Beggars they are with one consent,*
> *And rogues by Act of Parliament.*

Such "rogues" faced daily the danger of being placed in the stocks, tied to a whipping post, or thrown into prison.

The jugglers of that era were easily recognized by their costumes and accouterments. Many street magicians of the seventeenth century wore pocket aprons made of leather, tied around the waist. In the open purse or large pocket in front of the apron, the juggler placed the objects needed for his performance.

In Paris, nineteenth-century street magicians set up their tables in many of the squares and parks to practice their conjuring arts. Scene is Place de la Bastille on a Sunday afternoon in 1825. *(Sheridan Collection)*

The ragged-looking magician earned only a few shillings a day from his street performances. English law considered him a "Rogue" or "Sturdy Beggar." (Mulholland Collection)

Since he acted from a standing position and could be seen from every side, the conjurer used this device to hide the "loads" prepared for his illusions, or to get rid of objects which were supposed to "vanish." In France a word was even invented to describe this pocket apron—the *gibecière*.

In European dress of the sixteenth and seventeenth centuries, it was typical for men to wear a large flap or "codpiece" to cover up the opening in the front of their breeches. Some jugglers also used the codpiece as a place to dispose of their wares, though they must have looked rather peculiar producing cups and balls from the front of their breeches. Also used by the Anglo-Saxon juggler was the "budget," simply a small pouch or bag made of leather and hung from the belt. The English expression "a bag of tricks" probably referred to this accouterment of the street magician.

Later, conjurers gave up the leather aprons and budgets when they began using small tables to hold their tricks and devices. The portable folding table was equipped with a small bag or sack called a "servante" which swung easily in and out at waist level, but was unseen by the audience. Often the street magician would cover this table with a cloth, permitting him to hide fairly large objects beneath it.

Over the centuries, the style of dress changed along with the mode of presentation of the street conjurers. The costume originally worn by the medieval jugglers was indistinguishable from that of a tumbler, acrobat, or jester. A typical Italian juggler might wear brightly colored silks with a checkered or striped bodice, tight leggings, shoes with pointed toes, and a floppy cap. Sometimes strings of bells were tied around the ankles or sewn into his clothing, and their jangling helped announce his presence on the street. The Anglo-Saxon dress was simpler, consisting of a short jerkin with a collar, leggings, and slippers that tied around the ankles. In early prints and drawings, jugglers were sometimes depicted with a few buttons or ornaments attached to their clothing.

Some of the wizard-like costumes worn by the medieval charlatans and mountebanks were adopted by itinerant conjurers who later attended the fairs in Germany, France, and England. Like fortune-tellers, priests, and necromancers, these conjurers made their presence more imposing and added a sense of mystery to their shows by wearing long, dark robes. Occult signs and symbols were woven into their gowns in gold braid.

Up to the eighteenth century, the typical French conjurer wore a distinctive costume which was rather dilapidated, but colorful. One contemporary description of a juggler named William Cuckoe is quoted in *The Annals of Conjuring,* by Sidney Clarke. Cuckoe was portrayed as "an old fellow, his beard milke-white, his head covered with a round low-crowned torn silk hat, on which was a band knit in many knots, wherein stuck two round sticks after the juggler's manner. His jerkin was of leather cut, his cloak of three colors, his hose painted with yellow, drawn out with blue, his instrument was a bagpipe, and him I knew to be William Cuckoe, better known than loved, and yet, some think, as well loved as he was worthy." Cuckoe's appearance must have been eccentric even for those times, but his costume probably helped him attract the attention of numerous spectators and drew them to his show.

A European street magician produces wonders from his pocket apron, the *gibecière*. He used the trumpet to call a crowd and offered books and souvenirs for sale. *(Mulholland Collection)*

Later, during the eighteenth century when the status of the conjurer began to improve, the cups-and-balls performer dressed in a more stylish mode, wearing a frock coat and vest, with a cravat and jewels or gold chains. By the nineteenth century, the French street magicians were as well dressed as the most prosperous Parisian gentlemen—and needed to be, since they frequently performed for members of high society.

In order to present a complete repertoire of popular entertainments, Elizabethan jugglers and players formed troupes similar to those which had accompanied the troubadours in a previous era. Along with the conjurer or juggler, the road company might include a rope dancer, an equilibrist, an acrobat, or a contortionist. These troupes often used improvised platforms or mobile stages similar to those adopted by the Commedia dell'Arte players. Once on location, the players would set bare planks atop a few hogsheads, stand up two long poles, and stretch a cloth as a backdrop to the improvised "stage."

Other wagons resembled the types used by tinkers and gypsies, with brightly painted wheels, colorful curtains, and bells that jangled as the wagon moved. The side of the wagon would fold down to expose the stage, and a set of steps led from the stage wings to the ground. The style of these wagons was preserved over the centuries, and the magician John Mulholland saw one performance from such a vehicle in the early 1940s while traveling in Germany. According to his description,

It was a cleverly designed wagon, beautifully made of fine wood. It was large, and drawn by four horses. When the magician found the spot where he chose to give his show, the horses would be unhitched and tied out to graze, and the magician would unfold his stage. Two large doors opened at the end, and swung back out of the way. There in the end of the wagon was a tiny but most attractive stage. Steps were attached so that the magician could leave his stage from time to time to go among his audience; folding chairs, an unbelievable luxury, were brought for the spectators to sit on. The

The French *escamoteur* reflected his improved status in society by wearing fashionable wigs and expensive clothing. This nineteenth-century conjurer carried a short wand, a long bugle, and a traveling chest well-stocked with quack medicines and paraphernalia. *(Sheridan Collection)*

A crude outdoor stage, complete with stairs, lighting and curtains. Wandering magicians performed from platforms or stage wagons through the early 1900s. *(Sheridan Collection)*

stage was lighted by several specially designed and good-looking lanterns. In short, it was a folding theater on wheels.

With a stage this elaborate, the traveling magicians probably installed various implements and devices to help them carry out their illusions. It was a first step toward stage magic.

Many jugglers also performed in the courtyards of inns and taverns, or used spacious barns for their conjuring acts. Judging from scenes in old prints, many conjurers found it profitable to give shows inside the taverns, doing their card sleights or cups-and-balls tricks at the main eating table. Eventually, when a large enough crowd had gathered, they might go outside to the courtyard to perform the same tricks in public for a small fee.

Barn performers, on the other hand, had to attract a crowd before they began. Sometimes the juggler would walk the town playing a trumpet before the performance while someone announced that the upcoming show would—in the words of a playbill—"amaze and astonish the beholders!" There was probably no admission charge, but money would be collected by the magician's assistants both during and after the show. No doubt the trumpeting magician held an extraordinary appeal for the curious and restless children in town, and the tale of the Pied Piper may very well be based on the story of a magician rather than a musician.

Many conjurers, realizing that people were attracted by things that seemed most foreign, gave themselves strange-sounding names, used

An Italian magician producing yards of ribbon from his mouth. Scene is the courtyard of an inn. *(Sheridan Collection)*

A country barn performer produces songbirds from a hat. His assistant, seated at the magician's feet, did acrobatic stunts and plate-spinning. *(Sheridan Collection)*

long incomprehensible words in their patter, and introduced foreign tricks into their performances. Thus a French performer might have the name of an Italian, Egyptian, or German, and claim to be descended from all three nationalities. Also, these names were changed often, since the conjurer left behind many debts, as well as enemies, in his travels. His tricks, he might claim, were taught him by a "Chinee" or a "Hindoo," or borrowed directly from a master sorcerer such as Nostradamus, Paracelsus, or Agrippa. Simple devices such as a box or a set of balls might bear strange insignias or hieroglyphics as a subtle way of informing the audience that the conjurer had occult knowledge far beyond the understanding of these provincials. In addition, conjurers used many "strange terms and emphatical words to adorn their actions and astonish the

spectators"—combinations of Hebrew, Latin, and astrological terms. These terms seemed very impressive when combined with the performance of some mysterious trick.

For a description of the jugglers' tricks, we must look to the earliest books and pamphlets which provide descriptions and anecdotes concerning their art. As mentioned earlier, Reginald Scot's book, *The Discoverie of Witchcraft*, published in 1584, included a long chapter on "The Art of Juggling Discovered." Many authors borrowed directly from this chapter in writing books and pamphlets about the juggling arts. *The Discoverie* itself was reprinted in several editions, and authors who plagiarized from this popular volume added their own methods and suggested different effects for sleight of hand. Some of the earliest works in English describing the arts and secrets of the juggler included *The*

Art of Juggling or Legerdemain (1612); Thomas Ady's A Candle in the Dark or, A Treatise Concerning the Nature of Witches and Witchcraft (1656); Hocus Pocus Junior (1635) by an anonymous author; and Henry Dean's The Whole Art of Legerdemain or Hocus Pocus in Perfection (1722). These treatises provide faithful descriptions of the tricks practiced by itinerant magicians of the day.

In the "how-to" chapter of The Discoverie of Witchcraft, Reginald Scot described several tricks performed with cards, such as "How to deliver out four aces, and to convert them into four knaves" and "To tell one without confederacy what card he thinketh." And there is a long description of "How to tell what card any man thinketh, how to convey the same into a kernel of nut or cheirstone, and the same again into one's pocket, how to make one draw the same or any card you list, and all under one devise." Today, a magician would begin such a trick by saying, "Pick a card, any card."

Playing cards have long been used for the art of conjuring, but it is interesting to trace their origins to the times when they had a symbolic significance. The earliest cards used for gaming were probably introduced to Europe sometime during the fourteenth century. They may have been imported by the Moors or by gypsies from Hungary, or brought back by the Church's soldiers returning from the crusades. The early packs contained anywhere from sixty-two to ninety-seven cards and were hand-painted or printed on large pieces of thick paper, which were too unwieldy to be easily shuffled or manipulated by a juggler. The figures on these cards were symbols we now associate with the tarots—such as Death, the Wheel of Fortune, the Sun, the Devil, and so on—and those face cards which have since been incorporated into the modern deck, such as the king and queen. The old decks also carried pictures of the juggler—le bataleur—playing at cups-and-balls.

By the fourteenth century, Italian playing cards or tarocchini having four suits were being used by royalty for various pastimes. At first, the cards were much too expensive for a juggler to purchase, but by the sixteenth century a smaller version of the Italian deck was being printed on a mass scale. The conjurer quickly incorporated these cards into his act, and "card tricks" have remained an important part of the magician's repertoire ever since.

A tarot trump card showing The Juggler ("Le Bateleur" or "Le Bataleur"). The conjurer holds a wand in one hand and an egg in the other. On the table are cups, balls, knives, coins and the magician's purse. (NYPL Picture Collection)

A French conjurer cuts the deck, and the girl discovers her card. Street magicians have been doing card tricks since the sixteenth century. (Mulholland Collection)

Cards were also used by two other groups—gypsy fortune-tellers and gamblers—and Scot wanted to warn the public against false practices and cheating. One of his descriptions therefore tells "of cards, with good cautions how to avoid cousenage therein"—in other words, how to spot a crooked gambler. By revealing the tricks, Scot was not only guiding the juggler of the future but was also helping the innocent person who might be cheated by a card sharper.

The same volume reveals many kinds of coin tricks that could be done with or without the help of a confederate in the audience. In Scot's day, these tricks were done with "testors, counters, and groats." The testor was a normal coin; the counter, a plain piece of metal which resembled the testor in size and probably served as a poker chip; and the groat was a prepared or "doctored" coin. Today, prepared coins can by purchased in any magic shop, but in Scot's time the conjurer had to make his own coins or have the groats made by a metalworker. With a little practice, Scot says, one could learn "to put one testor into a stranger's hand, and another into (his) own, and to convey both into the stranger's hand with words."

Scot suggests that the conjurer used the following patter while carrying out this trick: "Hay, passe, presto vade, jubeo, by the vertue of Hocus Pocus, 'tis gone." The words were meaningless, but Scot believed it important to say them to convince the audience that the words did the "work," making the coin invisible and prompting it to fly from place to place.

Many of the tricks were ingenious simulations of self-abuse, which involved using trick swords or daggers to produce bizarre effects. Scot devoted an entire section to "desperate or dangerous juggling knacks, wherein the simple are made to think that a silly juggler with words can hurt and help, kill and revive any creature in his pleasure. . . ." The juggler would pick up a normal dagger, which he would pass around the audience for examination. Upon its being returned he would substitute a trick dagger of the correct variety (Scot gives designs for at least a dozen), and thrust it through his arm, stomach, tongue, nose, or head. Viewed from the correct angle, the knife seemed to go all the way through the selected part of the body. Furthermore, if the juggler surreptitiously applied some daubs of fresh calf blood, as Scot recommends, the effect

could be thoroughly ghoulish and quite impressive. Of course, the juggler did not allow his audience enough time to get over the initial shock before he pulled out the dagger—concealing the "trick" part of it all the while—and applied a healing salve to the injured part of the anatomy. It was this kind of trick that was reported by Thomas Coryat in 1608 when he saw the mountebank perform in Venice.

One of the most startling of these tricks was performed by a drunken juggler, and it backfired in a rather gory way. According to Scot, the trick attempted by the juggler was "to thrust a dagger or bodkin into your guts very strangely, and to recover immediately." It was specified that the juggler wear on the front of his torso a special plate which would keep the shape of his body even when he sucked in his stomach. Inside the plate were bladders filled with calf or sheep blood. The juggler was supposed to insert his sword in one side of the plate, suck in his stomach, and drive the sword through to the other side. When he relaxed, his stomach came to rest harmlessly against the *side* of the sword. According to Scot, "the said blood will spin or spirt out a good distance from you, especially if you strain your body to swell, and thrust therewith against the plate." And the juggler was advised to use "such a style with words, countenance, and gesture as may give a grace to the action, and move admiration in the beholders." Scot continues: "Not long since a juggler caused himself to be killed at a tavern in Cheapside, from whence he presently went into [St.] Paul's churchyard and died. Which misfortune fell upon him through his own folly, as being then drunken he had forgotten his plate, which he should have had for his own defense." It was a warning to jugglers of the future to make their preparations soberly.

Some of the "tricks" noted in *The Discoverie* would seem little more than party jokes today, but the juggler may have enjoyed playing the clown as well as wonder-worker. For example, a juggler would surreptitiously "rap a wag on the knuckles," and then claim that the foolish fellow had been struck by an imp or familiar for trying to cheat the juggler. Another, more profitable, ploy was for the juggler to take bets that with his arms extended wide apart he could move a shilling from one hand to the other. Having collected the bets, the juggler took a shilling in his right hand and laid it on a table, then turned around with his arms still extended and picked up the shilling in the left hand. Since his arms had remained wide apart, he proclaimed, he had fulfilled the conditions of the bet, and his creditors should pay up. Not what one might consider witchcraft.

There were a number of tricks which required the aid of a confederate. The juggler would say that he could guess whether a "counter" came up heads or tails—in those days, it was "crosse" or "pile"—just by listening to the ring it made as it hit the floor. His confederate, pretending to be a complete stranger, said that he would go behind a door and throw the coin while the juggler tried to guess each toss. When the bets had been collected, the confederate left the room and tossed the coin. After each throw he called out "What is it?" if the coin came up "crosse," and "What ist?" if it came up "pile." The juggler, knowing the signal, answered correctly every time. Elementary though it may seem, this kind of confederacy was the basis for many impressive feats of mind-reading and thought transference which have been demonstrated by magicians and mentalists to the present day.

An equally simple bit of confederacy, "to make one dance naked," probably made a strong and lasting impression on the audience. The juggler would focus the "evil eye" on someone in the audience and begin to recite numerous spells which sounded like curses or enchantments. After awhile, the spells would seem to take effect, and the person would begin to shake, stamp, cry, and fling away his clothes until he stood stark naked. (Scot mentions that if there are ladies present, the juggler can stop short his spells before the confederate becomes completely exposed.) Not knowing the arrangement between the juggler and the possessed person, many observers must have been convinced they were witnessing witchcraft in action. Here, too, the method of the juggler may seem obvious to us, but magicians can still dupe audiences by using confederates on stage or choosing them, supposedly at random, from the audience.

In *The Discoverie of Witchcraft* a number of jugglers' deceptions were left unexplained, as in the story of Brandon the juggler. While the story itself may be apocryphal, many jugglers must have known the technique for performing Brandon's trick, for a similar effect was later shown at Bartholomew's Fair.

According to Scot, Brandon appeared before a certain king who asked the juggler to perform some trick for him. Brandon complied. He pointed out a pigeon that was roosting on a nearby house, then drew an enlarged outline of the bird on the outside wall of the house. As the king watched, Brandon took out his dagger and plunged it into the center of his drawing—just where the heart of the bird would be. At once the bird fell from its perch and plunged to the ground. When the king's men went to investigate they found the bird stone dead.

The king, according to the story, was startled but not particularly pleased, being afraid that such powers could be used against man as well as bird, and he forebade Brandon ever to perform that trick again. Scot noted that if Brandon's feat had been performed by an old woman, probably a number of people would "cry out for fire and faggot to burn the witch." In the story it is not explained how the trick was done, but we can surmise that Brandon had casually arranged the entire set-up before the king arrived on the scene.

An impressive illusion explained by Scot was a decapitation trick called "The Decollation of John the Baptist." In effect it was a simulation of an actual beheading, but with a trace of Biblical allusion and a dose of medieval sanguineness. According to the Gospel of Mark, King Herod imprisoned St. John and then ordered that his prisoner be decapitated. In the Biblical story and in the jugglers' re-enactment, the severed head was placed on a platter for everyone to see. The jugglers' victims, however, always had their heads restored at the end of the trick.

To perform the Decollation, as it was sometimes called, the juggler set up a long table covered with a cloth reaching to the ground. He then asked his assistant to come forward and lie on top of the table. Underneath the head of the prospective victim, the juggler placed a large platter, and over this he drew a cloth. He took out a dagger, put his hands underneath the cloth, and cut off the victim's head. So, at least, it appeared to the audience. All that could be seen was the motion of the juggler's hands beneath the covering—and the aftermath.

The juggler lifted the platter with its burden, still covered by the cloth, and moved it to the opposite end of the table, revealing a brief

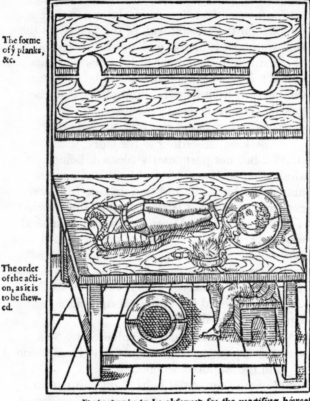

13. Booke.   The difcouerie

To cut off ones head, and to laie it in a platter,
which the iugglers call the decollation of Iohn Baptift.

The forme
of ý planks,
&c.

The order
of the acti-
on, as it is
to be fhew-
ed.

What order is to be obferued for the practifing hæreof
with great admiration, read page 349, 350.

The decapitation trick. During a performance, the
table was covered with a long cloth to hide the
seated assistant. Illustration is from Book XIII of
Scot's *The Discoverie of Witchcraft. (NYPL Picture
Collection)*

Stage version of the decapitation. Smoke pours from
the mouth of a "severed" head and the magician
uses a hefty meat cleaver instead of a sword.
Illustration from Albert Hopkins' *Magic; Stage
Illusions and Scientific Diversions* (1898). *(Mulholland
Collection)*

glimpse of the gory contents underneath.
Finally, the conjurer would lift the cloth from
the platter to reveal the victim's dripping head.

But there were more astonishments to
come. A chafing dish containing fire and
brimstone was placed in front of the platter, and
the head began to cough and choke. Then it
began to converse in a hoarse, sepulchral voice.
The audience, having feasted its senses on this
spectacle, continued to watch as the juggler once
again covered the head with a cloth, carried the
platter to the appropriate end of the body, and
under cover of the cloth restored the head as
easily as it had been severed. The victim sat up
at once, spoke for a moment or two about his

experiences in purgatory, and retired with a
bow while the juggler collected contributions
from the audience.

To us the entire spectacle may seem like a
Gothic horror, but it should be remembered that
the spectators in those days were somewhat
hardened by their daily experiences.
Throughout the seventeenth and eighteenth
centuries, it was fairly common for criminals to
be punished in broad daylight and in public
places, where the executions provided a warning
to any would-be criminals. Most people had
witnessed malefactors hanged, decapitated, or
even drawn-and-quartered. Under the
circumstances, it must have been a relief to see a

beheaded victim restored unerringly to life.

Putting aside matters of taste, we can see that the decapitation trick appeals on a level that is both primal and universal. Its effect is similar to that of the Indian basket trick or the Shinto miracle ceremony, and similar methods have been used by modern day magicians for "sawing a woman in half" or performing "the guillotine trick." People everywhere are intrigued by the possibility of life after death, and this kind of trick gives a physical rather than spiritual manifestation of that event. In a way, although a frightening scene, the decapitation trick has had a unique fascination that has survived the centuries. Most authors who used *The Discoverie of Witchcraft* as their source were certain to include The Decollation of John the Baptist for the enlightenment of their readers.

A Candle in the Dark by Thomas Ady was published in London in 1656 and included most of the tricks which were described in Scot's earlier book. In addition, Ady revealed the secret of the magic pen, which would write in ink of many colors. Ady had probably observed street magicians in his own time, for he recounted some of their exploits as an example to his readers.

One conjurer described by Ady was said to be accompanied by an imp or familiar. Ady described a cups-and-balls performer in London who had improvised an imp that would leap out during each act, apparently just to irritate the magician. The conjurer shouted angrily at the imp, demanding to know whether the little demon was going to vanish, or stay and perform some tricks. Finally, much to the amusement of the audience, the conjurer caught the imp, held it up by the feet, and beat the mousy creature until it began squealing pitifully. Then it suddenly disappeared and was not heard from any more during the performance. Ady provided some vague instructions for making such a familiar by using a ball of cloth, a coil spring, and the skin of a mouse.

In *A Candle in the Dark* there is a description of the decapitation trick preceded, in performance, by some imaginative blood-letting and wine-drinking, all done with the aid of an accomplice. Ady says that the conjurer would set up his table, covered with a long cloth, in the center of a village or on a busy street. When a curious crowd had gathered around the juggler, he took out a large jug of wine filled to the brim and apparently drank the contents in a single gulp. The performer managed to remain standing, though tipsily, and next took up a funnel, showing it to his audience to prove that it was empty. He requested the loan of a knife, and a young boy stepped forward to proffer his pocket knife. Making a joke about the size of the instrument, the magician added it would nonetheless do, and plunged the blade into his forehead!

While the gentlemen gasped and the ladies shrieked, the conjurer appeared to extract the knife from his brain and place a funnel over the cranial hole. In an instant, a reddish-colored liquid poured from the end of the funnel into a goblet, which the magician then passed around among the spectators. He informed his watchers that the liquid was not Anglo-Saxon blood but good French wine. Cautiously, a few spectators sipped it, and when they announced that the wine was perfectly fine vintage, the goblet was passed hurriedly from hand to hand until it was emptied.

The supply in his forehead having run dry, our magician would declare himself a bit dizzy on being so drained—but as consolation for those who had been unable to get a share of the wine, offered to tap another source. Spotting a large wooden post on the corner of a building, and taking up a gimlet for corkscrew, the conjurer "in a thrice" brought forth a new stream of wine out of the bare wood.

This time, the juggler noticed that the boy who had loaned him the knife was refusing to drink. When the magician asked why, the boy replied that it was not good wine since it came from a post. At this the magician swore that he would punish the youth for his insolence. He grabbed the boy, threw him on the table, covered him with a cloth, and proceeded to cut off the young man's head—in the usual manner adopted by conjurers.

But immediately the magician appeared to regret his actions and confessed that "the fault did not deserve death." According to Ady, the juggler then said the following spell: "By the virtue of hocus pocus, and Fortunatus his night cap, I wish thou mayst live again." His wish of course came true. The head was returned to its place, and the youth, restored to life, leapt up and ran away without a backward glance. The audience, relieved as well as astonished, contributed generously to the juggler's fund and, some time later, the juggler paid off the boy actor for his invaluable assistance.

Ady's book, like *The Discoverie,* was principally about witches, their habits and recognizable characteristics, and the chapter on sleight of hand was intended to show how the arts of the juggler or "Prestigiator" seemed to overlap the powers of the witch. From his observations of jugglers at their work, Ady drew the conclusion that "jugglers act first in sleight of hand, or cleanly conveyance; secondly, in confederacy; thirdly in abuse of natural magic." Witches, on the other hand, could be recognized because they would refuse holy water, despise the cross, or deny any of the seven sacraments.

The author of *A Candle in the Dark* also suggests a possible origin of the expression "Hocus Pocus," which even today is an exhortation pronounced by magicians whenever they want a magical event to occur. In the time of King James, according to Ady, the king's own juggler was called "Hocus Pocus." During each trick he used to say "Hocus pocus, tontus talontus, vade celeriter jubeo," which Ady defined as "a dark composure of words, to blind the eyes of the beholders."

The expression might have come from other sources however. Some linguists have pointed out that that "hocus pocus" sounds very much like the words of the Latin liturgy, "hoc est corpus," and might have been spoken by jugglers who were mocking the ceremonies of the Roman Catholic Church. Other historians of magic say that the words are derived from the name of an Italian priest or mystagogue named Okos Bokos, who practiced what was called "the vain and idle art" of juggling.

Whatever its source, "Hocus Pocus" was a common expression in seventeenth-century England. Ben Jonson, in *The Staple of News,* wrote that "iniquity came in like Hocos Pokas, in a juggler's jerkin, with false skirts, like the Knave of Clubs." And a poem in *The Witts Recreation,* published in 1640, supplies a gloating epitaph for the king's most excellent conjurer:

Here Hocas lyes, with his tricks and his knocks,
Whom death has made sure as a juggler's box;
Who many hath cozen'd by his leiger-deman,
Is presto conveyed and here underlain.
Thus Hocas he's here, and here he is not,
While death played the Hocas, and brought him to th'
pot.

The writer seems inordinately pleased that not even a juggler could escape death.

Other books describing only the art of legerdemain incorporated the name Hocus Pocus in their titles. *Hocus Pocus Junior, or The Anatomie of Legerdemain,* published in 1635, was the first English work devoted exclusively to the art of juggling. While borrowing heavily from *The Discoverie,* the anonymous author of *Hocus Pocus Junior* added his own list of rules for the conjurer, including the following: "First, he must be one of an impudent and audacious spirit, so that he may set a good face upon the matter. Secondly, he must have a nimble and cleanly conveyance. Thirdly, he must have strange terms and emphatical words to grace and adorn his actions and the more, to astonish the beholders. Fourthly, and lastly, such gestures of body as may lead away the spectators' eyes from a strict and diligent beholding [of] his manner of conveyance." In modern terms, this author was suggesting good stage presence, a lot of rehearsal, appropriate patter, and a mastery of the art of misdirection.

The author also recounted the history of magic, saying that it began with the Egyptians who made a practice of cheating and deluding people. According to the author, the Egyptians became notorious for these habits and the

A gypsy fortune-teller. She did card manipulations and cups-and-balls tricks while offering mystical predictions. Ladies in fashionable society consulted the soothsayers frequently. *(NYPL Picture Collection)*

English Parliament passed a statute forbidding anyone to transport Egyptians into the country. The immigration ceased, but the art of the "Aegyptian Jugglers" continued to flourish.

This brief history probably confuses the Egyptians with gypsies, who arrived in England during the fifteenth century and traveled in bands around the countryside. The gypsies were notorious for fortune-telling, cheating at cards, and thimblerigging, the last being a form of cups-and-balls with betting. The tribes of gypsies probably originated in India rather than Egypt, but they were confused with Egyptians because of their swarthy complexions.

The pictures in *Hocus Pocus Junior* are crudely drawn, but they do illustrate a number of tricks which Scot omitted. One was a Magic Barrel which could be filled with water. Upon command, it could be made to pour out several kinds of drinks and liquors. *Hocus Pocus Junior* also provides a diagram of a collapsible funnel and various step-by-step drawings which show how to perform cups-and-balls tricks. Finally, the author suggests that "by agility and nimbleness of hand you may make a piece of Hare-skin to stir and run about you as a live creature, and at last to vanish away, which will be imagined to be some Familiar that you deal withall." Information such as this goes to make up a pamphlet which is a genuine hodgepodge of old tricks and new devices.

The author welcomes the reader to this pamphlet just as one might be welcomed by a juggler to the scene of a village fair. In the opening lines of *Hocus Pocus Junior* we can hear the charlatan's patter, as he beckons us toward his open booth:

Courteous Reader, do you not wonder? If you do not, well may you, to see so slight a pamphlet so quickly spent; but lightly come, and lightly go; it is a Juggler's term, and it well befits the subject. Would you know whither it's bent? For the Fair again. It's a straggler, a wanderer, and as I said, as it lightly comes, so it lightly goes; for it means to see not only Bartholomew Fair but all the Fairs in the Kingdom also.

Clearly the juggler's patter as well as his art was well suited for the hustle and bustle of those early fairs.

Many other pamphlets were peddled at the great fairs held yearly in England and on the Continent. From the time the first entertainers began to flock to the fairs, and at least to the early nineteenth century, these locales were favorite places for itinerant conjurers to demonstrate their skill at sleight of hand and mechanical illusions. It is only fitting, in our search for street magic, that we should next wander to the fairground at the invitation of Hocus Pocus Junior to have our pockets picked, our noses offended, our eyes deceived, and our horizons expanded in the presence of illusion.

A street conjurer in military dress. He promises his spectator a steady income, tooth powder and a house in the country—all for the price of two coppers. *(NYPL Picture Collection)*

Conjuring at the Fair

Stalls line every street of the city, their shelves overflowing with jewelry, fine clothing, trinkets, metalwork, dolls, toys, candies, and thousands of other luxuries and necessities. The tradespeople call out their wares, shouting to be heard over the roar of the crowd. There are other shouts—"Make way! Make way!"—as armed guards push through the crush of people in pursuit of some felon who has violated the special rules of the fair.

On the main square the scene is even more chaotic. A foolhardy skydiver has ascended to the top of a steeple and is about to shoot down a long, sagging rope on his stomach. A dwarf stands nearby playing the bagpipes and manipulating two little dolls with his foot so they dance in time to the wailing music. All around are performers who want attention—a contortionist with his head twisted behind him almost touching his spine; a slack-rope performer swinging from a rope; an animal-trainer with dancing dogs; and an organ-grinder with a talented monkey. Even more alluring are the posters and placards advertising the wonders hidden in booths and stalls. Vocal pitch-men announce midgets and giants, a live mermaid, a child with three legs, a man with one head and two bodies, and a woman with one body and two heads.

To one side of the main square is a balustraded platform, six feet off the ground,

and behind it a huge placard painted in a dozen brilliant colors showing a solemn, two-dimensional portrait of a man with a bag in his hand. In the illustration the bottom of the bag is open, and there are a number of small objects being produced. In front of this portrait stands the man himself—dressed like a member of Parliament in a frock coat with ruffles, wearing an impressively curly and hoary wig. Now we can hear his oratory. If we come into his booth, he cries, we shall see a woman decapitated. We shall see an empty bag produce hundreds of eggs; a pig that understands the King's English; coins that fly of their own volition; flowers that spring forth from an empty bowl, and birds from an empty hat. "How is this possible?" he asks. There can be only one answer. Only one person is capable of such feats. It is the conjurer, the magician, the wizard, the sorcerer *par excellence,* the jewel of the fair. . . .

In all of Europe there was nothing to rival the confusion, excitement, and allure of the annual fairs. They were carnival, circus, side-show, market, and theater all rolled into one. The visitor, pushing his or her way through the crowd, had a good chance of losing or spending every cent in the melee, and the enterprising street juggler had a good chance of making his fortune on this common ground.

Though the tradition of the saint's day fairs was started during the Middle Ages, these

In a conjurer's tent at the fair. A magician pulls a rotten tooth by means of a single pistol shot. Illustration is from *The Whole Art of Hocus Pocus: Containing the Most Dexterous Feats of Slight of Hand* (published 1812). *(Mulholland Collection)*

festivals reached the height of their popularity during the seventeenth and eighteenth centuries, when their primary purpose was to provide amusement and pleasure for the people. Each fair was held in a specific location each year, either a part of a city or in the center of a particular town, and might last anywhere from three days to two weeks. Originally the fairs were for the benefit of the church or for a charitable cause, and a certain portion of the proceeds was allotted to the sponsor of the fair. Gradually the sacred and commercial purposes of the celebration became secondary while the entertainment value assumed first importance.

St. Bartholomew's Fair, probably the most famous of all the great English fairs, was founded in 1133 by a clever monk, probably a juggler, who performed miracles such as healing the sick and lame. Soon other fairs sprang up around England, each dedicated to some saint or worthy cause. Stourbridge Fair was instituted to help lepers, and St. James Fair in London was granted a charter to aid the hospital of St. James. Southwark Fair, later drawn by the English artist William Hogarth, was held in London for three days each September. Other popular fairs in England included Greenwich Fair, May Fair, and the fairs of St. Denis and St. Giles. Outside of England, the best known was probably the Fair of St. Germain in Paris.

Many kinds of street magicians attended these gatherings, and Bartholomew's Fair especially had a large and sometimes wild assortment of characters. Of course the mountebanks were on hand. With their boxes full of quack medicines, they stood on every corner praising their drugs and slandering the reputations of other so-called physicians and charlatans. Sometimes the mountebank had a trained dog or monkey on a leash and, as in years past, performed sleight of hand while murmuring Latin phrases.

"Southwark Fair," 1745, by William Hogarth. At right, a magician does tricks in front of a hanging banner. A fire-eater, smoke billowing from his lips, stands on a platform near the center of the crowd. Other sights include a dancing dog, a bagpipe player with foot-puppets, a peep show, slackwire artists and two dramatic companies (one in a state of collapse). (NYPL Prints Division)

Aside from such mountebanks, there were a number of ingenious sleight-of-hand performers who had distinguished careers at the English fairs. A full account of their many exploits was first collected by Sidney Clarke in *The Annals of Conjuring* (1929).

One of the best known of the conjurers was Isaac Fawkes, or Faux, who had a booth for private performances at Bartholomew and Southwark fairs in the 1720s, and eventually had his own theatre room at the Cock and Half Moon Tavern. The magical performers known as "the Younger Yeates" and "Pinchbeck" were immortalized in verses recalling these fairs:

There Yeates and Pinchbeck change the scene
To sleight of hand and clock machine,
First numerous eggs are laid, and then
The pregnant bag brings forth a hen.

And a showman called "Flockton," who traveled to many fairs between 1760 and 1794, even earned a review in a local newspaper: "Mr. Flockton, whose name can never be struck off Bartholomew roll, had a variety of entertainments, without and within. The King's Conjurer, who takes more money out of the pockets than he puts in, made the lank-haired gentry scratch their pates!"

Finally, there were a number of families performing as troupes at the fairs. The Gyngells, who traveled London and the provinces between 1788 and 1833, had a mixed show. Mr. Gyngell performed card tricks; Mrs. Gyngell sang; Joseph, their eldest son, was a juggler; Horatio danced; George, the youngest son, did fire tricks and danced the slack wire; while the daughter Louisa performed on the tight rope. A theater manager, Edward Stirling, vividly recalled seeing the leader of this team in action: "Monsieur Gyngell, emperor of cards, arch-shuffler, wizard-like held his pack, cutting, dealing, shifting in his delicate hands sparkling with diamonds (as we thought them, but which were cut glass in reality). With what a courtly air did Monsieur request the loan of a hat, merely to boil a pudding in!"

Most fair conjurers could boil a pudding—or an omelet or pancake—in a hat, and return the hat to its owner in perfect condition. But there were many other kinds of magic they knew as well. In fact the tricks performed by these conjurers were a strange assortment of the traditional, the inventive, and the bizarre. A

Isaac Faux (or Fawkes) doing the hen-bag trick. He showed the audience an empty bag, then produced a dozen eggs or balls from it. *(NYPL Picture Collection)*

The conjurer's booth. A clown and a trumpeter attract fairgoers to see "Faux's dexterity of hand." *(NYPL Picture Collection)*

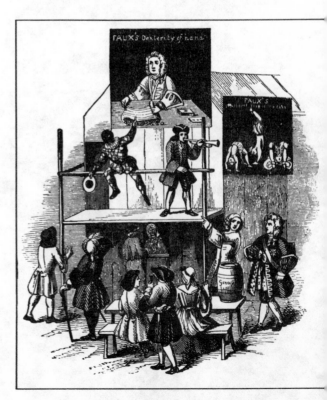

A conjurer finds an egg in a scarf, and a clown pulls silks from his throat at an eighteenth-century English fair. *(Sheridan Collection)*

conjurer might be advertised for one specialty—such as "the hen bag trick" or "the decollation"—but he would also perform sleights such as the cups-and-balls as a prelude to the main show. Sorcerers like the fire-eaters and sword-swallowers often performed on exposed platforms, while the more established conjurers had enclosed booths or tents and charged an admission price. These conjurers often hired "shills" who would rush forward to buy tickets. The purpose of the shills, of course, was simply to create a crush in the direction of the performer's booth. Once inside, the shills slipped out a side door and joined the crowd again, pushing forward and waving their money in the air.

Jugglers who could perform "salamandering" feats—eating, breathing, or handling fire—were especially popular at the fairs. The salamander was a mythical animal which was supposed to be able to endure any kind of fire or flame, and the fire-eaters at the fair truly seemed to have all the powers of such mythical beings, and more. The interest of the spectators became even greater when, during the eighteenth century, people began to hear of the mysterious cults of the Far East and

consequently associated the fire-eater with tales of men who could walk across hot coals or leap through flames. The salamanders at the fair seemed to know the secrets to these rituals, for they juggled heat and flame without any apparent harm to themselves.

A common trick was to eat blazing tow. The tow, fibers of flax or hemp, was formed into a ball and soaked in oil, then ignited. A long tendril of flame shot out from the little ball of stuff, and the fire-eater picked up this fearsome-looking object with a pair of tongs. Then he tilted back his head, opened his mouth, and placed the fireball on the tip of his tongue. To the spectators it seemed that fire was shooting from his mouth, while black smoke billowed around him. Now and then he would withdraw his tongue, pulling the fireball inside his mouth, send out a few puffs of smoke from between his lips, then display the ignited tow again.

Fire-eaters deservedly attracted a great deal of attention, and many acquired outstanding reputations. The seventeenth century diarist John Evelyn especially admired a performer calling himself "Richardson" who was known for his salamandering at English and French fairs. According to Evelyn, Richardson put brimstone

A mountebank swallows burning tow—fiber dipped in oil, then ignited. *(Mulholland Collection)*

coals, and soft glass which he had apparently swallowed for breakfast.

The conjurer also heated pitch and wax over some flaming sulfur until the mixture caught fire, then seemed to drink it down hot. His observer, Evelyn, remarked with a certain horror, "I saw it flaming in his mouth a good while." During the next act, the diarist noted the first sign of caution on the part of the fire-eater. Richardson, he observed, picked up a red-hot bar of iron in his teeth, and then tossed it around in his hands. But Evelyn perceived that this was something that even the talented Richardson could not do for very long.

A showman named Powell (like many such performers, his first name is unknown) was a popular figure in fire-eating society between 1750 and 1760. Like Richardson, he could cook food inside his mouth, but he preferred to roast a piece of beefsteak on his tongue rather than an oyster. He encouraged audience participation in the act by asking a spectator to blow on the coal until the steak was done. Powell also composed a soup by mixing melted lead, pitch, brimstone, and other combustibles in an iron

(sulfur) on his tongue, then took a hearty mouthful of glowing hot coals which he would chew and swallow. He followed this act by melting down a beer glass, then drinking the liquid glass from a ladle.

Such men, however, live not by glass alone, and Richardson chose to follow up his non-nutritious drink with a more palatable delicacy—the oyster. As might be expected, he had a novel way of preparing the shellfish. First he would put a live coal on his tongue, and on the coal he would lay an oyster in its shell. With his bellows Richardson would fan the coals again, and the oyster shell would begin to open, its inhabitant being unused to so much heat. When it was finally extracted from the conjurer's mouth, the oyster was found to be well broiled and ready for eating. On some occasions the chef would offer this treat to the hungriest-looking gamin in the audience, but more frequently he added it to the brimstone,

A fire king licks a red-hot bar of iron while his harlequin assistant heats up a second course. *(Mulholland Collection)*

ladle. He then set his soup on fire and, taking up a smaller spoon, began to eat out of the ladle. The potage blazed furiously even while it entered his mouth.

By the nineteenth century a woman had taken up the fine art of juggling fire at Bartholomew's Fair. Her name was Madame Josephine Giradelli, and she called herself "The Fireproof Female from Germany." Henry Morley, in *Memoirs of Bartholomew Fair* (1859), stated that "this lady put melted lead in her mouth, and spat it out marked with her teeth, passed red-hot iron over body, limbs, and hair, thrust her arm into fire, and washed her hands, not only in boiling lead but also in aquafortis (nitric acid)." This remarkable lady must have been confident she would not spill a drop, for she performed in an elegant gown and did not bother to wear an apron.

In the midst of all this fire and brimstone, there must have been a few accidents, but we have heard of only one—a fire king at Bartholomew's Fair who almost suffocated when a spectator thrust a bundle of lighted matches under his nose. The fire king was accustomed to smoke and fire, but the strong fumes of the sulfur matches almost overpowered the unlucky performer. The unruly spectator was arrested and subsequently prosecuted for bad behavior.

Almost as popular as the fire-eaters were sword-swallowers and pebble-swallowers. As with fire-eating, sword-swallowing was done with a certain ritualism, the performer extending his preparations as long as possible in order to heighten the suspense. He would sharpen his sword, test the fineness of its edge, and stab it into the wooden stage-platform to prove that the sword's point was as deadly as it looked.

Throwing back his head, the sword-swallower inserted the weapon into his mouth and thrust it downward gently until only the hilt protruded from between his lips. Then he turned around several times, showing the audience that the blade had in fact gone into his body, but without harming him in the least. Nonetheless, he turned very carefully.

Then his assistant handed him a second sword. After some delicate maneuvering of its deadly point, the swallower took it down in a single gulp. Soon after, he added a third to his diet of tempered metal, strutted about his stage staring directly into the sky, and then removed the swords one by one, sticking each into the platform.

A French performer of the eighteenth century known only as the "Sabre Swallower" displayed his talents at the Paris fairs and gave a regular show on the Pont Neuf, one of the main bridges in Paris and a gathering place for street performers of all kinds. According to one of his admirers, the Frenchman could also swallow an egg without cracking it, then bring it up again. He would gulp down nails and pebbles, then strike his stomach with his fist, and the audience could hear the small objects rattling around inside him. The climax of his show came when he swallowed a sword and at the same time put knives up his nose. In a congested voice he would boast it did not hurt in the least.

Madame Giradelli, the "Fireproof Lady," as depicted in *The Memoirs of Bartholomew Fair* (1859). Her right hand holds the "red-hot iron" which she "passed . . . over body and limbs." (NYPL)

A sword swallower on stage. He could safely swallow daggers, sabres and bayonets. *(Mulholland Collection)*

Water-spouting was also a favorite trick of street and fair performers. The water-spouter would swallow a large quantity of clear water and then spout it in various colors or produce several kinds of drinks from his mouth. Jugglers in ancient Greece had performed similar tricks, but of course they had been forgotten, and by the seventeenth century the water-spouters were considered a novel attraction. To us the trick may seem merely grotesque, but evidently many people found the idea of a "human fountain" appealing. In the engravings and drawings which portray the famous water-spouters, the figures are considerably romanticized. The colored waters and liquors flowing from their lips appear to be of the purest substance, the crowd is admiring, and there are sometimes even angels or cherubims in the pictures.

In the seventeenth century, several water-spouters in France became famous for their extraordinary abilities, and they probably performed at many of the French fairs. Blaise Manfre or Mandrède was a native of Malta, Jean Royer was a water-spouter from Lyons, and Floram or Florian Marchand was from Tours. Of these Manfre was the best known.

Manfre would begin his act by setting out several dozen small bottles and requesting a bowl of lukewarm water. After gargling several times to show there were no dyes in his mouth, he swallowed the contents of the bowl in a single gulp. Then, seemingly from the depths of his stomach, he produced two streams of liquid, one wine and one beer, and filled the bottles.

After drinking a second bowlful of water, Manfre regurgitated streams of red wine, brandy, rosewater, orange water, and white wine, enough to fill all the glass bottles again. Once a spectator had been found with the courage to taste these liquors, the bottles would be passed from hand to hand until everyone had verified the success of the transformation experiment. For a finale, Manfre would tip back his head, insert a mouthpiece equipped with several tubes, and squirt streams of vari-colored water into the air. It must have been an impressive sight as the rainbow-colored streams sparkled and glittered in the sunlight.

Manfre's act was so inexplicable, and the magician attracted so much public attention that the Cardinal de Richelieu became suspicious and ordered the water-spouter imprisoned. Richelieu suspected that Manfre had solicited some kind of supernatural aid in performing the liquid exercises, and he threatened to execute the conjurer unless Manfre could prove his innocence. In a private appearance, Manfre satisfied his captor's demands—and curiosity—and the pardoned performer was set free to wander the country spouting his fountain of many flavors.

Eventually he taught his arts to Floram

Blaise Manfre, the water-spouter of Malta. This portrait suggests that the power of angels aided him in his work. *(NYPL Picture Collection)*

Manfre as portrayed by the artist Hollar in 1651. After spouting into the crowd, Manfre filled goblets with drinks of many flavors. *(NYPL Picture Collection)*

Floram Marchand used a fitted mouthpiece to spout three streams of sparkling drinks. *(Mulholland Collection)*

Marchand, who called himself "Le Grand Boyeur." Marchand attracted the attention of two Englishmen, who brought him to London and sponsored his show. However, when they discovered the spouter's methods, they published *The Falacie of the Great Water-Drinker Discovered*, in which they described him as "a moist cheat" and revealed his secrets. It was undoubtedly from this primer that many of the English fair performers got their first lessons in water-spouting.

At many of the popular fairs there were magicians who used domesticated or wild animals in their shows. The conjurer considered himself much more than an animal trainer, for he claimed that his animals had special powers of intelligence and could read the minds or understand the language of the spectators. Whereas the trainer's animal responded to signals of the keeper's hands or voice, the "intelligent" animals of the conjurer seemed to answer the spectators, thereby proving that they had both the mind and the soul of a human being locked up in an animal body. That, at least, was the impression the magician wanted to give.

One intelligent animal who made a profound impression on English and European audiences was a horse named Morocco that performed during the seventeenth century. His master, Banks, would accept a coin from anyone in the audience, and his horse would stamp out the correct number of pence for that coin. When Banks and his pet performed in France, the horse reputedly evaluated the franc-note, giving the correct rate of exchange. According to one story, Banks was accused of owning a horse possessed by demons, and the master was forced to explain his animal's behavior to a council of churchmen at Orléans. Morocco is said to have acquitted himself beautifully. Upon appearing before the church fathers, he made a deep bow and took to his knees, and the clerics acquitted both Morocco and Banks on the grounds that no devil would kneel before the cross.

Another conjurer of Bartholomew's Fair had a Learned Goose which was supposed to be able to read numbers. The magician, who adopted the name "Fawkes," would lay some numbered cards on the ground in a semi-circle. A spectator would call out any number, and the goose would waddle over to the correct card and pick it up. This conjurer's show also featured a Learned Pig which would pick up playing cards in a similiar manner, choosing them by suit as well as by number. As a climax to the show, the magician could borrow a watch from anyone in the audience, give it to the pig, and the intelligent beast would return the timepiece to its owner.

As higher education became common in the animal kingdom, other generations of conjurers "discovered" learned dogs, performing cats, monkeys, and pigeons. In addition to those animals which performed in concert with their masters, there were many others—also deserving recognition—which appeared or vanished according to the will of the juggler. And there were some animals sacrificed on the altar of magic. The original Isaac Fawkes was an expert at producing wild beasts at Bartholomew's Fair. In 1726 an advertisement for his show announced that he would turn an empty bag inside out several times, then produce one hundred eggs out of it "and several showers of real gold and silver." Finally the supposedly empty bag would begin to swell, and several kinds of "wild fowl" would emerge from it and run around the stage or fly over the heads of the audience. The ad also claimed that "he throws up a Pack of Cards, and causes them to be living birds flying about the room. He causes living Beasts, Birds and other Creatures to appear upon the Table." Fawkes' creatures must have been faithful as well as superbly trained, for they evidently returned to the conjurer's menagerie once the show was over.

A learned pig, as advertised at Bartholomew Fair. He had the miraculous power to read, add numbers, match dominoes and tell time. *(NYPL Picture Collection)*

An outdoor conjurer at the fair does tricks with eggs, cups and cards. His assistant puts a padlock through his cheek, and a distant performer breathes fire from his lips. *(Mulholland Collection)*

A conjurer who advertised himself as "Lane" also had a way with birds, and according to his own claims he could perform tricks with eggs and fowl that would cheer anyone up. A rhyme of the eighteenth century, circulated by Lane himself, said:

It will make you laugh, it will drive away gloom,
To see how the egg it will dance round the room,
And from another egg a bird there will fly,
Which makes the company all for to cry,
'O rare Lane! cockalorum for Lane! well done,
Lane! You are the man!

Lane's act was so popular that he eventually rented his own room in London—a room large enough to hold spectators, dancing eggs, and flying birds.

Other magicians had the undesirable habit of mutilating an animal or two every showtime. A performer named Jonas, who was either German or Italian, came to England in 1766, and carried out the decapitation of a pigeon in a novel manner. Jonas announced he would "perform the pigeon, by giving leave to any gentleman to hand a live pigeon on a string, and Mr. Jonas will cut the head off by cutting on the shadow, so that the body shall fall on the ground, and the head shall remain on the string." This murder was frequently perpetrated in front of a large, applauding crowd of people who had no idea whether the decapitation actually occurred or whether it was an illusion. The trick of "cutting off the head of a bird by cutting its shadow" was frequently repeated at many conjurers' booths on the English fairgrounds.

By the early eighteenth century the showmen at the fairs in England and France had discovered a new branch on the flowering tree of magic—the mystery of mechanics! Magicians began to exhibit clockwork mechanisms which operated dolls or animal figures, and they even had full-scale human mannequins which would do such things as change their clothes, write, and tell fortunes.

It is significant that these early mechanical contrivances were first associated with magic and were displayed by conjurers at their fair booths. In many cases there were human operators hiding behind a curtain or inside the case that held the mechanism, but sometimes the apparatus was almost completely self-operating. The conjurer tried to give the audience the impression that the mechanism itself was alive; or motivated by some kind of intelligent relationship among its gears, springs, and levers. This appearance made it seem as if there were a demon inside the clockwork mechanism, and the principles of mechanics were so poorly understood by most people that they did not even try to find a rational explanation for the machine's actions. They would watch spellbound while a doll-like figure with painted wooden face and creaky arms went through the motions of picking a card or playing an instrument.

Thus the automata became immensely popular at the conjurers' booths. Isaac Fawkes, already famous for his dexterity, collaborated with Christopher Pinchbeck, a London clockmaker, in building a human-looking automaton. They came up with a "posture maker," a figure that could play the violin and other stringed instruments and could imitate the sounds of birds singing. One observer of Mr. Fawkes' show stated that the music heard was "just, regular, and tunable, the time well observ'd." The partner Pinchbeck, who had his own shop at the Sign of the Astronomico-Musical Clock in London, eventually opened his own show on the fairground, calling it "The Grand Theatre of the Muses." The mechanical apparatus in this "Theatre" became one of the most popular sights of the fair.

In France a number of inventive magicians exhibited mechanical devices at the Fair of St. Germain and other Paris fairs. In 1738 a nobleman, M. Jacques de Vaucanson, who had previously invented a mechanical loom, introduced a mechanical flute-player dressed in German costume. By 1741 he had added a second figure which played the Provençal pipe and beat on a small tabor, or drum. De Vaucanson also exhibited a mechanical duck which quacked, drank water, gobbled up food, and digested it, leaving evidence of its marvelous digestion in a bowl of water.

In 1747 there appeared at the Paris fairs "Le Fameux Paysan de Nort Hollande," who had, according to his billing, "a philosophical flower pot, in which he raises trees which grow in the presence of the audience and become covered with foliage, which falls to disclose ripe fruit, which may be tasted by the spectators." This illusion, which was later adapted for the stage by French magicians, is almost exactly like the "mango tree trick" performed by Indian street magicians. But in this case, "Le Fameux Paysan" probably used several kinds of apparatus to produce the effect of a growing tree.

One of the most skilled illusionists of this era was Nicolas Philippe Ledru, who called himself "Comus." He owned a famous automaton that would follow the commands of the audience in selecting a number of clothes. Another charming miniature figure had eyes that changed color, matching the irises of whoever stared at it. There was also a device that could guess the thoughts of anyone in the room, and would write out its message with a mechanical hand.

In a certain respect, the popular magicians who used mechanical devices were only carrying on the tradition of the earliest *tregetours,* those court performers of the Middle Ages who had won reknown by demonstrating amazing devices as well as sleight of hand. And yet the times had certainly changed. In *The Annals of Conjuring* the magic historian Sidney Clarke refers to the eighteenth century as "the age of philosophy and refined skepticism, as well as of mysticism and magic. . . ." The automata appealed to both the "modern" skeptic, who was curious about the technical innovations that were becoming possible, and the mystic, who was intrigued by the fact that mechanical objects appeared to take on life.

Could an automaton behave like a human being? Could inanimate objects like gears and springs and levers be combined in such a way as to "come alive"? What were the limits to the things these machines could do?

Two hundred years ago people were already asking these questions which are still with us today. In the presence of a computer that seems almost to talk and think for itself, we have forebodings of a machine which might someday be more human than mechanical. Any

action without an apparent cause leaves us with a feeling of uneasiness. If a door suddenly closes without anyone touching it; if an undisturbed plate crashes to the floor; if a steady light begins blinking with a distinct pattern—we are "spooked" by an eery feeling. And that impression remains with us until we have found the explanation. The audience at the fair must have felt much the same way when confronted with the inexplicable behavior of objects that seemed to take on life.

But the introduction of mechanical apparatus also began to change the nature of conjuring at the fair, and by the end of the eighteenth century the art of stage magic had begun to come into its own. Magicians discovered they could keep an audience entertained with a whole evening of illusions. They combined sleight of hand with mechanical apparatus, added some theatrical effects, and found spectators—even of the highest class—ready and willing to enjoy hours of fantasy. From the street magician to the conjurer at the fair and finally to the stage magician, the development of the art of magic made a smooth transition. And in the nineteenth century the arts of illusion continued to prosper in theaters throughtout the world.

As people began to desert the fairgrounds in favor of the theaters, however, the popularity of the fairs began to decline throughout Europe. By the mid-1800s, many of the fairs were closing down, and performers deserted their old haunting places as their profits declined. The sword-swallowers and fire-eaters closed up their stalls for the last time. The new conjurer, with a room of his own in the city, no longer put his hens in a basket and trudged to the fair. Even the mountebanks found busier corners from which to peddle their quack nostrums. It was in 1855 that Bartholomew's Fair in Smithfield closed down for the last time, signaling the end of an era.

Stage Illusions
and Street Diversions

tage magic was the final development in the natural evolution of street magic from a folk art to a theatrical profession. During the nineteenth century the methods of the stage magician—methods requiring special lighting, curtains, props, pulleys, and traps—continued to be developed and improved as the stage magicians refined their arts. But most of the sleight-of-hand techniques used by stage magicians had been developed previously by street magicians, and even mechanical effects came directly from the tradition of the tregetours and illusionists at the fairs. The art of stage magic was a flowering of the art of street magic.

Like the itinerant jugglers, stage magicians traveled the world, and many achieved unprecedented fame. In every land they were greeted as curiosities, tested by public opinion, and proclaimed the ruling potentates in the universe of illusion. Kings and presidents, premiers and prime ministers, the highest and the humblest—all showed an interest in the world's latest and greatest magicians, and the fame of these wonder workers preceded and followed them wherever they went.

What, then, of lowly street magic? Did it vanish altogether? Did it fade into obscurity?

Not at all. Street magic survived, but it took on many forms, some traditional and some completely new. In the 1800s, for example, it was still practiced by such itinerant magicians as the *escamoteurs* of France, clever cups-and-balls performers who set up their tables in the squares or on street corners and challenged the crowd to match wits with them. Performing by day rather than night, in the open rather than indoors, these surviving street magicians were part of the ambiance of city life. As wanderers and fantasists, magicians such as the *escamoteurs* were almost symbolic figures, representing freedom and romance to the nineteenth century audience. In fact the magic performed by the escamoteur was less significant than the figure itself, recognized by all French society (and especially the new bourgeoisie) as a carefree and picturesque individual. In sketches and paintings, popular novels and plays, the descendants of Hocus Pocus were praised, mimicked, and satirized, while the magicians themselves continued to prosper, depending solely on the generosity of the crowd.

There was also a new and less tangible form of street magic—the kind that pursued and enhanced the reputation of every stage magician and, in some cases, even the reputations of fortune-tellers, psychics, and charlatans. Perhaps the best description of this kind of street magic was provided by H. J. Burlingame, a perceptive historian of the magical arts, in an excellent book called *Herrmann the Great; the Famous Magician's Wonderful Tricks,* which was published

The conjurer and the eggs. The magician finds a gold piece inside a fresh egg, pockets it and thanks the egg seller. According to the story, she then cracks all her eggs without finding a single coin. Alexander Herrmann duplicated the trick, but left payment in the bottom of the poor woman's basket. *(NYPL Picture Collection)* in 1897. Burlingame was trying to define that certain something, the aura of magic and wonder which seems to surround the greatest of magicians and follows them wherever they go. He concluded, "There is ever an atmosphere of mystery about the magician, and for the most part it is not himself that makes it. It is the product of the fame of his art, and fame is the babble of tongues and . . . the echo of thought and talk, print and pictures."

It was this "echo" created by the magician and his reputation that became street magic of the new era. It was the babble of tongues in the street that made crowds press to the doors of a theater to see the wonders of a great magician. It was a magician's image on his posters and playbills, surrounded by colorful devils, or the fantastic names of his tricks, or the stories told about his life, which gave him the reputation for knowing the darkest, dimmest truths about the magical arts. To an audience the magician's fame was established before his tricks were even witnessed. What happened on the stage was only a portion of the mystery. The real mystique was in the street magic created by the conjurer himself—"the babble of tongues . . . the echo of thought and talk, print and pictures."

During the nineteenth and early twentieth centuries, there were many great stage magicians who were masters of this kind of street magic. It would be entertaining to look at each of the famous magicians who have performed since the early 1800s, to try to hear again the echoes and see the images which they projected in all directions, wherever they traveled. But of course that is impossible. There have been so many, each with his own mystery, a special image, an immutable mystique. Instead we shall look at only a few, hoping to understand how in times past the magic of the street combined with the reputation of a performer to create that superhuman figure known as a magician.

Louis Christian Emanuel Appollinaire Comte was sometimes regarded as a man who knew ghosts and demons as well as he knew the performing arts, for this magician seemed to be accompanied constantly by "spirit voices."

Comte was born of French parents in Geneva, Switzerland, in 1788, and he ran away from home at the age of fifteen. For several years he wandered through Switzerland, and finally began to support himself by showing off his special abilities in the art of "ventriloquism." Eventually he traveled to southern France where he met a magician billed as "David" who taught Comte a number of sleight-of-hand tricks to augment his ventriloquial performances. David also gave Comte some apparatus which the young man probably used in his first shows when they opened in Paris. On stage he was known as an artistic "illusioniste" who always worked out a way to flatter the ladies or embarrass the gentlemen. Off-stage, he had a reputation for bizarre encounters.

One day, he was passing through the city of Tours, France, when he heard a man crying for assistance. "Oh, help me! I'm being murdered," wailed the shrill voice, which sounded as if it came from just behind the door of a nearby house. A number of pedestrians stopped and listened with increasing horror as the man's voice became more and more shrill. A crowd gathered. Suddenly the voice started to fade away, as if the man were in the throes of death. The crowd surged forward and broke down the door. They burst into the house—only to discover that it was completely empty. No victim, no murderer, nothing! The man crying for help had vanished like a spirit. Comte seemed to be as bewildered as everyone else, but he did have the presence of mind to hand out playbills advertising an evening performance of M. Comte, ventriloquist and magician *extraordinaire.*

A portrait of M. Comte, with his head perched on top of a conjurer's cup. The mischievous magician was well-known for his ventriloquial tricks. *(Mulholland Collection)*

It was said that the same magician once rescued a group of travelers from a murderous brigand who, as it turned out, did not even exist. As the story goes, Comte was traveling at night in a carriage, accompanied by several other travelers who were complete strangers. The coachman came to a stop at a crossroads, and the people in the carriage heard a gruff voice cry out, "Your money or your life!"

Naturally the travelers were terrified, but Comte quickly came to their rescue. Putting his head out the window, he bargained with the unseen burglar for a couple of minutes, then told his fellow travelers the scoundrel outside would settle for nothing less than all their jewels and valuables. Of course the travelers gave M. Comte their possessions, which he handed out to the robber, and before any of them had time to regret their losses, the coach had already started on its way again.

They arrived late at an inn, and after discussing their adventures over a hot toddy, all the travelers went to bed. The next morning, M. Comte came down to breakfast carrying all their jewels and cash in his hands and soberly returned their possessions. The travelers were bewildered by this strange turn of fortune, until Comte frankly explained that he was a magician by trade, and that they had been hoodwinked. Relieved to have their valuables once again, the travelers laughed at their fears of the previous night, and each of them swore they would be in the audience the next time M. Comte was on stage.

It may seem improbable that people were so easily taken in by Comte's "spirit voices," but every magician knows that the best audience is the one least prepared for a particular effect. Also, Comte must have been the most ingenious of street performers. Well-dressed, cultivated in his manners, he did not seem capable of practicing deceptions on anyone. Until people realized he was a magician, they regarded him as a perfectly proper individual—perhaps a lawyer or a banker. And when the voices began to speak around him, Comte always seemed to be the one who was most astonished.

Occasionally he was the last person to be suspected when a spirit voice began to speak. One of his most famous episodes occurred at a farmers' market in Mâcon. Comte was going among the crowd, shopping for some household items and looking over the local livestock. At one stall a woman was selling a live pig, and Comte paused to assess the value of this animal. The woman said the pig was worth one hundred francs.

Comte argued that one hundred francs was much too high a price, and said he didn't think the pig was worth half that much. The woman reddened in anger and proclaimed loudly that her porker was in perfectly good condition, and she would not even consider a lower price.

"One moment," said Comte. "I am sure your pig is more reasonable than you." Then he turned to the pig and asked the animal, "Tell me, on your conscience, my fine fellow, are you worth one hundred francs?"

"You are a long way out," replied the pig. "I'm not worth one hundred pence. I am measled, and my mistress is trying to take you in."

By now a crowd had gathered to listen to the argument, and the spectators were amazed to hear the pig speak on its own behalf. Obviously the gentleman (Comte) did not seem to be at fault, so the crowd turned on the lady and berated her for owning a pig inhabited by demons. In fact, they begged her to take her pig to a priest and have it exorcised before it wreaked havoc in the town. The woman was sharp-tongued enough to defend herself and the honor of her pig, and Comte allowed the scene to continue merrily for several minutes before informing the crowd of his part in the conversation.

Such jokes gave him a widespread reputation for devilment but occasionally got him into trouble as well. It was said that Comte almost met his end in Fribourg, Switzerland, when a group of superstitious peasants overheard him talking with demons and prepared to throw him into a lime kiln. Just as they were about to toss the bewitched man into the kiln, however, they heard a voice speaking from the depths of the charcoal pit, saying they would all roast in hell if any harm befell M. Comte. Terrified, the peasants dropped the magician and fled from the scene, leaving Comte to rub his bruises and consider the perpetual absurdity of human superstition.

In each of these incidents Comte was of course using the skill he had acquired as a young man in the art of ventriloquism. Today we associate a ventriloquist's act with Edgar

Bergen and Charlie McCarthy, with vaudeville routines and stand-up comedy. But we would be just as accurate in associating this art with spirit séances, ghost voices, and spirit rappings, since many supposed mediums have used ventriloquism even in the twentieth century. When performed on a stage, ventriloquism is amusing and entertaining. But performed on the street in a casual situation, it can create the most uncanny effects. The secrets of the ventriloquist are hardly secrets at all: he simply learns to imitate voices without moving his lips and to suggest that the voices come from a particular direction. But the real secret is far more intangible—it means knowing the audience and understanding how the average person expects a voice to sound, whether it comes from a highwayman or a pig or some other source. It is also a matter of knowing what words to speak and how to react when the voice is suddenly heard. These are the real secrets of a great performance and the key to the mystery of M. Comte.

Bosco! In his portraits he looked like a devil. Short mustachio, wild hair, eyes dark and demonic. He wore a black velvet jacket fastened around the waist with a leather belt. His black satin breeches were trimmed with lace, and a large white collar encircled his neck. Bosco appeared on stage carrying a long wand tipped with a magical gilt ball.

In Paris Bosco was all the rage during the early 1800s. In his private salon he would begin each performance by polishing his wand with a silk handkerchief and striking three times on a great copper globe above the center of the stage. With each blow of the wand he intoned the magic words calling forth demons from the infernal regions: "Spiriti mihi infernali, obedite."

These words were introduction to some of the greatest cups-and-balls magic ever performed on stage. Improving on the old street magicians' routines, Bosco used five cups and a number of balls that would appear to expand to double or triple their original size. And his performances concluded with another bit of skulduggery borrowed from the fairgrounds: cutting off the head of a bird. Bosco decapitated a black pigeon, placed its head on the body of a white bird; then placed the white head on the black body; and presto!—two instant hybrids flew into the air. The other kind of street magic—the "atmosphere of mystery"—also

The great Bosco in stage costume. He wore a ruffled shirt and carried a magic wand topped with a gilt ball. *(Mulholland Collection)*

Bosco in evening dress. *(Mulholland Collection)*

added to his glorious reputation. For it was said that Bosco had a very bizarre history, and the story of his life added lustre to his career as a stage magician.

Bartolomeo Bosco was born in Turin, Italy, in 1793 to the noble family of Piedmont. He must have been a renegade within the noble household, for he learned the arts of pickpocketing at an early age and used his skill to impress his friends with legerdemain. He was only nineteen when he joined Napoleon's army as a fusilier in the Eleventh Infantry of the Line, and was just in time for one of the most ambitious and ill-fated ventures in the history of warfare, the invasion of Russia by Napoleon's Army.

During the campaign, Bosco was wounded at the Battle of Borodino. When the battle was over, Bosco was still in the field, lying among the dead and the dying. During the night, a Russian cossack approached the wounded soldier, and believing Bosco was dead, the cossack began going through the Italian's pockets and belongings. Though suffering from his wound and in great danger, Bosco could not resist the temptation to exercise his own skill as a pickpocket, and he managed to clean out the Russian's loot even while the Russian was looting him. It must have been a shock to the greedy marauder to arrive back in camp and find out that he'd been "done" (to use a pickpocket's expression) by a dead man. For Bosco it was a risky game. If his sleight of hand had been discovered at the moment when the cossack was searching him, it is certain that the great Bosco would never have made it to the Paris stage.

But in fact it was magic that helped Bosco survive the terrible ordeal of Russian imprisonment. The morning after the battle, he was picked up by the Russian medical corps, and his wounds were treated. Sent to a camp in the town of Tobolsk in Siberia, Bosco soon attracted the attention of the prison officials. Hour after hour, he amused them with the cups-and-balls and conjuring exhibitions—as well as pickpocket tricks. To assure themselves of continuing entertainment in that cold and desolate land, the officials took care to see that Bosco remained well-fed and in good health. Eventually he returned to Italy, studied medicine for a time, and then resumed the trade that had saved his skin—the fine art of legerdemain.

A contemporary of Bosco's, Jean Eugène Robert-Houdin, was one of the most influential figures in the history of stage illusion and modern magic. In 1845 Robert-Houdin opened a salon in Paris called the "Soirées Fantastiques," where he presented nightly shows including mechanical and sleight-of-hand illusions which were extraordinarily fanciful and artistic. The following year he gave a performance in the private gardens of King Louis Philippe and began to travel Europe with his "Evening of Fantasies."

Robert-Houdin's salon was full of endless surprises, and the superb magician was continually inventing new illusions or adapting old techniques to suit the romantic, psychic, and scientific interests of his audiences. When he retired as a public performer, the magician recounted many stories concerning his travels and adventures in a lively autobiography which he entitled *The Secrets of a Prestidigitator*. A young performer who was to call himself "Harry Houdini" read this book when still a boy, and the name "Houdini" was fabricated from his idol's last name.

Jean Eugène Robert-Houdin. The son of a clockmaker, he became the most popular stage illusionist in Paris. His memoirs include a number of street magic episodes. *(Sheridan Collection)*

Street magic was the original inspiration for Robert-Houdin. His father had been a clockmaker, and Jean Eugène would probably have followed the same profession all his life if he had not encountered a street conjurer and mountebank in his hometown of Blois. According to his memoirs, Robert-Houdin was only eighteen when he met the conjurer, but he could still recall vividly his first impressions long after he had become known as "the father of modern magic." In his autobiography he wrote:

One after-dinner, while walking along the side of the Loire, engaged by the thoughts suggested by the falling autumn leaves, I was aroused from my revery by the sound of a trumpet, evidently blown by a practiced performer. It may be easily supposed that I was not the last to obey this startling summons, and a few other idlers also formed a circle around the performer.

The performer called himself "Dr. Carlosbach," and he gave an engrossing demonstration of cups-and-balls tricks. Though Robert-Houdin watched every move of the conjurer carefully, the young man was unable to detect a single flaw in the performance. He was especially impressed when the ingenious Dr. Carlosbach pulled a nutmeg out of a boy's nose, for the sleight was so convincing that the boy started snorting and sneezing—to blow out any more nutmegs which might be lodged in his nostrils.

At the end of the sleight-of-hand performance, Dr. Carlosbach honored the citizens of Blois by telling them about his vermifuge balsam which he claimed would destroy vermin, flush out worms, and distill noxious odors from the body. He claimed the best way to halt daily decay was by a process of embalming. And what could be better adapted to such a process than the Vermifuge Balsam, invented by Egyptian sages of old, which had preserved mummies intact for untold centuries? The powerful elixir, said Dr. Carlosbach, would be dispensed free, but only to the people of Blois.

The townspeople, of course, rushed forward to grab the bottles. To their amazement, Dr. Carlosbach only started to laugh at them. His laughter was followed by a public apology:

"Gentlemen, [he said], do not be angry with me for the little trick I have played you; I wished thus to put you on your guard against those charlatans who daily deceive you, just as I have done myself. I am no doctor, but simply a conjurer—professor of mystification and author of a book in which you will find, in addition to the discourse I have just delivered, the description of a great number of conjuring tricks. Would you like to learn the art of amusing yourself in society? For sixpence you may satisfy your curiosity."

Robert-Houdin paid his sixpence for the conjurer's book but was disappointed to find that it told him almost nothing about the sleight of hand he had just witnessed. The next morning, he went to visit the tavern where Dr. Carlosbach was staying, to ask for some clarification. But the boy was told, by an enraged inn-keeper, that the professor of

Dr. Carlosbach, the street conjurer seen by young Robert-Houdin, may have resembled the performer in this engraving. The charlatan has mounted a chair to expound on the power of his medicines and magic. *(Sheridan Collection)*

mystification had left town already—and without paying for his room! There was nothing in the room he had occupied but a large bag which turned out to be full of sand. A showman to the end, Dr. Carlosbach had attached a placard to the bag with the words "The Mystifying Bag." It was the last trick he would perform in the town of Blois for a long, long time. Or so said the innkeeper.

Inspired by this elusive character, Robert-Houdin soon began to practice magic for himself. Like most young magicians, Robert-Houdin probably learned the cups-and-balls first, imitating the moves of the amazing Dr. Carlosbach. But he was already forty years old before he began showing on stage some of the great illusions he had learned or invented.

Throughout his career, Robert-Houdin prepared each magical effect with the care and precision of an expert clockmaker and mechanician. But he also had the adeptness to take advantage of any situation to perform his own kind of street magic. In fact, the most impressive trick ever performed by the magician did not take place in a theater at all, but in the garden of Louis Philippe of Orléans. Even the date—June 6, 1845—was an important factor in the success of the magic.

Robert-Houdin asked for six handkerchiefs from the audience—which was made up of the king's attendants and favored guests—and announced that these items would be invisibly transported to any place the king desired. The magician asked the spectators to write down a number of locations where they wanted the silks to be found. When their selections had been noted, Robert-Houdin collected the slips of paper and handed three of them to the king. His Majesty read aloud the three alternatives which had been selected at random—the candelabra on the mantel; the dome of the Invalides; and the roots of an orange tree in his garden. After some rumination, the king declared that the handkerchiefs should be found at the roots of the orange tree.

At once Robert-Houdin placed the handkerchiefs under a bell of opaque glass and said a few magical words. When he raised the jar, the handkerchiefs had vanished. In their place was a white turtledove, with a ribbon tied around its neck holding a small key. The magician noted that the reason for this messenger bird's appearance would soon become clear. A moment later he announced that the king would now find the handkerchiefs at the chosen spot. Immediately the king sent one of his servants to uncover the roots of the orange tree, and the messenger promptly returned with a small, rusty box in his hands.

"Well, Monsieur Robert-Houdin," said the king, "here is a box. Am I to conclude it contains the handkerchiefs?"

"Yes, sire," replied the magician, "and they have been there for a long time."

"How can that be? The handkerchiefs were lent to you scarce a quarter of an hour ago."

"I cannot deny it, sire; but what would my magic avail me if I could not perform incomprehensible tricks? Your majesty will doubtlessly be still more surprised when I prove to your satisfaction that this coffer, as well as its contents, was deposited at the base of the orange tree sixty years ago."

Robert-Houdin told the king to unlock the box. This could by done with the key hanging from the neck of the bird which had appeared under the bell jar. Fitting the key to the lock, the king opened the lid of the box and pulled out an envelope which carried the wax seal of Count Cagliostro—a notorious necromancer and soothsayer who had lived in France before the Revolution. Already amazed at this find, the king proceeded to open the envelope—which smelled of magician's sulfur—and opened a message signed by the great charlatan of the previous century. The message read:

This day, the 6th of June, 1785, this iron box containing six handkerchiefs, was placed among the roots of an orange-tree by me, Balsamo, Count de Cagliostro, to serve in performing an act of magic, which will be executed on the same day sixty years hence before Louis Philippe of Orléans and his family.

The prophecy had been fulfilled to the letter. The king was unable to find any clue to the trick, but he knew a number of reasons why it should be impossible. The note from Cagliostro seemed genuine, yet Robert-Houdin was too young to have known the soothsayer personally. The only way the two magicians could have arranged the trick was through some mystical connection that bridged space and time. As for the handkerchiefs, they had been chosen from the audience at random. In fact the choice of a location had even been arbitrary, since the king himself had made the final selection of a spot where the handkerchiefs were to be found. And how did one explain the bird with the key around its neck which appeared under the bell jar . . . ?

As far as we know, King Louis Philippe never learned how the trick was performed though he must have puzzled over the enigma many times. In his memoir the conjurer does not reveal how he carefully manipulated the situation for ultimate surprise—how he prepared the envelope, the casket, and the bird with a key around its neck. But we can be fairly certain of the procedure. In selecting a site for the "discovery," Robert-Houdin simply substituted three slips of paper for those submitted by the audience. The choice of locations was his. He assumed that the king would not choose the dome of the Invalides, which was too far away, nor the candelabra on the mantle, which was within easy reach. Therefore the magician had an assistant waiting to rush the six handkerchiefs to the base of the orange tree. On the way the assistant slipped the silks into the prepared envelope containing Cagliostro's note (written by Robert-Houdin). The sealed envelope was placed inside the box, and the container buried at the roots of the tree. Meanwhile, Robert-Houdin stalled for time by saying magical words over the bell jar and distracting the audience with the live turtle-dove.

Another, though lesser, public figure mentioned in the memoirs was a certain Belgian customs official who was also exposed to the magic of Robert-Houdin. The trick which the magician called "second sight"—that is, mind reading—worked as perfectly on the street as it had on stage.

During the Soirées Fantastiques, the magician's son Émile would be blindfolded and turned around with his back toward the audience. His father would then ask the boy to describe certain members of the audience and announce what was in their pockets. From the spectators' viewpoint it seemed that Émile had the uncanny ability to read minds, for he invariably described the person and the possessions with perfect accuracy. This ability came in handy when Robert-Houdin tried to cross the Belgian border in 1846.

The magician's carriage was stopped at the frontier town of Quévrain, and the customs

Cagliostro (1743–1795), a notorious necromancer and charlatan. It was his letter, with seal and signature, that Robert-Houdin found at the roots of the orange tree. (NYPL Picture Library)

officials told Robert-Houdin that he would have to unpack all his equipment and pay duty on it before he could cross the border to enter Belgium. The magician argued that he needed this equipment for his show, and he could not afford to lose time unpacking all his valuable apparatus. Finding that the lower officials would not budge, Robert-Houdin asked to see the director of customs immediately.

As it happened, the director was more interested in discussing magic than helping the conjurer into his country, but Robert-Houdin saw a way to turn this interest to his advantage. He offered to show the burgher some examples of his art and mentioned that his son Émile had the unusual power of second sight.

The director appeared doubtful. Émile was a few yards off down the road, kicking a stone back and forth, and did not seem at all concerned about the conjuring profession. Robert-Houdin called out to his son:

"Émile! Can you tell us what this gentleman has in the left breast pocket of his suit?"

"Certainly," replied the boy, kicking the stone again. "He has a blue-striped handkerchief."

The customs director seemed surprised, but went on to ask whether the boy could tell him what was underneath the blue-striped handkerchief. When this question was passed along to the talented Émile, the boy replied, "There is a green morocco spectacle-case, without the spectacles."

At this point the director admitted that the boy's performance was "very curious," but went on to ask what was under the spectacle case.

"It is a piece of sugar which the gentleman saved from his cup of coffee," Émile replied, when his father had passed along the message.

"Ah! That is too fine." the director exclaimed. "The lad is a sorcerer."

Evidently the customs director had heard enough. He quickly made arrangements for Robert-Houdin and his equipage to cross the border with only a small tariff. The bill was paid, and Robert-Houdin entered the nation of Belgium with his talented son and small company of travelers.

Robert-Houdin's secret was simple enough, and the greater credit should go to Émile for his extraordinary memory. During his many months of stage performance, the father had perfected an elaborate word code with Émile. By the way he phrased his questions, Robert-Houdin could communicate the answers to his son. When he first met the customs director, Robert-Houdin did some deft pickpocketing, discovered what was in the pockets of the customs official, then returned the items in their original order. Using the prearranged code, Robert-Houdin told his son about the handkerchief, spectacles, and the lump of sugar which he merely assumed was left over from the gentleman's afternoon coffee.

As for the customs director, it is interesting to speculate what the gentleman might have been hiding in his other pockets. A note from a mistress? Some mention of a bribe? A smuggled jewel? Judging from the quick way he moved

the magician over the border, the customs director certainly did not want the boy with second sight to look in any more pockets. Better, by far, to have the sorcerer and his apprentice continue on their way.

Alexander Herrmann could make a living person rise ten feet in the air or a small card rise a few inches out of a glass bowl. He could make a man vanish from the heart of a burning pyre or a delicate wine glass disappear from his fingertips. He could catch a flying bullet between his teeth or find a tiny jewel nestled in the heart of a salad. He was a master of the art of stage magic, but street magic followed him everywhere.

Or so it seemed. Everywhere he went, unusual and extraordinary things happened to him. He seemed to have no control over these events, so he accepted them as a matter of course. He was like a man who sees flying saucers every day and becomes so accustomed to the sight that he no longer considers a flying saucer anything extraordinary. Alexander Herrmann seemed eternally in the presence of a demon who played at magic, and he simply allowed the demon to have its way.

Alexander Herrmann was born to magic. His father, Samuel, had been a sleight-of-hand artist in Germany and France, and the profession was taken up by the eldest of his sons, Carl. Alexander Herrmann, born in 1844, joined Carl's popular magic show as soon as he could play the part of assistant, and he learned many of the principles of the conjuring arts while traveling with his older brother.

Alexander started his own show in 1861 and traveled continental Europe and the British Isles billing himself as "Herrmann the Great." His show was large and well-publicized, and he usually performed with the assistance of his wife Adelaide. Though Herrmann traveled around the world several times, he made his home in the United States in 1876, and he was beyond doubt the most popular magician in this country during the latter part of the nineteenth century.

Herrmann once remarked to a friend, "I learned in America the value of making the press talk about a public performer." To make the press talk, Herrmann looked as well as acted the part of a magic-maker. A reporter named Henry Ridgely Evans, later an historian of magic, was working as a reporter for the *Baltimore News* when Alexander Herrmann walked into the city office of the paper, and he never forgot his first impression of the great magician. With his jet-black goatee, his piercing eyes and long dark cape, Herrmann was the perfect image of the devil. Of course the analogy was not wasted on the eager reporter, who soon discovered that the man in devil's clothing could get money from a coat pocket, turn a watch into a turnip, get a hardboiled egg out of a person's nose, and of course draw a rabbit out of a hat.

Evans, the young reporter, was assigned to follow the miracle worker from place to place around the city, and he witnessed some memorable demonstrations of the fine art of impromptu street magic. One incident, involving Herrmann and a surly streetcar conductor, was duly reported the next day in the *Baltimore News.*

In the center of Baltimore, Herrmann boarded a streetcar and found himself a seat. But when the conductor came round to collect the fare, Herrmann simply refused to pay. He insisted that he had already paid the conductor

Alexander Herrmann, better known as "Herrmann the Great." Despite his sober appearance, he did street magic that delighted his friends and astonished the public. *(Mulholland Collection)*

with a five-dollar gold piece, and the man in uniform now owed him change.

"Here," cried Herrmann suddenly, "the gold coin is sticking right out of your scarf." Herrmann took the gold piece out of the man's clothing, then looked at the conductor again and said sternly, "And worse than that, you've robbed me."

Herrmann stuck his hand into the conductor's vest pocket and took out a huge bundle of dollar bills. The bewildered conductor did not even have time to reply before Herrmann flung the bills into the air, scattering them all over the streetcar. There was an immediate uproar as people jumped out of their seats and scrambled for the bills.

To their disappointment, the riders soon discovered that the greenbacks were fakes. Where the portrait of a president should have been, there was instead a picture of a devilish looking character with a black goatee and the caption "Herrmann the Great." The bills also invited one and all to attend the magician's performance at Ford's Opera House that evening. As for the harassed conductor and the driver of the streetcar, both were given free passes to the show.

Herrmann was again in the news when he was arrested for pickpocketing in Union Square, New York. According to the story, he was standing among a crowd of people watching a Hindu magician perform a few tricks. In front of Herrmann were two boys completely enthralled by the entertainment, and one of the boys was wearing a gold pocket watch on a long chain. Herrmann waited until a policeman approached, then reached into the boy's pocket and lifted the watch.

The boys and the policeman all saw Herrmann with the watch-chain in his hand, but he had acted so quickly that the watch itself had already vanished by the time they caught him. The policeman arrested the culprit and hauled him off to the police station, with the two boys along as witnesses. They went at once to the police sergeant to explain the case.

Herrmann of course protested his innocence and charged that the whole situation was a frame-up. The magician righteously insisted that the two boys were thieves themselves and had already stolen some items from the policeman.

"That one took his badge, I am sure," said Herrmann, pointing to one of the boys. It was not until that moment that the policeman noticed that his badge was missing, and he looked at the two boys suspiciously.

When the boy insisted that he had never touched the policeman's badge, Herrmann told the youth to check his pockets. The missing badge was found tucked away in the boy's hip pocket.

"As for this other fellow," said Herrmann, "I suppose he is the one who stole the officer's pistol."

At these words the policeman clapped his hand to his holster—which he found to be empty—and a look of puzzled disbelief came over his face.

Meanwhile the second young man frisked himself and—feeling a weight in his coat pocket—produced the missing weapon and gingerly handed it over to the officer.

"Begging your pardon," continued Herrmann, "I think it is high time the policeman searched himself for that missing watch."

The officer was conscientious in his search, and in a moment he produced the gold timepiece and mutely handed it over to the sergeant.

"You see, sir," concluded Herrmann, addressing the sergeant, "I am the only honest man among them all."

Herrmann handed over his professional calling card, which the sergeant perused only a moment before concluding the hearing. Said the sergeant:

"You did this pretty well, Mr. Herrmann. But in the future, you'd better not joke with policemen." And the case was dismissed.

Of course the sergeant's words had little effect on the irrepressible demon that followed Herrmann from place to place, and he continued to bewitch, bother, and bewilder law enforcement officers at every opportunity. To Herrmann things like money, coins, and jewelry were merely props for his continuous street show. Wherever he went, the magician made precious objects change shape, color, size—or vanish completely. Unlike a stage show, these incidents were not announced with a program or introduced by the opening of a curtain. People didn't even know what was happening until events began to go awry.

Once Herrmann encountered a woman on the street who was selling hardboiled eggs from a basket. Herrmann bought two for a nickel and broke them open. Inside each egg was a shiny quarter.

"Hah! I'm in luck today!" exclaimed Herrmann, pocketing the quarters. He promptly bought several more eggs, and when he broke them open found a half dollar in each one.

"Well, ma'am," said Herrmann, "I like those eggs so much I think I'll take them all. How much will that be?"

"For the good Lord's sake," replied the woman, "you couldn't buy another of those eggs for all the money you've got." She hoisted her basket of eggs to her shoulder and set off for home.

It probably did not take her long to find out that the remainder of the eggs contained nothing more precious than hard-cooked yolk. But the woman would also have discovered in the bottom of her basket enough money to pay for twice the number of eggs she destroyed. And to repay her for the amusement she had unconsciously afforded Herrmann the Great.

As with many of Herrmann's tricks, the incident with the egg vender certainly never made headlines. But it was not meant as a cruel joke either. The fact is that Herrmann saw the chance for street magic in every situation, great or small, and like a restless adventurer could not resist the temptation to try out his dexterity and

The bullet-catching feat. When the marksmen fired, Alexander Herrmann caught the rifle bullets on a plate. He performed the trick many times on stage and outdoors—once, in a Havana bullring. *(NYPL Picture Collection)*

match wits with anyone he encountered. Far from being malicious, Herrmann was known for his generosity and kindness, his worldly knowledge and urbane manners, but he was like a wandering Dr. Faustus who could not resist using his magical powers to tease people and expose their folly. Herrmann once confided to a friend, H. J. Burlingame, "Few people have any idea how much fun a magician can have by the exercise of his art for his own amusement." For Herrmann street magic was both art and amusement, and the best spectator of all was the magician himself.

In time his friends came to recognize that Herrmann lived in a world of fantastic coincidences and remarkable encounters. When he met Ulysses S. Grant, Herrmann pulled a cigar out of the president's bushy whiskers. When he visited the Marquis of Acapules, Herrman found a pair of partridges in his own hat, and offered them to his host for the main dinner course. When he met a pioneer in San Francisco, the burly frontiersman soon found that his own bowie knife had flown out of its sheath and stuck itself into his bowler hat.

For one friend Herrmann produced an entire snack of pumpernickel bread, Apollinaire water, and limburger cheese. These items came, respectively, from a coat pocket, the bottom of a chair, and the inside of his friend's coat-tails. When the owner of the cafe complained about the smell of the cheese, Herrmann found a bottle of perfume in the proprietor's pocket, uncorked it, and set it out on the table.

Herrmann raised a wine bottle to pour a drink, and the bottle vanished. He raised a full wine glass to propose a toast, and the glass vanished. Gold rings turned up in salads. Petty change was turned into silver dollars. Familiar objects, steady habits, easy assumptions became jumbled and confounded in the presence of Herrmann the Great.

Usually the people who witnessed these acts were so amazed that they were incapable of explaining the recurring phenomena. The age of witchcraft had ended long ago. Even psychics and mediums were being exposed in the press. Yet magic traveled with Alexander Herrmann around the world—magic made up of surprises, mysteries, extraordinary stage illusions and street diversions. As H. J. Burlingame expressed it, Herrmann created his own atmosphere of mystery, the product of the fame of his art and "the babble of tongues." He was a conjurer who created magic on the street as well as the stage, and he used his magic to bring bafflement, pleasure, and endless amusement into the daily lives of others.

Alexander Herrmann died on December 17, 1896, on his way to an engagement in Bradford, Pennsylvania. In that year a young man who called himself Harry Houdini was traveling with a side show, performing card magic and escape tricks. The newest addition to his act was a straitjacket escape that would one day be performed in front of tens of thousands of people outdoors, above city streets, in the greatest performance of street magic of all time. But in 1896 Houdini was unrecognized, and he struggled to eke out an existence in the side show circuit. He dreamed of some day being as famous as the great Alexander Herrmann. He could not have realized that some day the name "Houdini" would be a household word, while names such as Alexander Herrmann, Comte, Bosco, and even Robert-Houdin would be remembered by only the few.

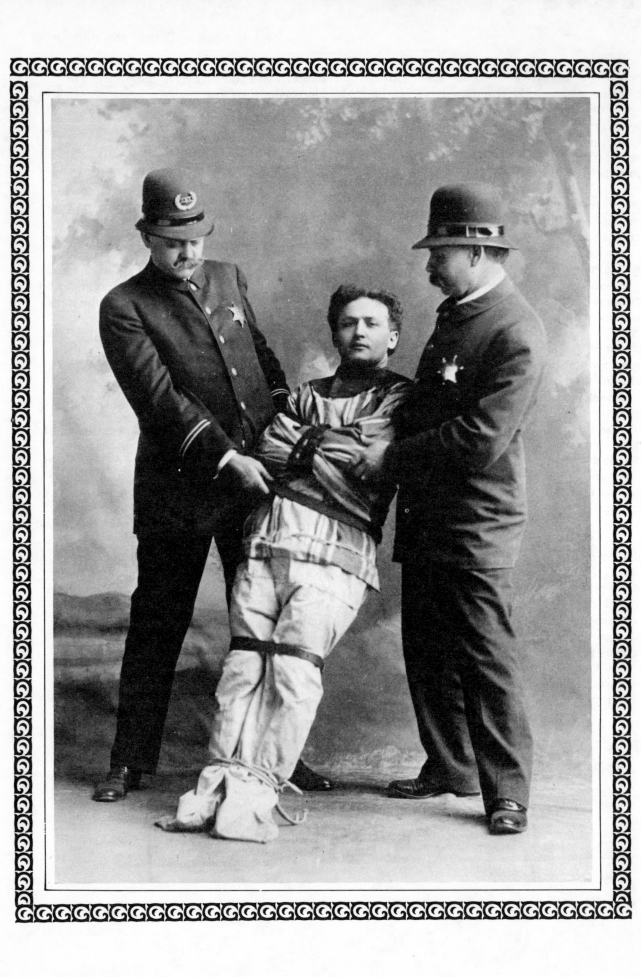

The Age of Houdini

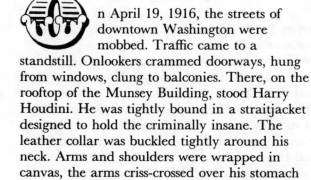n April 19, 1916, the streets of downtown Washington were mobbed. Traffic came to a standstill. Onlookers crammed doorways, hung from windows, clung to balconies. There, on the rooftop of the Munsey Building, stood Harry Houdini. He was tightly bound in a straitjacket designed to hold the criminally insane. The leather collar was buckled tightly around his neck. Arms and shoulders were wrapped in canvas, the arms criss-crossed over his stomach and strapped to his back with leather belts. One man tied a heavy rope around the magician's ankles and knotted it tightly. Almost immobilized, Houdini leaned forward to check the knots, then nodded his approval and said a few words to his assistants. The famous escape artist had to be lifted bodily and carried like a package to the edge of the roof.

The men laid Houdini on his side on the high balustrade. Strapped into his bonds, he looked down at the crowd filling the streets and avenues in every direction, as far as the eye could see. From that sheer height he could not make out features, only the sea of raised faces and the flotsam of waving hats and handkerchiefs. And he could hear a distant roar as they cheered. It was all music to his ego. Houdini relaxed, waiting for the first shock of tension in his legs as the assistants lowered him over the edge.

Down in the street, the crowd went silent as the body of the magician slid over the parapet of the Munsey Building. In a moment Houdini hung free, swaying gently back and forth, head-downward, high above the pavement. A guy-rope went taut, and the floating body steadied in the air.

Like a descending sarcophagus, Houdini was lowered until he hung one hundred feet over the pavement. People glanced at their watches as he began his escape. Houdini began to writhe in his bonds, struggling against the thick canvas, straining the unbreakable leather straps. He twisted upward until, amazingly, his body was almost doubled, then dropped down and hung still as if exhausted. People checked their watches. One minute. How long could he endure that incredible position? How would he be rescued if something went wrong? Some feared this might be the moment of failure for Houdini. After all, he was forty-two years old.

Another minute went by. But during that short time, Houdini managed, miraculously, to slide the arms of the straitjacket over his head. This only seemed to increase the tangle. His efforts became violent. He twisted and turned as if wrestling with some unseen animal. Was he panicking? He seemed to be chewing desperately at the leather bonds. The rapt audience suddenly realized that this was Houdini's secret. He did not tear free from the

The picture is posed but the straitjacket genuine. Sleeves were tightly buckled in back and a heavy leather collar was fastened around Houdini's neck. *(Mulholland Collection)*

straitjacket. He just unbuckled it—with his teeth!

A moment later, the straitjacket slipped from his arms and fell into the heart of the crowd. The escape had taken two minutes, thirty seconds. Arms spreadeagled, body released, Houdini acknowledged the cheers of the audience. An infectious joy seemed to ripple through the crowd. Straitjackets might hold maniacs and criminals, but not the incredible Houdini.

Houdini's escapes were the greatest street magic ever performed. From the early 1900s, when he first became known throughout the world, until his death in 1926, Houdini gave people the magic of acts which stretched human powers to their limits. The great literary critic, Edmund Wilson, wrote of Houdini, "It is thrilling, even in a juggler or a trapeze performer, to see some human faculty carried to its furthest point, to a point where its feats seem incredible." Houdini thrilled audiences time and again as he allowed them to witness a lone man demonstrate a miracle. The crowd came to a standstill, the people of the world watched in awe because the magic of the escape was irresistible. Yet there were no stage tricks involved, no hidden apparatus or deft sleight of hand. There was only a man using his human powers as though they were miraculous. His reputation as a miracle worker increased with every year of his life, until it was no longer a reputation but a myth that was part of the age. Finally people even came to believe in the myth of Houdini.

Harry Houdini was a myth created partially by the magician himself and partially by the "babble of tongues"—as H. J. Burlingame would have called it—and the currents of public opinion which ran through his life and deeds. He was born in 1874 in Budapest, Hungary, and his family moved to Appleton, Wisconsin, shortly after his birth. His real name was Ehrich Weiss (or Weisz), and he adopted the pseudonym of Houdini, adding an "i" to "Houdin," after reading the memoirs of Robert-Houdin and studying that magician's famous tricks. He adopted the new name at the age of seventeen, when he had already firmly decided what his career would be.

There were four children in the Weiss family, though only Ehrich and his brother Theo became involved in the world of magic.

Their father, Samuel Weiss, was a rabbi with a small congregation in Appleton, and he struggled to support the family on a meager income. Ehrich's mother Cecilia was a tolerant woman who provided Ehrich with strong encouragement, even as he developed that remarkable and strange alter-ego called Houdini. The family eventually moved to the Upper East Side of New York, where Samuel died in 1892. After his father's death Houdini did his best to provide for his mother. He loved her dearly, and his extraordinary affection for her was openly expressed by his gifts, in letters, and even in public statements.

Early in life, Ehrich must have realized that his family would always be impoverished, but he also believed in his own ability to make it to the top of that risky mountain known as show business. The first time he left home, Ehrich was only twelve years old, and he carried a shoeshine kit rather than a magic wand. Ehrich eventually made it to New York and, when his family, too, moved there, worked for a time as a tie-cutter. However he soon put his shears aside and started a magic show in collaboration with his brother Theo, calling their act "The Brothers Houdini." In the show Houdini produced a flower from his buttonhole, a red silk handkerchief from the center of a candle flame, and he performed a number of card tricks. But the most popular act was an escape trick called "The Metamorphosis" which the brothers performed together.

In this trick the two brothers appeared to change places magically. Theo, with his hands tied, crawled into a sack that was roped shut, then placed in a padlocked trunk. Houdini pulled a screen in front of the trunk, stepped behind the drape, and clapped his hands three times. An instant later the screen was pushed aside by Theo. When Theo opened the trunk and the sack, Houdini stepped out. As the audience saw it, the whole "metamorphosis" took no more than a few seconds. The success of this early trick inspired Houdini to invent escapes of a similar kind.

"The Brothers Houdini" traveled throughout the Midwest, acting in the sideshows and dime museums popular during the 1890s. The dime museums, like country fairs and carnivals, featured many of the traditional street entertainers, and the Brothers Houdini performed alongside midgets, contortionists, fire-eaters, sword-swallowers, and freaks of all kinds. The Houdinis performed six to twenty shows each day, but earned barely enough to keep themselves alive. They were constantly moving, since the dime museums offered patrons a continual change of fare.

In 1893, when Harry Houdini was only nineteen, the two brothers performed at the Chicago World's Fair. There Houdini learned a new adaptation of some ancient street magic—a sleight which he was to call "the East Indian needle trick." The act was performed by a Hindu conjurer who had attracted a crowd on the midway. The magician, who of course called himself a "fakir," appeared to swallow a dozen needles, gulping visibly as he took each sliver of steel in his mouth. He then swallowed a small ball of cotton. Pausing only a moment to digest these articles, the fakir reached in-between his teeth and pulled. Out came the twelve needles evenly threaded on a long string.

Houdini realized that many in the audience actually believed that the fakir swallowed the needles and cotton. Among the spectators there was always someone willing and ready to explain how the Hindus acquired masterly control over their powers of digestion and regurgitation. The young Houdini also knew that people were fascinated by the element of danger involved in this experiment. It was more gruesome than swallowing swords or daggers because there were twelve—a whole dozen—of the tiny needles, each capable of inflicting terrible pain.

But any magician knew that the Hindu probably had a safe as well as foolproof method of doing the trick. After the crowd dispersed, Houdini approached the self-proclaimed fakir and offered to exchange a few secrets with him. It is not known exactly what exchange was negotiated. Houdini was probably shrewd enough to acquire more information than he gave away, but he may have told the fakir a knot-tying secret or a card trick. In return, he learned the method of needle swallowing—a trick which was to add to his image as a wonder-worker for the rest of his life.

Many years later, a number of magicians began imitating the needle trick, and Houdini claimed he had exclusive performing rights. All imitators, he said, were using sleight-of-hand methods and therefore were impostors who had no right to demonstrate this magic as if it were genuine. Houdini claimed that he was the only performer who actually swallowed the needles, and he announced his willingness to appear before a committee to prove his claim.

At his request a group of observers were assembled. Houdini swallowed a small cork ball and encouraged each investigator to search his mouth. When the committee found nothing there, Houdini asked the investigators to touch the outside of his throat, where they could feel the shape of the cork ball lodged in his esophagus. Then Houdini gave a live demonstration of how he brought the ball from his throat into his mouth. Houdini said he controlled the needles exactly as he manipulated the cork ball, and his demonstration should prove the trick was genuine. Incredible as it may seem to us, the members of the committee accepted the logic of this explanation, and they gave Houdini exclusive performing rights to "The East Indian Needle Trick."

However, at nineteen Houdini was still just an unknown sideshow performer, and even needle-swallowing did not win him any lengthy theatre engagements. By 1894 he and Theo had returned to New York, where they performed in dime museums around the city and in the side show at Coney Island. In June of that year, Houdini met Wilhelmina Beatrice Rahner, age eighteen, and he and "Bess" were married within ten days of their first meeting. After that, Bess took Theo's place in "The Metamorphosis," while Houdini's brother left to start his own side show act. For several years Bess was Houdini's only assistant as he struggled to win the attention of vaudeville managers and theatre owners. Throughout those years Houdini searched incessantly for new effects and novel ways to strengthen old routines.

Some of his best ideas occurred to him in unexpected places. The idea for the straitjacket escape came to him early in his career while he was taking a visitor's tour of an insane asylum in Nova Scotia. According to his own account, Houdini was shown around the institution by a Dr. Steeves, whom he met while giving shows in the Canadian provinces. As the doctor led him by one of the padded cells, Houdini saw a man in a straitjacket lying on the cushioned floor turning and twisting to get free. Hardly considering the man's plight, Houdini was most

Harry and Bess Houdini with the side show company. They shared the bill with clowns, acrobats, animal trainers and stuntmen. The young Houdinis are seated on the end at right. *(NYPL Theatre Collection)*

fascinated by the tortuous-looking device which kept the inmate tightly bound. As he watched the struggle, Houdini noticed that the man might have been able to free his arms if he had twisted his shoulders and allowed some slack to form in the canvas jacket. But of course the trapped man was no escape artist, and he only succeeded in tightening the straitjacket as he continued to struggle.

Even as Houdini completed his tour of the asylum, he was thinking of the strangely awesome effect of seeing the man in the straitjacket. Years later he wrote:

Previous to this incident I had seen and used various restraints such as insane restraint muffs, belts, bed-straps, etc., but this was the first time I saw a straitjacket, and it left so vivid an impression on my mind that I hardly slept that night, and in such moments as I slept, I saw nothing but straitjackets, maniacs, and padded cells! In the wakeful part of the night, I wondered what the effect would be to an audience to have them see a man placed in a straitjacket and watch him force himself free therefrom.

It was from this original conception that the idea of the straitjacket escape was born. Within a short time he began performing the release on stage. When he was sure of its success, he practiced the escape outdoors, hanging head-down from high buildings in the presence of tens of thousands of spectators. His street performances were seen in Kansas City, New York, Baltimore, St. Louis, Minneapolis, Washington, D.C., and in dozens of other cities in the United States and around the world.

What was the allure of this escape? What was the strange vision that kept Houdini dreaming of "straitjackets, maniacs, and padded cells"? Many people would have been horrified to see an insane man struggling for his life, trying with all his might to break the leather and canvas which bound him. But unlike most people, Houdini considered the struggle as a theatrical possibility and a logical problem. He realized objectively the tremendous emotional impact of seeing a man escape from a restraint of this kind. "The word straitjacket alone," said Houdini, "conjures up to the mind pictures of violent maniacs and thoughts that tend to gruesome channels."

Early in his career Houdini discovered that the release was not effective theatrically unless it was performed in full view of the audience. In the original stage presentation, Houdini had himself strapped into the jacket and then went behind a curtain to make the escape. He expected the effect would be most "magical" this way. To his surprise he learned that concealment was a mistake. When he came out from behind the curtain with hair disheveled and clothing torn, he met with only light applause. The audience believed there was an assistant concealed behind the curtain who simply unbuckled the straitjacket. Houdini confronted a dilemma. Either he should drop the escape from his repertoire or else he would have to perform it in front of the audience and reveal the method of release.

The next time, he tried it without the curtain, and the straitjacket escape made a hit. By accident Houdini had stumbled on a new approach to the art of performing magic. Instead of concealing the secret, he revealed it. Yet the impact of the release was so strong that people literally could "hardly believe their eyes." Some called him a contortionist and said his body was double-jointed. Others would insist he was only a charlatan, claiming the straitjackets were rigged to make the release easier. Many were content to call him simply a "magician," using that word in its vaguest sense to describe a man whose physical powers could not be explained.

To say Houdini performed magic was a convenient way to describe his actions. But the real mystery of the man always remained a question. Why did he do it? Why would any person in his right mind allow himself to be strapped inside a straitjacket, then hang upside down above a city street? Was it for publicity alone?

These are questions which still remain unanswered. But many people have tried to explain why audiences regarded Houdini with awe—and what made him perform as he did. Houdini may have filled a symbolic role, representing each person's desire to fling off the fears, cares, and responsibilities of daily life with a dangerous act of courage. There is no question that Houdini acted out the role of hero, defying any challengers to equal his acts. There was a kind of national pride in Houdini that became particularly evident as the United States prepared to enter World War I. Houdini was one of those Americans who believed in his own greatness and set out to prove it, and his success made him a symbol of strength and determination.

There are also Freudian interpretations of Houdini's motives, and a number of psychologists have attempted to explain the way his acts appealed to the subconscious. Anyone studying Houdini's life sees at once the deeply felt relationship he had with his mother. A number of psychiatrists have gone on to interpret his escapes from boxes, bags, and ropes as the archetype of the child releasing itself from the womb. The Freudian interpretations become even more heady when one considers the Chinese Water Torture Cell, one of the last tricks Houdini developed for the stage. In this escape he would be suspended head-downward in a water-filled cabinet and attempt to release himself from this uncomfortable prenatal condition while the audience waited breathlessly to see him emerge alive and dripping wet.

Whatever their validity, these interpretations do not explain the most important element of Houdini's performance—the magic. Houdini was not just tussling with a piece of canvas. Rather he was escaping from something that was a part of the unknown. The people of the Middle Ages called that "unknown" by the name "demons." Modern psychiatrists might call it "compulsions." It lies both without and within the human being. But when a person engages in a visible struggle with such an unknown—with no clear explanation for his feats—then his character seems mysterious and his actions seem like magic.

Though the straitjacket escape was

invariably a crowd-stopper, Houdini probably achieved greatest fame for his jail breaks and underwater releases. These, too, were a kind of anarchistic street magic performed outside the boundaries of any conventional theater, often without the official consent of the police, and they gave Houdini an unparalleled reputation for courage and daring. With the straitjacket escape he had often defied local laws, for the packed crowds and jammed traffic could paralyze the center of a city for hours, and the police would have to rush to the scene to control the enthusiastic mob. Defiance of the law was carried even further as Houdini released himself from handcuffs or from jails designed to hold the most devious criminals. Certain that cells and handcuffs were unbreakable, confident police in dozens of cities sent their challenges to Houdini. He rarely failed to meet them.

On his first trip to England in 1900, when Houdini was struggling to build up his reputation as a stage performer, he stunned the detectives of Scotland Yard by escaping from a pair of sturdy British manacles. The manager of a London theater was present when the Scotland Yard detective placed Houdini up against a solid pillar and handcuffed the magician with his wrists behind the pole.

A "staged" handcuff escape. The escape king wears padlocks, handcuffs, iron balls and steel chains. Police officials searched Houdini and checked the locks. *(Mulholland Collection)*

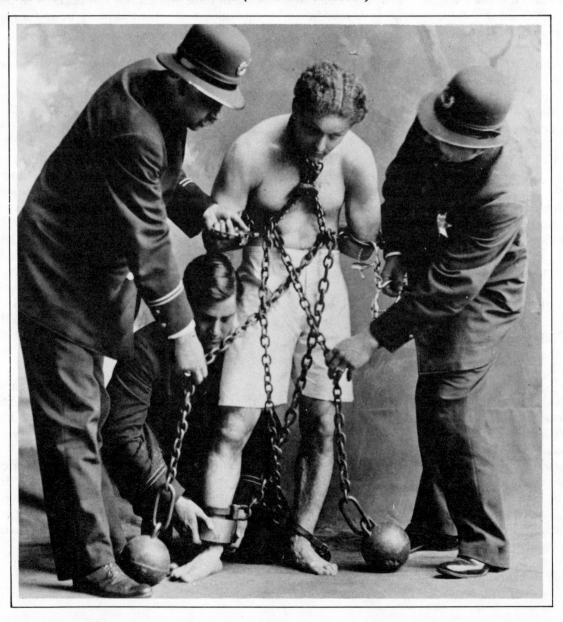

Detective and theater manager turned to leave the room. Before they opened the door, Houdini was free. The contract for the show was signed that day.

Throughout his career, Houdini escaped from handcuffs of every imaginable size and description. Some were bizarre, medieval-looking contraptions with bolts, screws, and heavy chains. Others were standard police handcuffs with intricate internal mechanisms supposedly impossible to open without a key. If Houdini had been a criminal there would have been no way to hold him—as police in every country soon realized.

Houdini's challenges to jailers and wardens brought him opportunities to make astonishing, well-publicized escapes. In 1906, he was stripped

The release. Publicity photos like these drew challenges from all over the country. (Mulholland Collection)

and locked in a single cell in "murderers' row" of the United States Jail in Washington. Houdini succeeded in escaping easily from his own cell, then shifted each of the prisoners to different locations by unlocking in turn each of the cell doors. Reporters and photographers were amazed to see Houdini escape in only twenty-seven minutes. But prison officials were rather chagrined to find their rooming assignments had been shuffled, and they immediately set out to improve security precautions in the prison.

In Boston Houdini was stripped, searched, and placed in Cell 60 of the Tombs. Houdini escaped from Cell 60, broke into Cell 77 (where his clothes were), dressed, then ran across the prison yard and climbed over the wall. The newsmen were still waiting for Houdini's surrender when the phone rang. Houdini was calling from his dressing room at the theatre. He graciously agreed to stop by for photographs.

One of his most successful escapades was release from a prison van in Moscow. The mobile cell was designed to transport prisoners to Siberia, and Russian police had made certain it was virtually impossible to escape from the vehicle. Lined with zinc and steel, the transport cell had only one door fastened on the outside with a heavy padlock. The only opening was a tiny barred window on the door which allowed the police to peer in at the prisoners.

After searching Houdini carefully, the police placed him in the van and locked the door. In less than half an hour he was out. People's reactions to Houdini's escapes often varied, but in this case the police were infuriated. They subjected him to another thorough search, then examined his manager as well.

When Houdini's jailbreak attempts were successful, he would ask the police to sign statements declaring the challenges had been met. The Moscow police, however, were so outraged they refused to sign a statement of any kind. Fortunately the event was witnessed by delighted journalists, and Houdini collected enough news clippings to testify to the validity of the escape.

Occasionally Houdini did have trouble meeting a challenge. He declined to attempt an escape from the Wayne County Jail when he learned that all the cell doors were controlled by an automatic locking device linked to a single electrical switch located in the warden's office. As always, Houdini inspected the cell block before accepting the challenge. This time he declared it was impossible for anyone to escape from a cell in that prison. Other "escape artists" later tried it, but as Houdini had predicted, they failed.

According to one story, Houdini was once outwitted by a shrewd jailer. After the usual frisking, the escape artist was placed in a normal jail cell equipped with a conventional keyhole lock. In front of witnesses the jailer closed the door and then retired to another room to wait for the magician to complete his work. The minutes ticked by. After an extraordinary amount of time, Houdini emerged with a calm but sheepish expression on his face. The jailer

was delighted. It had taken Houdini nearly two hours to escape from a jail cell that had been left unlocked!

As the story goes, Houdini later admitted he had tried to open the cell door by picking the lock. Of course the tumblers inside refused to budge. Houdini was about ready to give up when he discovered by accident that the door was only latched shut. The jailer had been perfectly correct in thinking Houdini might be defeated by his own ingenuity.

In his jailbreaks and handcuff releases, Houdini often made use of small picks which were concealed on his body or in his clothing, though too cleverly hidden for any inspector to find. But the escapes were not simple by any means. To meet his challenges Houdini had to learn almost every kind of lock, handcuff, and key in existence. He made hundreds of different varieties of picks and visited locksmiths, museums, jails, and manufacturers to examine every conceivable device that had ever been used to hold a human being.

Often he was challenged with situations which included neither bars nor fetters but traps that were ingenious and sometimes bizarre. In one case Houdini was bound up inside a giant "sea monster"—probably a cross between an octopus and a whale—which had washed up on the shore near Boston Harbor. Houdini recalled it as one of his most risky escapes. Since the monster had been washed with arsenic as a preservative, the inside was filled with the fumes of the poison. The escape king was almost overpowered before he managed to break free.

In 1907 the University of Pennsylvania promoted the home team by tying up Houdini inside a huge football especially prepared for the occasion. Houdini escaped in thirty-five minutes. But he ran a risk when he allowed a brewer in Leeds, England, to imprison him in a water can filled with beer. Houdini, a lifelong teetotaler, was thoroughly drunk after a few seconds in the vat, and he almost blacked out before his manager broke open the can and released him. What was meant as a semi-comic publicity stunt nearly cost him his life.

Though he accepted many challenges, the greatest of all was made by Houdini himself. It was a daring escape, the crowning achievement

With shackles on wrists and ankles, Houdini steps into a wooden packing crate. Moments later, the crate was nailed and chained shut, and the escape king thrown overboard. *(Mulholland Collection)*

of a lifetime of street magic. He called it the underwater release.

On July 7, 1912, a Sunday morning, Harry Houdini arrived at Pier Six on the East Side of Manhattan. The papers had announced that he would be handcuffed, nailed in a box, and thrown into the East River. Newsmen and photographers were on hand, and crowds lined the shore on either side of the pier.

The assistants were in the final stages of preparing the packing case as Houdini stepped onto the pier. Suddenly police appeared. Houdini was using city property for a public performance. It was not allowed. The stunt would have to be called off.

Houdini would not be deterred. He quickly made inquiries. The owner of the tugboat Catherine Moran said he would be willing to tow a boat with Houdini, his assistants, and his equipment far out in the East River where he would be beyond the city limits. In a few moments Houdini had made an agreement with a captain, and the newsmen began boarding the boat. The shackles, chains, and wooden packing crate were carried aboard, and Houdini gave the signal to start. The Catherine Moran pulled out into the current and dropped anchor just off Governor's Island.

Houdini looked like a sideshow strong man in his nineties-style bathing suit. He was in superb physical condition. Preparing for the dive, he stopped to pose for photographers. He looked grim but determined.

Heavy irons were clamped around his wrists and ankles, the bonds connected by a heavy chain. The newsmen on board realized at once that Houdini would have to free himself from all his shackles if he was to escape. If he tried swimming with the chains on, their weight would drag him to the bottom.

Houdini stepped into the packing case. It seemed too tiny to hold him. Constructed of heavy beams, with thick iron bands at each end, it was only two feet high, three feet wide, and thirty-four inches long. Houdini crouched down inside—with barely room to move. The lid was nailed shut, thick ropes tied crosswise and lengthwise. More steel bands were fastened in place, and two hundred pounds of iron weights were attached to the sides.

From shore all eyes were on the wooden chest as the crew slid it over the side of the boat and lowered it into the water. The time: 11:44

a.m. The heavy chest sank into the water. A few seconds later, it rose until its top was level with the surface of the river. Holding Houdini, the cask drifted away from the Catherine Moran.

Seconds ticked by. Swimmers tensed, ready to go to the rescue. A rowboat full of men started off from the tug. Along the shore the crowd waited expectantly. Suddenly there was a shout. A head appeared above the water, more than fifteen feet from the submerged chest. The rowboat sped off in pursuit, and in a moment Harry Houdini was brought in over the side, dripping wet but smiling. Minutes later, the chest was hoisted from the East River onto the deck of the boat. None of its boards had been loosened, and all the bindings of rope and steel were in place. Yet the man inside had escaped, to the cheers of the Sunday spectators.

Was it magic? Or only a stunt? Was Houdini really a wonder-worker? Or only a clever safecracker? These questions would be asked many times, even long after his secrets were known.

The real secret, the key to the mystery, was death. To every spectator death was feared, unknown, and unknowable. As they watched the sealed chest slip into the water, the Sunday morning strollers realized they were seeing a magician perform a trick. They also knew that something might go wrong, that the trick box might turn into a casket. If so, there was nothing anyone on shore would do to save him.

In his diary Houdini once wrote, "It is the element of danger that interests people. People do not wish to see one killed, of course, but they are more interested in a stunt when they think there is danger attached to it." He added a sentence that seems oddly contradictory: "Human beings don't like to see other human beings lose their lives; but they do love to be on the spot when it happens." Houdini was grappling with the fact that people came and watched to see whether he, Houdini, could live through each experience—which was almost the same as saying they came to see him die. This must have been a disturbing thought, and certainly not a reflection that would give a performer any great respect for the desires of his audience. Yet Houdini knew his spectators would not settle for packaged danger or pretended risks. They wanted the real thing, and he was willing to give it to them.

Time and again, Houdini faced the

ultimate mystery. Like previous exploits, the underwater escape performed that Sunday in 1912 was repeated many times before many audiences, and each time people wondered whether he would survive. Whether he hung by his feet from tall buildings or leapt into deep rivers, Houdini created thrills out of people's hidden fears and traumas. Each time he walked into the jaws of death and emerged, he demonstrated the miracle of survival. Yet each survival seemed more mysterious than the last—each mystery brought him closer to that incomprehensible thing called magic.

Houdini had a long and curious association with occult magic. Early in his life, Houdini and his wife Bess incorporated various mind-reading routines into their side show act. As an employee of Dr. Hill and his traveling medicine show, Houdini gave "spiritual séances" during which he would reveal the thoughts and secret desires of people in the audience, and receive messages from their deceased relatives. Upon arriving in a town, he would go through the local graveyard, study old newspapers, and chat with the town busybodies to acquire information about his audience. By the time Houdini got to the stage, he had a precise knowledge of the local history and gossip, and he could call forth all sorts of reasonable-sounding messages from the grave. He could also recall murders and scandals, and even suggest the outcomes of some love affairs and business deals. Houdini quickly learned that impressionable audiences can be either entertained or hoodwinked by an adept performer who pretends to have knowledge of the occult.

In his later years Houdini drew upon all the methodology he had learned as Dr. Hill's featured performer to expose many of the fake spiritualists and mediums popular in the early twentieth century. Mediums were supposed to be able to hear spirit voices and interpret signals from the dead, but Houdini soon became convinced that most, if not all mediums were frauds. Later he joined a committee sponsored by *Scientific American* to investigate the practices of famous mediums and see their evidence of spirit visitations.

Spirits, it was said, made their presence known by rapping on tables or walls, writing on blank slates, causing a curtain to blow or a ghostly image to pass across the room. Séances were carried out at night in darkened rooms with several people seated around a table, their hands clasped and legs touching. Seated next to a supposed medium under these conditions, Houdini never failed to discover the sleight-of-hand and ventriloquial methods used by these so-called psychics to produce their illusions.

He attacked them with a vengeance, publishing books, letters, and articles condemning spiritualists who accepted fees for their bogus services. During the twenties, Houdini demonstrated on stage many of the false methods used by mediums to give the impression of spirit rappings and ghostly movements. In many cities he would visit the local mediums before the show, then expose their methods one by one, demonstrating to a popular audience exactly what he had observed. And in 1926 Houdini testified before a committee of Congress, supporting a bill which outlawed any kind of fortune-telling for fees.

Ironically, Houdini's strident condemnation of the quack mediums and his appeals to public reason evidently aroused a greater interest than ever in the spiritualist movement. As soon as one medium was exposed, people began searching for another whose manifestations could not be explained, and even the energetic Houdini was unable to keep pace with the growth of a fraudulent profession. Some people completely misunderstood the intentions of the famous magician, believing Houdini himself was capable of dematerializing his body or communicating with spirits. A famous Washington medium, Mrs. Jane B. Coates, testified during the Congressional hearings that "a mystic is a person who has evoluted [sic] certain senses within themselves which bring them knowledge from the world beyond." She added, "I think Mr. Houdini is one of the greatest mystics in the world."

Another of the ardent believers in Houdini's supernatural abilities was Sir Arthur Conan Doyle. The same author who created that master of reason, Sherlock Holmes, had become a confirmed spiritualist, and it was he who suggested that Houdini dematerialized, turning his body into separate tiny atoms in order to pass through solid material and make his escapes. Houdini, always sensitive to accusations that he was a charlatan, was enraged by Doyle's theories, and he firmly denied them in print.

While Houdini had no illusions about his own powers, he did have a strong desire to achieve some kind of spiritual communication to put him in contact with his mother after her death. In a private séance with Lady Doyle (wife of the author) in June of 1922, and in many of the séances he attended in later years, Houdini tested the mediums by asking them for specific kinds of messages from his mother. Each time these mediums failed him, the renewed grief only increased his sense of bitterness and loss. While he was never so foolish as to pay the mediums for their services, his attacks on their methods were partial retribution for the personal pain and sorrow they caused him. Yet he tried to maintain his objectivity and consider fresh evidence.

I am not an irretrievable skeptic [he wrote]. I am not hopelessly prejudiced. I am perfectly willing to believe, and my mind is wide open; but I have, as yet, to be convinced. I am perfectly willing, but the evidence must be sane and conclusive.

During his lifetime, Houdini found no evidence of spirits that was either sane or conclusive. But even on his deathbed he opened the way for further controversy by giving a message to his wife Bess. If there were any conceivable way for spirits to speak, he said, then he would confirm that message from the beyond.

It is not surprising that one of the surviving myths about Houdini is related to the circumstances of his death. According to the movie-fiction version of Houdini's life, the magician died on stage while trying to escape from the Chinese Water Torture Cell—that is, suspended head-down in a glass-walled cabinet filled with water. The truth about his death is less dramatic, but deeply ironic. In October of 1926, Houdini was playing in a theatre in Montreal. After the show, he was approached in his dressing room by several McGill students who simply wanted to talk to the famous magician. One of them asked Houdini whether it was true he could take a hard punch in the stomach without being harmed. Houdini, who was lounging on the dressing room sofa, said it was true his abdominal muscles were well-developed, and he was not likely to be injured by a punch in the stomach. At this, one of the students came forward and—before Houdini had time to brace himself—punched him several times. The other students rushed forward to stop their friend, but the attacker drew back when Houdini told him to stop. Houdini insisted he was all right, but he asked the students to leave him.

Actually he was in terrible pain. Unknown to himself, Houdini had been suffering from appendicitis, and the injury made his condition critical. During the next two days he lived with the excruciating pain while continuing to perform in Montreal. Somehow he managed to make the train-ride to Detroit, but he collapsed after his first show in that city and had to be rushed to the hospital. He died in bed on October 31, 1926.

In years following, his friends gathered at the anniversary of his death to receive any messages he might send from beyond the grave. Houdini had shown caution in giving the "correct" message to his wife Beatrice—and to her alone—for there were many who claimed to have received word from him. The myth of spiritualism that he had been unable to suppress during his lifetime had a fresh start with his death. What could be better proof of the spiritualists' cause than Houdini himself speaking to them from the world beyond? Houdini did not speak, but his name has become part of our language—standing for mystery, showmanship, and representing forever the uncanny ability to escape from the inescapable.

Houdini with a spiritualist medium. The speaking trumpet was used during séances to create "spirit voices." Some mediums co-operated with Houdini to demonstrate fraud. *(Mulholland Collection)*

Street Magic
and Kindred Spirits

Did street magic end with Houdini? Most assuredly not. It is all around us. It continues to creep into our lives, insinuating itself at the corner of our perceptions. There are now traditional street magicians, and also street magic of a new kind being created constantly in print, pictures, and in the electronic media. Today magic is very much alive.

At the beginning of this book, street magic was defined as a kind of popular entertainment in the guise of magic or illusion, performed outside the boundaries of conventional theater. Certainly street magic is not occult magic. Yet the entertainment of the street magician would not have survived had it not been for the related arts of the occult magicians and soothsayers of a bygone era. Even in the distant past there was a street magic created in print and pictures—a magic of the imagination, if you will—as people strove to record the events they found fascinating or inexplicable. As we have seen, it is not easy to search out the street magicians of the past, and perhaps there are many more who should be included. Agrippa, Nostradamus, Paracelsus, Cagliostro, John Dee, and Johann Faustus were among the priests, scholars, and soothsayers of the past whose works are celebrated as the arts of astrology and the occult. Some of these men may have been no more than famous—or infamous—charlatans

who hoodwinked the public, but they certainly did it with finesse. More importantly, they did it with all the accouterments of magic, the robes and tomes, crystal balls and mystic symbols. Whether they were great minds or petty pretenders, they helped to keep the spirit of magic alive through the ages.

And what of the mediums, the gypsy fortune-tellers, and the demonologists of more recent years? All have played an important part in keeping the magical arts in good health, and some may have influenced the course of history. Many people in positions of power have consulted spiritual and mystical advisors who presumed to wield prophetical rather than political power. Jeane Dixon, the Washington seeress, is a contemporary example of this genre of magician.

Though she has been predicting the outcome of political and foreign affairs issues for more than twenty years, Dixon still has as many "misses" as "hits." Of her ten predictions for 1968—including the suggestion that Johnson would die in office and Humphrey succeed him—not a single one came true. Yet she also predicted China would go communist, Marilyn Monroe would commit suicide, and Robert Kennedy would be shot, and it is the "true" prophecies that are remembered by the public.

A number of magic-workers of recent history have been miraculous healers. Born in

"Stepping into the unknown," Philippe Petit walks the high wire between the towers of the World Trade Center in Manhattan. Petit began his career as a street magician and juggler. *(Jean Louis Blondeau)*

1877, Edgar Cayce was an American seer who would treat patients by entering a deep trance-like state in which the cures were revealed to him. From the early 1900s until his death in 1945, this religious mystic prescribed thousands of drugs and surgical procedures as well as home remedies and general treatment.

More recently, the remarkable Brazilian Arigō performed major surgery on patients who were seriously ill, using only a kitchen knife and household implements for the surgical procedures. During the operations, he would take on the character and even the accent of a deceased German physician, Dr. Fritz, and he treated hundreds of patients every day without accepting payment of any kind. Factual accounts, including documented cases, of Cayce and Arigō are so convincing that one is tempted to call them "magicians" of a new era, an era when the secrets of nature may be learned. Yet many of their feats duplicate the quack cures and sleight-of-hand "healing" promulgated by charlatans of the past.

Far less convincing historically was the entire Spiritualist movement which began in the mid-1800s in the United States and England and continued into the twentieth century. The movement was as much a religion as an avocation, and its supporters were kept constant in the faith by séances and preachings. The mediums exposed by Houdini and other investigators were largely the protégés of the Spiritualists. In addition the movement had many fringe groups which studied particular phenomena such as hauntings, faith-healing, mystical religions, and so-called "spirit" photography. During its heyday, the Spiritualist movement was joined by many notable figures including Edgar Allen Poe, William James, Sir Arthur Conan Doyle, Lewis Carroll, William Butler Yeats, and Aldous Huxley.

Where does make-believe end and occultism begin? How do we distinguish a soothsayer in the temple from a mind-reader in a side show? The task is not an easy one. It is a problem that would not even be worth solving, were it not for the damage that can be done by an unscrupulous charlatan. For a fraudulent medium, exercising strong psychological control over a believer, can extort considerable profit by promising the client fame and fortune. Worse, the clever mystic can make people believe they

have re-established spiritual contact with their loved ones, or give them expectations for the future which produce bitterness and despair when they turn out to be sheer speculation.

Today, in New York City there are still many gypsy fortune-tellers—those classic figures with turbans, beads, and crystal balls—who actually convince people to spend hundreds, sometimes thousands, of dollars having their palms read and their fortunes told. Although the methods of the prosperous gypsy ladies have been repeatedly exposed, people still lose fortunes every year to these fraudulent mystics.

But magic is a part of many aspects of our present lives—the more one looks for magic, the more one sees. It is somewhat artificial even to make a distinction between performing magic, occult magic, and what we have called street magic, because the three are so interdependent. Modern stage magicians often say they have nothing to do with the occult sciences, and they deplore charlatans who pose as miracle workers. Yet even the effects of stage magicians are not produced solely by technical dexterity. A trick may be carried out by physical means, but the end to these means is psychological—an impact on the minds of the audience. When people see a powerful stage magician, they do not just ask the dull question, "How does he do it?" Rather they say, "That's wonderful." The art seems wonderful because it appeals to something unconscious and hidden in the human psyche, a primal instinct rather than a sophisticated understanding. It is when the stage magician begins to explore the psychological as well as the physical aspects of the entertainment that the magic begins to grow and become strong. Stage magicians in the past have never hesitated to exploit the occult sciences, using mumbo-jumbo patter, signs, and symbols to appeal to their audiences. Most stage magicians still rely on the old approaches and the usual "spiels," not realizing that audiences are seeking a new magic.

On the other hand, occult pretenders have often exploited the methods of stage magic. When Houdini was investigating mediums, he found that many were accomplished sleight-of-hand performers, ventriloquists, and illusionists. With careful technical preparation and superb staging, mediums could make a tin horn sound, a ghostly vision pass in front of a curtain, or a child's voice speak from the grave. Often the mediums used assistants who hid under the table or were included in the séance group and performed much the same function as stage assistants.

Their manifestations were convincing, and they worked in the presence of a highly susceptible audience more inclined to believe in the power of the medium than to challenge the minor inconsistencies that showed up during the performance. Many of the mediums were extremely skilled, and some of their methods were difficult to expose. If something went wrong during the séance and the spirits failed to appear, a medium could always claim there was a hostile presence in the room. Houdini was so often accused of being "hostile" that he began wearing disguises to the séances he attended, simply to conceal his identity. Even when he exposed the spiritualists as frauds, however, he often had trouble making the public believe in his findings. His stage demonstrations of mediums' practices were meant to prove conclusively that the spiritualists were using old stage tricks to deceive the public.

At the same time it must be admitted that we do not know everything there is to know about the human psyche, nor do we understand the psychological effects of so-called hypnotism, autosuggestion, and that unknown factor called extrasensory perception (ESP). Both performers and psychologists realize that audiences can be strongly influenced by a controlling personality, and it is not easy to see the limits of that influence. A prophecy of doom, for example, can definitely influence one's personal outlook and quite possibly affect one's life. But it is more difficult to measure or explain the subconscious factors involved in "second sight"—when a mother senses that her son has been killed, or a person about to take a trip has a premonition of disaster.

In statistical and psychological terms, these events are extremely difficult to interpret, even moreso because they are often in the form of anecdotes recounting events that have already occurred. Investigators such as J.B. Rhine, who carried out the studies of ESP at Duke University, and other "parapsychologists" who have attempted scientific studies have tried to control some of the numerous variables and interpret data relating to psychic ability. But the controversy rages on.

Interest in occult magic has soared in recent years. Today there is renewed enthusiasm for astrology, demonology, and witchcraft, accompanied by greater involvement in mystical and pseudo-mystical religions such as Buddhism, Hinduism, and Gnosticism. There has even been a revival of extreme forms of mystical and spiritual arts such as snake-worship, Voodooism, and worship of such mystical leaders as Baba and Maharaj Ji. Again, it is difficult to define the manifestations of spirituality among these cults, as distinguished from the psychological effect of their rites and ceremonies. Or, to put it more bluntly, to separate illusion from reality. The practice of yoga, for example, does not give one magical powers, yet continued practice of the spiritual and mental exercises can produce results that seem miraculous to a Western observer.

Snake-worship and Voodoo ceremonies seem to be the work of inflamed imaginations, yet there is no question that worshipers can enter a state of trance or ecstasy where they actually feel in the grip of demonic possession. It is impossible to say how much these worshipers are affected by group reaction, and how much by autosuggestion, sensory deprivation, and just plain frenzy, but it is certain that there are states of consciousness other than what we would call normal.

Besides those who are involved in such mystical cults and ceremonies, there are many more who are fascinated by them. The fascination increases as one hears of strange rituals or learns of mysteries supposedly based on arcane secrets. As always, we are intrigued by the things that seem most inexplicable.

Yet there are wonders and illusions we encounter every day that seem less bizarre only because they are more familiar. Films, for example, are a series of still pictures which give the illusion of motion because they pass rapidly in front of a lighted bulb. Then there is the greater wonder of electromagnetic waves, not fully understood even by physicists, passing invisibly through the air at variable frequencies to be picked up by illusion-machines called radios or televisions.

We have immense trust in this magic, believing that we can tell the difference between a factual film and a fictional movie, believing that the announcers will cue us in to the truth or falsehood of what they are showing. Orson Welles was violating precisely this trust when, in 1938, he broadcast a radio program called "The War of the Worlds," announcing that a spaceship had landed in New Jersey and the Martians were invading. The result? Listeners panicked. Thousands called the station or the police, and at least one person climbed to the top of a New York building and reported to bystanders that he could see the spaceship with little green men emerging. Listening to this program today, we understand it is a patent fiction. But it was not announced as fiction. Instead it interrupted a regular program and was announced as news. A trusting public accepted it as reality. Gradually we are becoming more sophisticated about the media, realizing the illusions created on TV may give little indication of political, social, or physical realities. But we are only beginning to learn how completely the media can transform our lives.

Illusion is inseparable from daily life. Language itself is an illusion, creating characters, actions, gods, and demons out of the letters of ancient alphabets. We can say, "A ghost crossed the room." Or we can explain, "A film projector flashed a white, human-shaped image on the wall, which appeared to be the image of a ghost." The first statement tells of magic; the second, of mechanics. Yet a writer, speaker, or story-teller can play with magic and mechanics to convince a reader an illusion is real. In fact this is one of the ongoing problems of psychic investigators. Their findings can always be "written up," but how much will people believe? And how much should we believe?

Largely because of television, stage magicians do not have the popularity they enjoyed during the nineteenth and early twentieth centuries, when they used concealed technology to produce amazing illusions. The stage magician has been robbed of his stage. Where he once attracted a mass audience to a show that had general appeal, he must now compete with film. The magician's repertoire, limited by the size of the stage and condition of his equipment, has given way to a medium where anything can happen. People cheered when Houdini made an elephant vanish from a stage, but in a film an elephant can vanish every minute. Performing magicians were robbed of another "platform" when vaudeville began to go out of business. Like Houdini, many magicians got their start in traveling sideshows, and suffered when the dime museums and circuses began to disappear. For a time, magicians appeared frequently on television, but there were many problems working with this medium. Tricks that seemed grand on the stage were less significant on the screen, and the magician's repertoire had to change rapidly so the mass audience would not be bored by seeing the same tricks. Also, a magician's trick could be duplicated by tricky camera work just as cleverly as it was done by sleight of hand.

Today there is renewed interest in stage magic—an interest which invariably accompanies any resurgent enthusiasm for occult magic. In 1974 "The Magic Show" opened on Broadway, the first full-stage magic show to have a continuous engagement in many years. Though embroidered with a thin story line and enough music to make it a "musical," the show's real attraction was its staging of illusions which had almost been forgotten. During the same year, magic stores across the country noted their sales of books and equipment had started to climb. Young people especially were becoming interested once again in the old, forgotten, but never tired tricks of the great entertainers. It may be that a generation which has grown up with the magic of media will make a full-scale return to the lively arts.

What, then, of street magic? The English fairs have closed down, as has American vaudeville, leaving both countries without a showcase for the lively entertainments of itinerant performers. Indian fakirs, true ones and pretenders, continue to do some of the old tricks in the streets of Indian cities. But they, like the magicians of Japan and China, have been influenced by Western styles to the point where the ancient, traditional tricks are almost forgotten. In the United States there are a few street magicians performing in New York, Los Angeles, and San Francisco, but they may soon go on to other media.

As in past eras, street magic is still the art of entertainment, but it has perhaps taken on new forms to keep pace with the times. It is still an elusive art, an uneasy combination of the outdoor stunt and indoor stage act and undefined rumors that circulate everywhere. It includes sleight-of-hand performers, stuntmen, charlatans, promoters, and prophets—each of them participating in the world of illusion. For all we know, it may even include genuine psychics.

As we move into the shadows of magic, there are two modern entertainers who require special attention, if only because their names are so much in the news. They are the alleged psychics or mentalists "Kreskin" and Uri Geller.

In a sense they are more entertainers than occultists because they seem to use their reputed powers principally for public performances and demonstrations rather than for private séances or other mystic purposes. Kreskin is said to be able to read thoughts and receive numbers and messages which are sent by people in the audience or—in some cases—people who are hundreds of miles away. Geller has given numerous demonstrations to show that he can bend nails, keys, coins, and silverware by the power of his mind. It is also said that he is capable of making objects dematerialize and causing things to move by unconscious control of mind over matter. Both Kreskin and Geller have been given extensive coverage in the media, with performances witnessed by millions via television. They are firmly in the tradition of seers and mystics of the past, but unlike their predecessors their private demonstrations become public at once through the miracle of TV—which is both stage and street of the modern performing world.

To the public, of course, the big question is whether these men actually have psychic powers. Both Kreskin and Geller have complicated the issue by denying their abilities can be termed "psychic" in the literal sense. Kreskin says instead that he establishes an "extremely sensitive rapport" with his audience which allows him to receive certain messages and sensations. As a sender, he claims to use a combination of "reverse telepathy" and suggestibility to make people perform according to unspoken commands. As a "receiver," he sometimes utilizes "automatic writing," allowing his hand to write freely some message which is apparently transmitted through channels of the subconscious.

Geller, on the other hand, thinks there is some force or power being channeled through him, and he often expresses surprise when he sees this force at work. Obviously both individuals make claims which are highly controversial. But their performances have been seriously studied by researchers of psychic phenomena as well as popular audiences.

Kreskin gives frequent demonstrations and lectures on the topic of what is commonly called "hypnotism." Selecting one or more spectators from the audience, he uses various means of psychological suggestion to induce his subjects to perform while in a trance-like state. Kreskin has successfully shown that a subject can be made to feel hot or cold, to hallucinate powerfully, or feel strong emotions of fear or anger. Frequently the entertainer has some definite point to prove by example.

In one instance he induced a number of people to "see" flying saucers. Under the influence of his suggestion, the subjects put on their coats, went outside, and observed a number of glowing, colored objects in the sky which they described in explicit detail. They were so excited they attempted to call the police and run toward the spaceships, yet they had no recollections of their hallucinations once Kreskin released them from the suggestion. This performance was witnessed by a number of scientists researching unidentified flying objects, and they admitted some "sightings" would have to be re-evaluated, taking into consideration the possibility of autosuggestion. Kreskin has shown convincingly that most people are extremely susceptible to many kinds of suggestion, and he has used his demonstrations to attack myths regarding hypnotism and mesmerism which are hangovers from the nineteenth century. "Suggestion," says Kreskin, "for my specific purposes of entertainment, is the presentation of an idea to an individual, or group of individuals."

Kreskin is a sleight-of-hand magician and uses many stage techniques to create illusions in front of an audience. He has even described his method of predicting newspaper headlines, which he does by studying local and national news stories and guessing at the probable outcome of events. As Kreskin admits, such tricks as guessing cards, numbers, and messages

Kreskin the magician claims to have the power to send and receive telepathic messages. His magic is reminiscent of fortune-telling and mind-reading practiced by early street magicians. *(WNEW-TV)*

can be done with numerous methods known to stage magicians, and spiritual phenomena such as table-tiltings and slate-writings are old tricks of the master illusionists. Yet Kreskin draws the line between mentalism and magic, confiding that some tricks are done only by telepathic means. Most magicians doubt his claims, however, and say he is no more "psychic" than an accomplished stage performer with a mentalism routine.

In reality Kreskin's greatest strength probably lies in the field of human psychology. Unlike many magicians, he has chosen to explore the psychological dimensions of entertainment as well as the mechanical and technical aspects of creating illusions. Though his facade is ingenuous, he is masterful in winning the sympathy of an audience, perhaps equally masterful in getting people to communicate things which they do not mean to reveal. His influence may be very strong in manipulating the mental as well as emotional reactions of his subjects. Depending on one's degree of skepticism, this complex relationship between performer and audience can be looked at in a number of ways—as a form of mass appeal, psychological manipulation, or even psychic communication. Kreskin manages to portray his own powers as extraordinary without sounding outrageous.

Unlike Kreskin, Uri Geller is most famous for displays of psychokinesis—moving objects by power of the mind. He specializes in bending metal objects, either by rubbing them with his fingers for a short time or simply having them within range. According to observers, Geller always seems surprised and excited when knives begin to bend or spoons break in half, and he says he has no idea what causes these phenomena to occur. During his televised appearance in England, housewives all over the country reported their silverware was bent, broken, or otherwise damaged by Geller's powers. A friend of Geller's, Andrija Puharich, surmises that such occurrences may be caused by an extraterrestrial influence he calls "Spectra," working through Geller but not directly under his control.

Geller also seems to be able to repair watches by holding them in his hands, but without touching the internal mechanism. One investigator inserted a piece of tinfoil in the watch spring, then sealed the timepiece. Geller was able to start the watch, and it continued to run perfectly. When the owner opened his watch, he found the tinfoil had been torn apart as the watch started again. Given clocks and watches which are in working order, Geller is said to be able to move the hands forward or back—again, without exposing or touching the mechanism.

There are numerous fantastic tales of Uri Geller and his work. He has been observed by hundreds of credible witnesses, including reporters, scientists, psychologists, parapsychologists, medical doctors, and magicians. The people who have seen him perform "psychokinesis" experiments probably number in the millions. Books and articles about "the amazing Geller" continue to proliferate, and 1975 saw the publication of the mentalist's autobiography.

The public seems to have an overwhelming interest in Geller's "power." At a time when technology appears to control our lives, and emotional and spiritual values are rationalized, Geller represents a mystical link with an extraordinary spiritual world. The publicity surrounding this performer is not enough to satisfy the general curiosity, and each of his feats seems like a message from outer space. People clamor to know whether he really has psychic power, and there seem to be no easy answers. Personally, Geller has all the characteristics of a precocious and egocentric performer—at least according to those who have interviewed him. Recently he has even begun to accept a mystic's thesis that there is some extraterrestrial power acting through him, though Geller explains that the powers act most effectively when he is in the presence of others rather than alone. Every observer has noted that he seems excited and amazed when things begin to happen around him, as if every occurrence were a kind of self-discovery.

At the moment Geller has joined the list of psychics, seers, and wonder-workers whose names are legendary. The truth about Geller may never be known, just as the biographies of Cagliostro, Nostradamus, and Agrippa contain many obscurities which have not been clarified by passage of time. But like the occultists of the past, he satisfies an ever-present need for mystery and stimulates our curiosity about the limits of magic. He is not a street magician, and yet he has helped to create street magic—the magic that is felt in the air, questioned in the mind, and accepted at a level beyond recognition or consciousness. He has created a controversy of magic which may never be resolved.

As in ages past, the art of juggling is closely related to street magic. The most famous contemporary street juggler is Philippe Petit. It was Petit who, in 1974, walked a steel cable stretched between the twin towers of New York's World Trade Center, a walk that was more than a quarter of a mile above the street.

A Frenchman born in the village of Nemours, Petit began performing as a street juggler more than ten years ago, and he is able

Uri Geller demonstrating his power to bend and break silverware. He takes street magic into the realm of psychic phenomena and fascinates modern audiences. *(NY Daily News Photo)*

to compare and contrast his experiences in the dozens of countries he visited during his travels. During an interview, he told of some of his experiences.

"I started to learn magic by myself when I was six years old. I had a little box of tricks and things—and I very quickly got a taste of perfection. Which is unusual for a kid. Usually the kid likes to do the trick in half a minute without even reading how it's done. I liked to do things well when I was young, and that taste grew up so that when I was twelve, thirteen, fourteen, I was a very good magician. I was doing things in front of my mirror to perfection."

His instructions on magic, however, also insisted that it was important to learn juggling. Petit took the advice of the author-magicians, and by the time he began performing on the street he was doing a juggling and mime act mixed with some magic. He first went on the street at the age of fourteen or fifteen, and he developed his act until he felt it was "perfect," a complete performance in itself.

During his years as a street performer, Petit has learned to handle the usual problems with children, dogs, policemen, wind, cars, drunks, and people who want to fight. "At the beginning of street juggling," he says, "I was very hard on people. When a man was sitting at the first row of my circle reading a newspaper, I went with my torch and I burned his newspaper. Now, I have changed. If a man is reading his newspaper I stop my act. Silence. I put my hat in the middle of the circle, and I tiptoe over, look over his shoulder, and I read with him."

Street magicians throughout history have amused people with their pickpocket tricks—and Philippe Petit has often entertained audiences in this way. But this sleight of hand can be as risky as it is amusing. "I was pickpocketing once at the corner of 42nd Street and Broadway, which is the worst place in the world. The stealers are there, and they steal your watch, they steal your wallet. But they don't like people stealing in front of the audience and showing them the tricks."

Police, too, can create problems. Petit has had to deal with officers of the law in many countries, and he has developed his escape tactics to a fine art. "I can *smell* a policeman," he says. "And I am very fast. I have three hundred people around me, and I can escape in between five and eight seconds. Sometimes I can trust the audience to protect me. I go into the audience, and the audience closes the circle again, and the policeman looks and there is nothing. During these ten years I have been constantly escaping the police, and the real reason is I don't want to be caught. I don't want to spend the night at their house. I want to spend it at my house."

Petit has found that police in many parts of the world react to him in different ways—but audiences, too, will differ from country to country. Of the nations where he has performed, Petit says he prefers Russia, Australia, Italy, and the United States—each for different reasons.

"Russia—people are very educated about the arts. When you are four years old there, you go to a ballet school, a juggling school, or maybe a mime school. So when they see something good they are the first ones to appreciate it. The Russian people are very human—very like children.

"Australia is a new country, and people are still building their houses, their roads. So when they see someone in the street, for them it's strong, it's sharp, it's—I don't know how to explain—there is a kind of natural sympathy between the man who works in the street and the Australian man. I had the whole country behind me when I was in Australia.

"Italy also, because of course Commedia dell'arte came from Italy. The Italians carry with them the joy of dance and singing. They almost dance with joy themselves when they see someone in the streets.

"America is different because in America I have a little bit of all the world. If you take five people in my crowd you have all civilizations, all races, all colors, all ages. So I am not working to New York, I am working to all the world at the same time. I have a piece of the earth in front of me."

Philippe Petit began to practice walking the tight-wire—what he calls "high walking"—when he was fifteen. It was impulse that led him from magic to juggling to high-wire walking, but impulse to him was a powerful force, and he practiced the arts to perfection. In 1971 he stretched a wire between the spires of the Cathedral of Notre Dame in Paris, and in

Philippe Petit juggling lit torches in a Paris street. Today, as in past centuries, the art of juggling is closely allied to sleight-of-hand conjuring. *(Jean Louis Blondeau)*

Blindfolded, Petit gropes his way along a 110-foot cable in Allentown, Pennsylvania, during a heavy rainstorm. *(Wide World)*

1973 he walked between the towers of the Sydney Harbor Bridge, Australia.

Then, New York! On the morning of August 7, 1974, early-morning commuters noticed the speck of a tiny figure suspended in mid-air between the 110-story towers of the World Trade Center. It was Philippe Petit, walking the high wire.

Petit says the idea came to him more than six years before, when he saw a newspaper photograph of what was to be "the tallest building in the world." Early in 1974 he and some friends began making technical preparations for the walk, and during the three months preceding the feat, they made more than two hundred trips to the building, disguising themselves as construction workers in order to gain access to the towers. Petit even rented a helicopter to fly over the building while it was still under construction. On August 6, he and his friends spent the night in the World Trade Center. Using a five-foot crossbow, they shot a fishing line from one tower across a space of 131 feet to the second tower. Then they strung the cable and fastened it in place, with guy-lines to hold it steady. It was about 7:15

a.m. when Philippe Petit stepped out on the wire carrying the long, curved pole of a tightrope walker and wearing the thin black clothing which was his street-juggler's costume. He was 1,350 feet above the earth! He began to walk—and the years of preparation, the risks, and the technicalities were forgotten.

"It was too high for a human being, you know, in that space. It was like an unknown world.

"I wasn't afraid, because afraid is a different sentiment. I was getting into the unknown. That's quite dramatic to say, you know, but that was my feeling. I was very happy when I was in the middle of that wire because I was something unique. You will never be twice in your life in the middle of a wire between the tallest towers in the world. This will be very ephemeral, very quick. So I was breathing this instant. The preciousness of the instant itself—that's what I was trying to catch, because it would disappear so quickly."

Street magic? To the thousands of people who watched that day, and the millions more who witnessed it on television, the event seemed almost inconceivable. Philippe Petit walked the sky, and he held hands with death. Later he told the press, "I was not scared because it was a precise thing." And of course it was, in technical terms. It was a skilled performer on a well-strung tight wire, performing the art he knew best. To make the moment all-too-familiar, even the cops were there, first haranguing him to get off that wire and get back to normal life, later praising him for his stupendous feat of courage.

Yet in some ways that event was very imprecise. What happened to Petit when he stepped out on the wire is something he still cannot explain, except to say, "It was too high" and "I was getting into the unknown." What happened to the people who saw him was not precise either. It was a mixture of delight and awe with an overwhelming sense of danger— and escape. They watched him as others had once watched Houdini, with the fear of death in their hearts and with the creeping sensation that possibly, just possibly, he was exploring the unknown. The feelings he aroused, the unexpected sensations he created that day may never be clearly interpreted. Yet we know that whenever someone explores the unknown, he walks the borders of that imprecise boundary called magic.

Street Magic Today

y own introduction to street magic was completely accidental, as such introductions should be. It was summertime in New York City, and I was enjoying what New Yorkers call the "ambiance" in Central Park. At the southeast corner of the Sheep's Meadow there is a broad, tree-lined sidewalk which leads from the park road north to Bethesda Fountain. As usual on a Sunday afternoon, the sidewalk was crowded with strollers, bike riders, venders, and various hawkers and performers. But what caught my eye was the large crowd gathered around the base of the Walter Scott statue.

The crowd, as it turned out, was watching a magician. The conjurer had mounted the pedestal of the statue and was performing a number of tricks with cigarettes, ropes, and cards. As I looked on, more people gathered around the fringes of the audience.

The magician was young, dark-haired, dressed entirely in black. He performed with ease, expertly judging the response of the crowd. As the performance continued, the audience—a broad mix of many ages, nationalities, and races—responded warmly to each new illusion, and often greeted the "finish" of a trick with spontaneous applause and laughter.

The show, completely in mime, lasted about ten minutes. When the magician wished to have the assistance of a spectator, he merely signaled the person forward with a gesture. His own movements, with the absence of explanation, were almost dream-like, yet he was able to excite a variety of responses ranging from hilarity to astonishment. When the act was finished and the applause of the crowd had been acknowledged, he stepped down from the improvisational stage and passed his black bag among the spectators.

The performance struck me as both stylish and oddly mysterious. I stayed for several shows, which he repeated with brief intervals in-between, until a new crowd would gather. Like many spectators, I was curious, and I later approached him to ask about his profession.

The answer was much longer than I had expected. As it turned out, the contemporary street magician had a long and interesting story to tell. It was the story of his experiences, his craft, and finally the history of an art called street magic.

Jeff Sheridan is a street magician in the traditional sense, taking his place among the conjurers, *tregetours*, and *escamoteurs* of history. When he began performing in 1967, Jeff Sheridan was the only street magician in New York, but in more recent years a number of magicians have begun performing in various locations around the city.

Jeff Sheridan, street magician. *(William Biggart)*

Every summer, Sheridan returns to the same spot in Central Park, the Walter Scott statue where I first saw him. Like the *escamoteurs* of Paris, he has become a familiar sight, a part of the landscape and the city. People who once regarded him with suspicion now bring their friends or children to see the magician. Even the police respect his territory and realize that people enjoy having him there. Like other good street performers, he has helped make the city a better place to live, and the public has supported these performers even when the city has chosen to discourage them.

For Jeff Sheridan the decision to perform in the street had social and political ramifications as well as a personal meaning. At the time he started in magic, there were few opportunities for a young magician to have his own stage show or to develop a personal style of magic. Nightclub managers were not interested in a performer who had a mime style like Sheridan's. They wanted lively, funny patter, and a curvaceous girl cut in half. But Sheridan's interest lay elsewhere. At the age of nineteen he had already developed a personal style of magic, and he was not ready to give it up.

Sheridan began practicing sleight of hand when he was ten years old, learning tricks from books, catalogues, and other magicians, and rehearsing in front of a mirror. His family moved from New York to Puerto Rico for a time, and when he returned to the Bronx, Sheridan joined a boys' club called FAME, Future American Magical Entertainers. The club was sponsored by the city of New York and met in an old, dilapidated gymnasium. Sheridan dropped out of high school and started to give private performances plus nightly shows at the Seahunt Supper Club, an all-black nightclub in the Bronx. Later he began to work in the Xerox room of a firm on Wall Street—a dull, mesmerising occupation he resolved never to try again. He finished high school by taking night classes and continued practicing magic whenever he could.

"When I was younger," says Jeff, "I felt a little embarrassed about being seen on the street. I was afraid that some relative would see me and think what I was doing was somehow improper. They felt that you had to do certain things to make a living, and being a street performer was certainly not one of them. The

Central Park, New York, on a Sunday afternoon.
(William Biggart)

Producing card-fans, Central Park *(William Biggart)*

options I had as a magician were actually very limited. I soon found out there wasn't much work for a visual performer. The vaudeville circuit, the cabaret, and the music hall faded a long time ago. For me the most logical thing to do was to turn to the street."

Each spring, when the snow melts from the ground and the weather turns warm, people return again to the park. "There are people I've never met before and will probably never meet again," says Jeff. "But in some way I've been able to enter and affect their lives. I would like to be a Pied Piper. But I don't want to drown anyone."

Like a Pied Piper, the street entertainer carries his own mystique which cannot easily be transferred to the stage. He seems to have escaped from reality, to perform in a time and

space where he doesn't necessarily belong. People expect to see a magician on stage, on television, or in a movie. But not at the foot of a statue or in the middle of a sidewalk.

Strangest of all are those instances when people believe the magic Sheridan performs is not sleight of hand, but a magic more mystical than physical. Sometimes they inform him that what he is doing is not manipulation but a secret art. They do not want to know the secret. They only want him to know they understand— what he is doing is beyond the comprehension of most people.

"I don't know how to answer them," he says. "I mean, this is the twentieth century."

"So what do you say?" I asked him.

"I don't say anything. If that's what they believe . . ." He shook his head.

Jeff Sheridan's discovery of the street audience was completely accidental. One afternoon in 1967 he was in Central Park near the Bethesda Fountain, which at that time was a gathering place for the under-thirty counterculture. A camera crew was making a documentary film, and Sheridan decided to liven up the scene by performing a few sleight-of-hand tricks. (Being a magican, he always carries a pack of cards.) In a short while, a large crowd gathered round him. Quite unexpectedly, he had discovered an audience.

What was discovered by accident soon became, for Jeff Sheridan, a new way to explore magic and to practice his art in a distinctive, individual way. Only later did he realize that he was, in fact, part of a tradition that had lived for thousands of years.

In New York and many other cities of the United States, the late sixties and early seventies were times when street life was "a-changin'" in many ways, change initiated by the war and enacted by people who were searching, radicalizing, making music, making protests, bearing witness, or just acting. Street activity of every kind had political overtones, sometimes with suggestions of anarchy. Mime troupes gave anti-war plays, satirizing the idiocy of political leaders, mocking corrupt values, or entertaining the children of the streets and ghettos who would never gain entrance to the so-called "legitimate" theatre. Crowds of young people—for it was left to the young—set about the self-conscious and often difficult task of "humanizing" parks, squares, and street corners. Authorities frowned. Police asked to see your

"license." But while the city fathers may have regarded the aberrant behavior of the city's children as radical and dangerous, they could not put a stop to it. The nature of street life was actually being changed by collaborative effort.

Most importantly, it became possible for performers to use the city environment with greater freedom than ever before. If the guitarist could make music from the curb, so could the violinist, flautist, or drummer. Street theater was not only a group effort by a mime company, it could also be performed by independent actors, jugglers, dancers, and—what concerns us here—magicians. The street movement of the sixties opened up a new performing area and revealed a popular audience, making it possible for street people to be show people as well.

We owe a debt of gratitude to these entertainers, who have helped change life in the city by transforming not only the environment but also our self-image as pedestrians. Amidst the dirt, hubbub, and strangulating traffic of a city throbbing with elements of self-destruction, the street performers offer pedestrians a moment to pause, watch, listen, to form a circle with

Magic on Fifth Avenue *(William Biggart)*

others, and to block out everything else except the performance. Whether a musician with a flute or an acrobat on a unicycle, the performer's concentration is on something far different from catching the bus, meeting a client, or rushing to some close-out sale. The street entertainer is a visitor from a world of no appointments. What he offers the audience is not only a moment of entertainment but also a moment of calm, the chance to pause and share an experience while escaping tensions created by an inhospitable environment.

Not all performances are suited for street entertainment, and the performer must be willing to take a certain number of risks. He must endure the condescension of those pedestrians who believe only bums and beggars ask for money on the streets of a commercial metropolis. The performer must adapt his style to an environment full of conflicting sounds and movements, blaring horns, squealing tires, and inattentive spectators. He must be willing to perform for spectators who will only stand still for a few minutes, and he must have the talent to capture them in that short period. To face all these problems takes some degree of courage.

Each street performer can choose a location to suit a personal mood or style, attract the largest possible audience, and reap the greatest profits. For obvious reasons, street shows are a fair weather, summertime amusement, although some start early in the spring and continue through the warm days of autumn. Generally, the impresario must find a location out of the mainstream of traffic but also visible to a large number of passersby. The parks are the most popular acting areas. On any weekend, we find in Central Park dozens of outdoor entertainers who do not brave the street scene during the week. In general, policemen have become more tolerant of street people, and performers who return frequently to the park can be confident they will not be "hassled." In time, pedestrians come to expect these minstrels in the same locations each week, and some admirers will return frequently to see them.

In summers past, Keith Berger could always be found in the Grand Army Plaza at the corner of Fifth Avenue and Central Park South. A talented mimist, he performed in white-face, wearing an all-black costume, and played the role of mechanical man. Nearby one

might find Steve Hansen, a puppeteer, or Cecil McKinnon of the Pickle Family, an accomplished juggler. A steel drum player took up his post at the southeast corner of Central Park, but on weekends the hollow tones of his drum rang out from a position on 42nd Street near Fifth Avenue. Along Fifth Avenue there were violinists, and a pair of instrumentalists played baroque music in a doorway near Brentano's. On Lexington Avenue a bagpipe player wearing kilt and tartan sent a Celtic melody swirling over the heads of passersby. Every year they and other performers appear again—a sign that all is well and spring is here.

There are also many other street artists who play Artful Dodger, constantly moving about the city, disappearing for days at a time only to return again suddenly to a choice location. Until recently, one of these vanishing adepts was Philippe Petit, whose name became immortalized when he walked a tightwire stretched between the towers of the World Trade Center. Previous to that ultimate street performance, he might have been found anywhere in the city during the summer or winter, juggling balls or twirling his hat, or doing both while riding a unicycle. He seemed oblivious to the coldest weather, gave a prolonged hyperactive performance, and rarely passed the hat he manipulated so deftly. (Since his courageous aerial stroll, he has forsaken the streets and now occupies a more permanent place under the aegis of the Ringling Brothers & Barnum and Baily Circus.)

As a street magician, Jeff Sheridan has performed in numerous locations throughout the City. The base of a statue helps form a backdrop and sets the stage for his magic. But the magic changes in character, depending on the location. In front of a modern stainless steel sculpture, the trick of the cut-and-restored rope looks almost surrealistic. In front of a fountain, the effects seem casual, the magician guileless. In the center of a crowd, total concealment of a trick is usually impossible, yet there is a stronger sense that the magic is a shared experience. And there is always the opportunity for the magician to be outrageous—to approach a pedestrian and startle the person with an exploding puffball; to stand on the steps of St. Patrick's Cathedral and flaunt "the Devil's playing-cards," as those pasteboards were once called; to surprise store-

owners, unnerve picnickers, or turn schoolchildren into helpless gigglers.

Despite the casual itinerary, Jeff Sheridan haunts two favorite locations during the summer months. One is the Walter Scott statue in Central Park, where he performs on Sunday afternoons. During weekdays, he takes up a position near the Sherman statue at the southeast corner of the Park. Sometimes he will move farther downtown along Fifth Avenue.

On a busy day, he may draw thousands of spectators. Since there is no music or loud ballyhoo to accompany this magician's performance, he must attract his audience in a visual, and highly visible, manner. It is difficult to say exactly how a crowd receives the silent message that a show is about to begin. For awhile, the magician fans a deck of cards, casually knots a rope, or plays with a cigarette. Then his manner changes, he strikes a pose, and the people who have stopped to watch suddenly begin to pay close attention. The show is about to begin.

On a weekend in the park, there are amusement-seekers of all kinds—families with children, dope pushers, fashion models, drunkards, business people, pimps, street gangs,

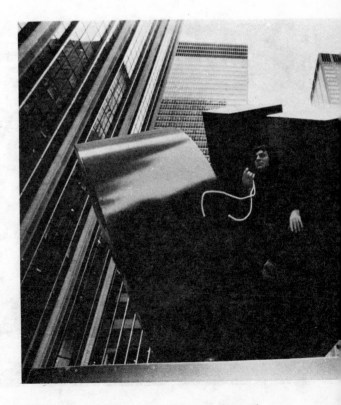

The cut-and-restored rope (William Biggart)

so-called hippies, senior citizens, self-conscious lovers, potential rapists, out-of-work actors, workers, loungers, entertainers, off-duty cops, wary thugs, and children who in time will grow up to assume all these definitive roles. Study such faces. Look into their eyes. Try, if you can, to interpret and decipher the wrinkles, planes, and furrows of outward appearance, to find written there some clue as to the magic that appeals to the innermost soul. What is the conclusion? One can only surmise that bragging magicians are correct—for they have always claimed that magic appeals to everyone, all people in all walks of life.

Well, so does music, of course, and even a soft pretzel has a particularly universal appeal on a lazy afternoon. But if we are not mistaken, there seems to be in the faces of these people something more than mere amusement. Their expressions reveal dreams, perhaps a sense of covert astonishment, and, occasionally, wonder. In the children's expressions there may be awe. In the adults', a mesmerised quality that turns quickly and unconsciously to delight in the presence of magic.

Why do they stop walking? Why do they stand and watch? It's all a joke, isn't it? They're just being hoodwinked. The cigarette does not actually vanish. The rope is not cut in half. The cards do not appear out of thin air. The watchers know these things, but their eyes tell them differently, their minds refuse to provide that instantaneous explanation which we have come to associate with rational thought. Logic has deserted us. Foolishness has taken over.

The children are curious. They want to know how the magician does that stuff, and the best way to find out is to press closer. Yet fear holds them back from approaching *too* closely. Clinging to the side of the statue, their eyes fixed on the magic-man's hands, the children are ready to jump back if he should notice them in any way. When he isn't looking, a girl sneaks forward and peers into his bag while her timid friend hangs back, waiting for a report. But the reconnoiter is unsuccessful. The magician spots the culprit and shoos her away.

For technicians, entertainers, or fellow magicians in the audience, the interest centers on the style and moves of the performer. They note that he raises his hand as he throws down the cards. They watch the direction of his fingers as he passes the deck from one hand to the other. They wonder what device is used for a particular kind of "vanish," and evaluate the impact of each effect.

"The children are curious. . . ." *(William Biggart)*

The majority of Sunday observers wish neither to be enlightened nor informed. They want entertainment, and in some cases, want to be show-offs participating in the entertainment. Without malice, they enjoy seeing the embarrassment of a friend or an anonymous spectator singled out to hold a rope, a sponge ball, or the magician's black bag. They are innocently delighted when a giant gold coin comes out of someone's ear or a stray ace of spades is found in a child's pocket. To the average spectator it doesn't matter that the performance has been practiced, that the moves—even when bystanders are included—are carefully calculated by the magician, programmed to create the desired impact. At precisely the same moment in each show, audiences respond identically to what they see and what they don't. Spectators are manipulated more easily than the cards in the magician's hand, but they do not feel the slightest imposition.

On a weekday—during the noon hour—the crowd is quite different from the leisurely weekend audience. When Jeff Sheridan performs on Fifth Avenue during the lunch hours, his magic must appeal to harried business people rather than casual pleasure-seekers. Few people smile, faces are tense, and pedestrians avoid looking into each other's eyes.

In the chaotic environment at the city's center, the street magician manages to create his audience. Out of the manic crowd he draws individuals one by one with his magic, and then springs them free. Involuntarily, they notice him, wonder what's his angle. With growing curiosity, they begin to watch. For only a moment, the office crises vanish, promotions are unimportant, responsibilities nil. The spectators hardly realize what they are doing or what attracts them, though at first they are sure it can be nothing important. They watch the production of a card, lighting of a cigarette, disappearance of a puffball—in reality, the most insignificant events. But as they give magic their full attention, gradually their faces undergo a change. Some of the tension passes away. Control is sacrificed, replaced by a shake of the head, or, more daring yet, a smile. Eyes that once avoided contact now scrutinize the conjurer as though he were the single most important client in all commercial life. Then people glance at their watches. A few throw coins. Then join the crush once again.

Noon-hour, midtown Manhattan *(William Biggart)*

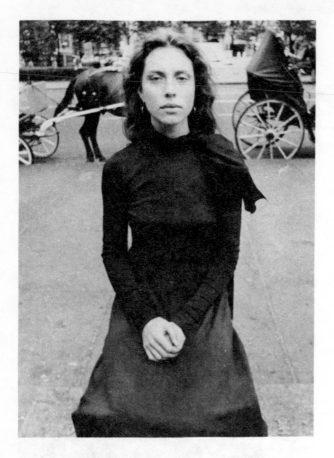

The vanishing head, performed in Grand Army Plaza, New York *(William Biggart/Model: Anne Stahl)*

For Jeff Sheridan, the conceptualization of the art of magic is like the images of a surrealist painting. On canvas, disparate objects, figures, and forms are brought together in new relationships—unlike their normal, everyday context in reality. Sheridan does not think only of a "trick." He considers how props and objects can be posed in new relationships, lending a "surreal" quality to the performance.

In the presence of Surrealism, we register distinct impressions, but uneasiness begins to creep in as we realize that contextual relationships have been distorted. The world portrayed on the canvas contains objects from our own world and yet is completely different. We seek to enter the new context which is portrayed, to establish the connections and understand the laws that determine its being, but our attempts are frustrated by the familiarity of the images. Relationships among those images are neither logical, functional, nor predictable.

In this sense, surrealism is something that can be presented by the magician. Working with familiar things, he can link apparently unrelated events with a single motion. In our natural, familiar world, we may clap our hands together

and hear nothing more than a loud, sharp sound. In the magician's surrealist world, the clapping of hands may cause an object to vanish.

But to many people magic is only tricks, and in this respect it differs from any other form of visual art. In a work of art the enigma always remains concealed, and by examining a canvas we do not hope to find the "trick" behind the visual experience. We merely examine the form presented. But in magic the trick is presented as the main attraction, while method is concealed. There are no real enigmas in the sleight-of-hand arts. There are only secret compartments and deceptive movements, strings, pulls, and trapdoors. Once those are explained, the mystery vanishes. But those who attempt to explain a work of art only encounter more mysteries, and explanations begin to take the form of aesthetics, philosophy, and religion.

Magic tricks are psychological as well as mechanical, for the performer is playing with the senses of his audience as well as his devices. Much has been written by magicians on the uses of psychology in conjuring, with many hints to other artists on how to make the most of their magic. But it was the historian H.J. Burlingame who wrote an analysis of the magician

Alexander Herrmann which seems most appropriate to the art of street conjuring. "The capability to win at the start the sympathy of the public, in order that the audience without exception be willing to follow the intentions of the artist, cannot be acquired, and yet the chief help [for] the prestidigitateur lies in just this mood of the public. . . . The charm of this art does not lie in the power to surprise the spectator with ape-like rapidity, but the capability of making him go home with the feeling that he has spent an hour in a real world of wonders. . . ." To accomplish this, says Burlingame, the magician must convince the audience that he can do as he pleases, and he must simultaneously suggest two ideas. First, that what they see is really happening. Second, that such an event is impossible. Through their awareness of the unresolvable contradictions, the spectators gradually realize an extraordinary sensation—being in the presence of an illusion.

Early in his career, Jeff Sheridan discovered that the life of a street conjurer suggests to many people an unusual, romantic kind of existence. With his few props and belongings, he can travel wherever there are people and sunshine, pull out his deck of cards, and begin a performance. People see the street magician as

Card fans and productions *(William Biggart)*

someone in tune with the seasons, but toughened to all the accidents and mishaps of the city. And his dark figure suggests romantic characters out of the past, wandering adventurers and fortune-seekers, carefree gamblers, circus performers, country travelers.

Most people long, in some way, for that impossible freedom. In everyone there is the child who wanted to run away and join a circus, tumble with clowns, walk the tightrope, or swing from a trapeze. In time, these fresh impulses are packed away in storage rooms of the imagination, locked tight with keys thrown away, as the guessing, scheming child becomes molded into an adult with fixed ideas and conventional ambitions. But not completely. In every person there is a sense of play, of wonder, which can be renewed.

In a magician there is the desire to make

the fantasy become real, to surround himself with wonders, illusions, and magical things. Nothing ordinary is worth considering. Magic is not mundane or explicable. The world is turned upside down by the Mad Hatter, and even plain Alice can drink from half-teacups. The fantasist has the single-minded and frivolous desire to practice deceptions until they seem to come true.

Street life tends to reinforce rather than deny the sense of fantasy and romance. A crowd goes by, and Sheridan finds that someone—who could it be?—has left him a flower. He empties his black bag at the end of the day and there, among Uncle Sam's legal tender, he finds brightly colored stones that a donor—child? hippy? idiot?—has offered up in payment for a moment of amusement. One day, a girl who had watched for a long time asked the magician

if he would agree to be the father of her baby. Another time, he received a letter from Europe, thanking him for a street performance long forgotten, a moment of entertainment that changed the visitor's perception of this country and its people. Day after day, he meets strangers who ask whether he believes in psychic power, whether there is such a thing as occult magic—and even some who believe that his act is no mere imposture but a demonstration of the real power of mind over matter. Many more who talk to him are trying to answer for themselves the riddle of why he is there, who he is, and what are his secrets. Underlying many of their questions are other, more revealing queries. "Is this what you really do? Is this all you do? Is this your life?" And when he says, "Yes," he notices that a certain look comes into their faces. They half smile, and a light comes into their

eyes, as if remembering something wistful, dim, half-forgotten. . .

For many reasons, this is a treacherous age for a conjurer to champion fantasy. While the techniques of magic—some old, some new—are easy to discover, it is difficult to apply them in new ways, to conceptualize illusions that are boldly imaginative, haunting, and mysterious. The performer must know more than the how-to side of magic. He must realize who he is, just what he can offer. He must be able to develop the tricks as they have never been done before, create magic that is so personal that, finally, the illusion cannot be separated from the illusionist. A magician must practice "vanishes," "passes," and "productions," and also unfold the enigma in a way that is dramatic and pleasing.

Unfortunately many amateur and professional magicians learn the old tricks without adding new elements to them, and there are many who themselves seem to fear the anarchy of their art. Some prefer to imitate the old magicians—or even vaudeville routines— and "Xerox" the tricks that were glorious when they were fresh, mysterious when the masters presented them for the first time. But what does the audience want now? Psychics? Blood-and-gore producers? Card sharpers and salesmen of magic? Magicians are all of these things. But the greatest, in times past, were illusionists who created almost a visionary experience, and laid a feast of vanishing riches before those who visited their castles.

No one is able to buy the most precious element—the art of presentation. When the magician begins with a private vision rather than a popular product, with an inspiration rather than a technique, then he himself will find all the magical props and history of conjuring at his disposal, and he will bend these elements to his will. One technique, rightly chosen and ingeniously applied, may be the key to turn vision into reality.

In recent times, magic shows have had to compete with a multitude of equally astonishing media—television, film, and other electronic presentations. But we are witnessing a return to old-time magic, not only to the mysteries of the occult, but also to mysteries of the lone performer capable of producing something out of nothing.

(William Biggart)

(William Biggart)

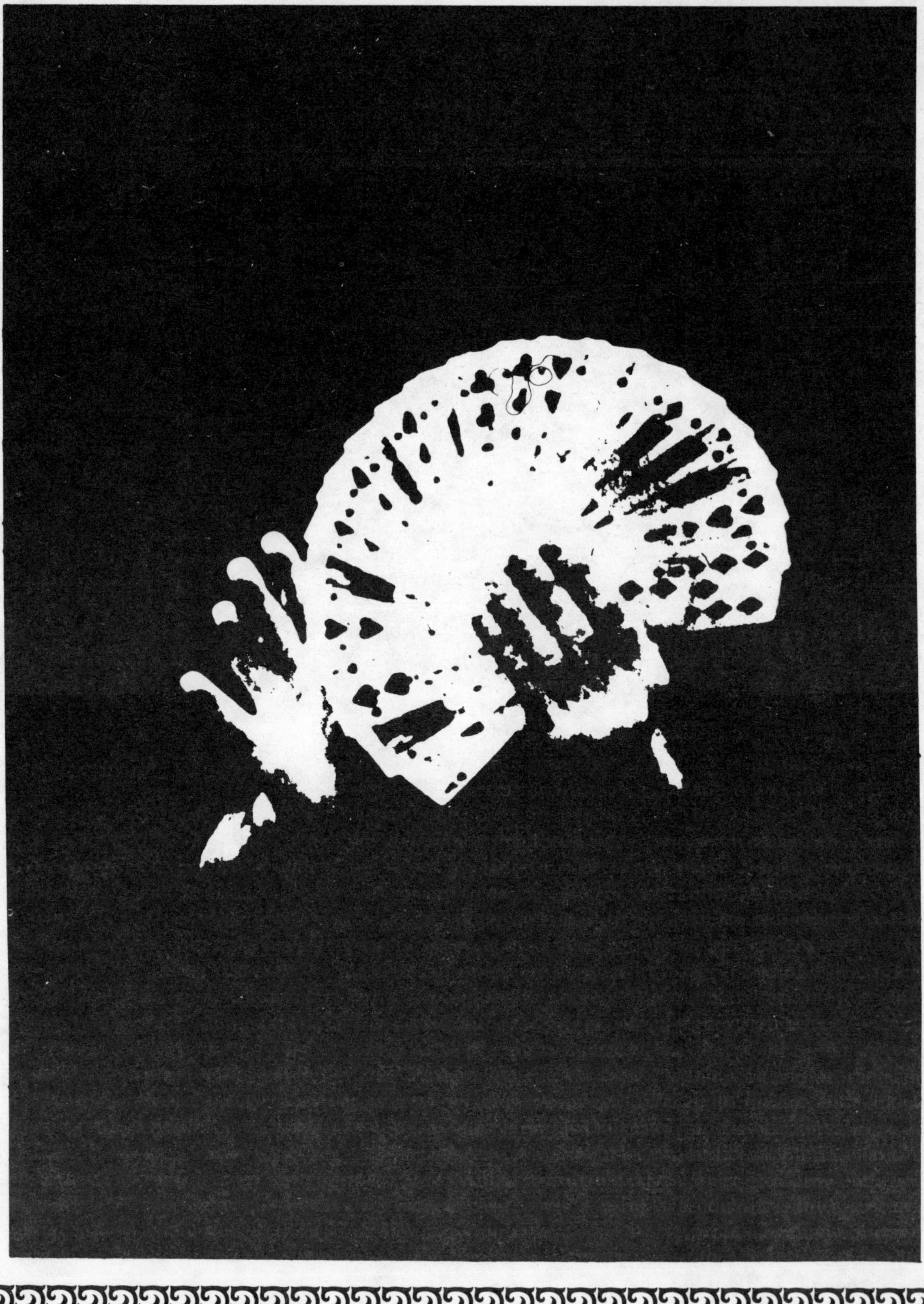

Vanish

From the cups and balls performers of ancient Egypt to a man who makes cards vanish in New York City is a long distance to travel under the heading of street magic. But throughout history, the magicians who entertain with arts of illusion have presented people with symbols of magic. The symbol is not a thing but an act—it is the process of something appearing, vanishing, or changing form. Magic is an ever-changing enigma which we are only permitted to glimpse occasionally. For ancient peoples it had something to do with the forces that made life begin and end. In medieval Europe it was connected with demonology and witchcraft; in the Orient, with reincarnation and Vedic philosophies; in the modern world, with psychic science and extraterrestrial life. To each generation there is the street magic of its time, and the best a magician can do is play on the symbols of that magic. A ball that vanishes, a spoon that bends, a card that appears in the hand—these are truly minor occurrences. They become impressive only when we think of the mystery they suggest.

But street magic is amusement and entertainment as well as mystery. The cosmic powers—if they are ever revealed—may turn out to have a profound sense of humor equal to that of the cups-and-balls conjurers and the wonder-workers at the fair. The joke, of course, is on us, human beings knocking around in an unknown universe and trying to comprehend everything with our five senses and limited intelligence.

Throughout history magicians have shown people just how inadequate these senses are. It is not a reassuring discovery, and people have been both awed and frightened when confronted with the unknown. At the same time magic has helped us sharpen another, more precious sense—the sense of wonder. It is often romanticized, rarely understood, but definitely worth having. For without a sense of wonder, there would be no magic.

In searching for the history of street magic, we have tried to recover, wherever possible, that sense of wonder, to discover its meaning. Yet it continues to be elusive. Perhaps that sense is best known to children and becomes weakened as we grow older. Perhaps, too, it begins to fade as civilization acquires age. We would hope not. For magic and wonder are not things for primitive cultures and unsophisticated intellects. Nor are they qualities which can be cheapened by advertising slogans and hardsell commercials. True, we now have "magic" formula cleansers and the "wonders" of modern technology. But there are greater wonders which remain pure, concealed in nature, and ready to surprise us. Street magic reminds people of those wonders, but at best the feats of an entertainer can only be a suggestion of magic. The real magic, the underlying mystery, will always elude us.

Selected Annotated Bibliography

The puzzle of street magic had to be pieced together from many sources, some only tangential to the subject itself. The following list is by no means complete, but includes some of the books and articles which amused and entertained as well as informed the search for living magic.

Ady, Thomas. *A Candle in the Dark: or, A Treatise Concerning the Nature of Witches and Witchcraft.* London, 1656.
  "Hocus Pocus," the King's own Conjurer, is first mentioned here, and Ady tells how to draw wine from the forehead, work with a confederate, and manipulate coins and cards.

Baldwin, Samri S. *Secrets of Mahatma Land Explained.* Brooklyn: T.J. Dyson, 1895.
  For showbiz Baldwin adopted the style of a "White Mahatma," and this book explores the land that gave a mystique to his career. Includes "fakir" tricks, mesmerism, spiritualism, and related entertainments.

Black, Ishii. "Japanese Magic." *"The Magician" Monthly*, Volumes X-XI, September 1914-May 1915.
  Authoritative descriptions of Japanese conjuring by a magician who adopted many traditional tricks for his own use.

Burlingame, H.J. *Herrmann the Magician: His Life, His Secrets.* Chicago: Laird and Lee, 1897.
  An appreciative biography of Alexander Herrmann and his street magic, with a fine attempt to define the allure of the magician and his art.

Christopher, Milbourne. *Panorama of Magic.* New York: Dover, 1962.
  Christopher's private collection makes beautiful scenery for this paperback summary of stage magic.

————. *The Illustrated History of Magic.* New York: Thomas Y. Crowell, 1973.
  Probably the most comprehensive history of stage magic yet published; thoroughly researched, with more illustrations than *Panorama*.

————. *Houdini: The Untold Story.* New York: Thomas Y. Crowell, 1969.
  A complete factual account of Houdini's life.

Clarke, Sidney W. *The Annals of Conjuring.* Published serially in *The Magic Wand* magazine, 1924-1928. Also published, London: George Johnson, 1929.
  A scholarly and comprehensive review of the history of magic through the early 1900s with

astute evaluations of individual performers and developments in magic.

Coryat, Thomas. *Coryat's Crudities.* New York: Macmillan, 1905. Reprinted from the original published in Glasgow: James MacLehose, 1611.
A curiously self-mocking travelogue, with sympathetic descriptions of sights in many cities, including mountebanks in Venice.

Dare, Paul. *Magie Blanche et Magie Noire aux Indes.* Paris: Payot, 1947.
A personal account of the tricks seen by Dare in India, with some well-considered lore about snakes, black and white magic, and the possibilities of hypnotism.

Evans, Henry Ridgely. *The Old and the New Magic.* Chicago: The Open Court, 1906.
Evans was overly preoccupied with people like Cagliostro, the charlatan, and Trewey, the inventor of shadowgraphy, but this casual history includes many anecdotes and stage techniques. An introduction by Paul Carus traces the "old" magic to the "new."

Fischer, Ottokar. *Illustrated Magic.* Translated and edited by J.B. Mussey and Fulton Oursler. New York: Macmillan, 1955.
Fulton Oursler includes sensitive portraits of magicians of his own time, and Fischer reviews techniques and devices used in sleight of hand, mind-reading, ghost-production, and "fakir" tricks and illusions. Unfortunately much amended in translation from the German.

Frazer, Sir James George. *The Golden Bough, A Study in Magic and Religion,* abridged edition. New York: Macmillan, 1974.
Frazer's *magnum opus* catalogues rites, myths, and superstitions, and in so doing provides a key to the symbols used by priest and conjurer alike.

Frost, Thomas. *The Lives of the Conjurers.* London: Tinsley Brothers, 1874. Reprinted Detroit: Singing Tree Press, 1970.
A scholarly view of the history of conjuring, drawing on ancient sources, personal observations, and interviews with showmen and travelers.

Gibson, Walter B. and Morris N. Young. *Houdini on Magic.* New York: Dover, 1953.
A potpourri of writings by Houdini, including escape secrets, spiritualist tricks, and notes on historical figures in magic. Gibson and Young are biographers, and chapters have informative introductions.

Gibson, Walter B. *Secrets of Magic: Ancient and Modern.* New York: Grosset and Dunlap, 1967.
What looks like a children's book turns out to be a very complete presentation of great magic illusions, told in the style that made "The Shadow" famous.

Hopkins, Albert A. *Magic, Stage Illusions and Scientific Diversions, Including Trick Photography,* with an introduction by Henry Ridgely Evans. New York: Munn, 1898.
A how-to book on the mechanics of creating illusions, including levitations, suspensions, and vanishing acts. Turn-of-the-century schoolboys probably snapped this one up, but it has lasting value for stage engineers.

Huggins, Wilfred and Fred Culpitt. *Secrets of the Street Conjurer.* London: G. Johnson, 1943.
A slim volume with few secrets, though it does include Tom Reid of the Pimlico Market Place, whom we wish we had met, and Solly Marks, who had a lunch-hour pitch on Fetter Lane.

Hughes, Pennethorne. *Witchcraft.* London: Penguin, 1973.
A slapdash, entertaining review of witchcraft, noting sleight of hand where used by witches, wizards, and priests in the past.

Keel, John A. *Jadoo.* New York: Julian Messner, 1957.
The American journalist called himself "a professional cliffhanger" and did everything from trying out burial alive to spotting the Abominable Snowman (from a distance).

Kellar, Harry. *A Magician's Tour Up and Down and Round About the Earth: Being the Life and Adventures of the American Nostradamus, Harry Kellar,* edited by his faithful "familiar," "Satan Junior." Chicago: R.R. Donnelley, 1886.
Kellar was born in Erie, Pennsylvania, and became one of America's outstanding stage magicians. Includes anecdotes of India, Africa, and other lands where he astonished the people—and they him.

———. "High Caste Indian Magic." *The North American Review,* Volume CLVI, Number 3. New York, 1893.

Kellar never did discover the secret of the levitation he witnessed, but many of the lesser "fakir" mysteries are exposed.

Kellock, Harold. *Houdini: His Life Story; from the Recollections and Documents of Beatrice Houdini.* New York: Harcourt, Brace, 1928.
Written shortly after Houdini's death and includes the minutiae of a public figure. Bess's memories are full of warmth and wonder.

Kirby, E.T. "Popular Entertainments." *The Drama Review,* Volume XVIII, Number 1, March 1974.
Documents tribal origins of jugglery, fire-eating, miming, conjuring, and other entertainments.

Kreskin. *The Amazing World of Kreskin.* New York: Random House, 1973.
Self-promotion, of course, but Kreskin has given much thought to the psychology of illusion and suggestibility of audiences.

Lynn, Professor H.S. *The Adventures of the Strange Man.* London: published by the author, 1873. Reprinted, Leicester: 1878.
The strange man plays tricks around the world, interviews itinerant jugglers, and hoaxes the stern Mormon, Brigham Young.

MacKay, Charles. *Extraordinary Popular Delusions and the Madness of Crowds.* London: 1852. Reprinted Boston: L.C. Page, 1932.
An intriguing, skeptical review of mass delusions, including fear of the devil, belief in the philosopher's stone, and witch mania.

Maskelyne, Nevil and David Devant. *Our Magic,* second edition. Berkeley Heights, New Jersey: Fleming, 1946.
Probably the best analytic treatment of the craft of performing magic, with a generous interpretation of the psychological effects of conjuring.

McKechnie, Samuel. *Popular Entertainments through the Ages.* London: Sampson Low, Marston, undated.
Pieces together the itinerant lives of mimes, minstrels, and strolling players; fills in with literary references; and concludes with circus, sideshow, and slapstick routines. Richly illustrated.

Morley, Henry. *Memoirs of Bartholomew Fair,* with facsimile drawings engraved upon wood by the brothers Dalziel. London: Chapman & Hall, 1859.
The great fair is explored in detail from origin to delapidation, with superb woodcuts.

Robert-Houdin, Jean Eugène. *Memoirs of Robert-Houdin, Ambassador, Author, and Conjurer, written by Himself.* Translated by Lascelles Wraxall. London: Chapman & Hall, 1860. Reprinted with an introduction by Milbourne Christopher, New York: Dover, 1964.
First memoir by a stage magician, offering high adventure and sound perceptions on magic. The authenticity of some of the passages is in doubt.

Scot, Reginald. *The Discoverie of Witchcraft.* London: 1584. Reprinted New York: Dover, 1972.
For the first time in English, the methods behind dozens of tricks, exposed in the rich language of a sixteenth century scholar. Shakespeare may have gathered lore on ghosts, spells, and witchcraft from this abundant source.

Tarbell, Harlan. *The Tarbell Course in Magic.* New York: Louis Tannen, beginning 1944.
Can anyone follow the multi-volume "course" from beginning to end? Many lessons here for future street and stage magicians.

Yva, Yvon. *Les Fakirs et Leurs Secrets.* Paris: Gallimard (L'Air du Temps 178), 1963.
Gives both the Indian and European views of the fakirs and attempts to distinguish the real cult from the legends surrounding it.

Index

A

Aaron, 4
acetabularii, acetabulum, 7
acrobats and acrobatics:
    China, 34
    Elizabethan, 66
    Europe, 49, 64, 66, 74–75
    India, 17, 24
    Middle Ages, 47, 49, 60
    United States, 104, 131
Adventures of a Strange Man, The
    (1878), 28
Ady, Thomas, 65, 69–70
Agrippa, 64, 113, 119
agyrtae, 7
alchemists, xi, 47, 53–55
Alciphron of Athens, 7–8
animals, tricks with
    bees, xii, 37
    beetle, 48
    birds, 4, 7, 8, 11, 26, 36, 57, 64,
        82, 84, 90, 93, 99
    butterflies, 41–42
    cat, 82
    crocodile, 6
    dog, 32, 74–75
    fish, 9, 35, 36, 43–44
    frog, 9, 39
    "gargoyle," 38
    goat, 32
    guinea pig, 11
    horse, 37–38, 82
    lion, x, 7, 48
    mice, 9, 11
    monkey, 41, 74, 82
    ox, 7
    pig, 32, 73, 82, 89
    rabbit, 71, 96
    snakes, 3, 4, 26, 28, 33, 37, 51
    various, 2, 3, 9, 25, 36, 39, 82
Annals of Conjuring, The (1929), 60,
    70, 85
Apuleius, 7
aquafortis (nitric acid), tricks with,
    79
Arigó, 114
Arjun Singh, 23
Around the World with a Magician and a
    Juggler (1891), 19
"Art of Juggling Discovered, The,"
    55, 64
Art of Juggling or Legerdemain, The
    (1612), 65
Artha Sustra, 25
Assize, Rochester, England, 55
astrology, 3, 64, 115
Athenaeus, 7

Autobiography of Benvenuto Cellini, 52
automatic writing, 117

B

Baba, 115
Bacon, Roger, 54
Badrayana Vyas, 17
"bag of tricks," 60
baksheesh, 25, 28, 31
Baldwin, Samri ("The White
    Mahatma"), 29, 30–32
Baltimore News, 96
"Banks," 82
barn performers, 63
Bartholomew's Fair (St.
    Bartholomew's Fair), 67, 71, 74,
    76, 79, 82, 85
Basak-Nag, 27
baskets, tricks with, 16–17, 26, 28,
    30–32, 34, 36, 50, 69
Bateleur, Le (Le Bataleur), 65
Beebe, William, 17
beggars, 13, 36, 59–60, 131
Beni Hassan, 6
Bergen, Edgar, and Charlie
    McCarthy, 90
Berger, Keith, 131

Bey, Rahman ("Egyptian Miracle Man"), 16
bhaghats, 25
Black, Ishii, 36–37, 41
black magic, xi, 1, 25, 53
Black Mass, xi
Bombay Rawm Sammi, 31–32
Bosch, Hieronymus, 50
Bosco, Bartolomeo, 90–91, 99
brahmin, 20
Brandon the Juggler, 67
brimstone (sulfur), tricks with, 77–78, 93
"Brothers Houdini, The," 102
Buddhism, Buddhists, 40, 115
"budget," 60
bullet-catching trick, 95, 98
burial alive, 15–16, 21–23, 38
Burlingame, H.J., 19, 87–88, 99, 102, 139

C

Cagliostro, Count de (Balsamo), 93–94, 113, 119
calcularius, xi
Calcutta Medical Journal, 23
Candle in the Dark, or A Treatise Concerning the Nature of Witches and Witchcraft, A (1656), 65, 69, 70
cards, playing, 65
cards, tricks with, 48, 59, 63, 65–66, 71, 76, 82–83, 99, 103, 117, 124, 128–30, 132, 134–36, 140–41, 145
Carlosbach, Dr., xiii, 92
Carroll, Lewis, 114
Caunter, Reverend Hobart, 30–32
Cautares, John, 55
Cayce, Edgar, 114
Cellini, Benvenuto, 52–53
charlatans and charlatanry, ix–xi, 23, 46, 48–49, 53–55, 57, 74, 87, 92, 94, 105, 111, 113–14
Charles IX, King, 59
Chatterbox, The, 86
Chaucer, 48
Chinese Water Torture Cell, 106, 113
circulatores, 7

Clarke, Sidney, 60, 70, 85
clowns, 46, 77, 104
Coates, Mrs. Jane B., 111
cobra, 26–29
codpiece, 60
coins, tricks with: 7, 65–67, 73, 82, 86, 96–97, 99, 135
Commedia dell'Arte (Comedy of Masks), 51, 61, 120
Comte, M. Louis Christian Emanuel Appollinaire, 88–90, 99
Coney Island, 103
confederacy in tricks, 57, 66, 67, 70
contortionists, 47, 49, 61, 72, 103
Convinsamy, xiii, 19, 20
Coryat, Thomas, 49, 66
Coryat's Crudities (1611), 49
"counter," 66, 67
Cratisthenes of Philias, 7
Cree Indians, 3
"crosse," 67
Crosset, Francis de, 17
Cuckoe, William, 60
"cunning men," 53
cups-and-balls, tricks with, xiii, 6–11,˙38, 48–50, 61, 63, 65, 71, 77, 83, 87, 90–92, 145

D

Dare, Paul, 32
"Dark Ages," 51
Davenport Brothers, 18
"David," 88
Dean, Henry, 65
decapitation tricks, 2, 6–7, 37, 67–69, 73, 138–39
"Decollation of John the Baptist, The," 67, 69, 77
Dedi of Dedsnefru, 7
Dee, John, 113
demonology, 115, 145
Dervishes, 13, 14
demons, 52, 89, 95, 105, 115–16
devil, 1, 47, 52–53, 65, 82, 96
dime museums, 102–3, 116
Diopeithes of Locris, 7
Discoverie of Witchcraft, The (1584), 55, 57, 59, 64–69
Dixon, Jeane, 113
djorghis, 25

dolls, tricks with, 3, 10, 44, 84
Doyle, Lady, 111
Doyle, Sir Arthur Conan, 111, 114
drum, magic, 25, 40
Drury Lane Theatre (London), 36
Duke University, 115
dumbis, 13

E

East India Company of the United Netherlands, Report of the, 34
East Indian needle trick, 103
egg tricks, 11, 31–32, 36, 45, 56, 65, 73, 76–77, 79, 83–84, 86, 96–98
Egyptian Hall (London), 17, 27
equilibrist, 61
escamoteurs, xiii, 52, 62, 87, 125–26
escape tricks, 2, 36, 99–110
Euclides, 7
Eunus (Eunios), 5
Evans, Henry Ridgely, 95
Evelyn, John, 77–78
"evil eye," 67
Exodus, 4
extra-sensory perception (ESP), xi, 115

F

fairs, 57, 71–85, 116, 145
fakirs, ix, xi, 13 (def.), 14–23, 31–32, 103, 116
"Fakir of Ava, The" (Harris Hughes), 18
Falacie of the Great Water-Drinker Discovered, The, 82
"Fameux Paysan de Nort Hollande, Le," 84
"familiar," 50, 54, 66, 69, 71
Faustus, Johann, 113
Faux (Fawkes), Isaac, xiii. 76, 82, 84
"Fawkes" (pseud.), 82
"feast of lanterns" trick, 43
fencers, 59
fire-eaters, xi, 74–75, 77–79, 85, 103
fire, tricks with, 2, 5, 13, 36, 38–39, 43, 56, 74–75, 77–79, 83, 85, 102–103

flageolot, 16
Flockton, 76
flowers, tricks with, 25–26, 37, 39, 42, 48, 73, 84, 102
flying saucers (unidentified flying objects), 117
food, tricks with
  beef, 7
  bread, 6–7, 26, 99
  cake, 26
  cheese, 99
  fish, 6, 41
  milk, 4, 7, 35
  nutmeg, 92
  nuts, 65
  omelet, 76
  oyster, 78
  pancake, 76
  pudding, 76
  steak, 78
  turnip, 96
  various, 25
Ford's Opera House, 97
Fortunatus, 69
fortune-tellers and fortune-telling, xi, 7, 53, 60, 66, 71, 87, 113, 118
"Franklin's Tale, The," 48
Frazer, Sir James George, 2
Fritz, Dr., 114
Frost, Thomas, 30
fruit, tricks with
  almond, 25–26
  apples, 25, 37, 40
  cherries, 9
  fig, 25–26
  grapes, 48
  mango, 25–26, 84
  mulberry, 25
  tamarind, 26
  various, 35, 84
Future American Magical Entertainers (FAME), 126

G

gali-gali men, 4
gamblers, 66
Geller, Uri, 117–19
giocatore di busolotti, xiii

Giradelli, Madam Josephine ("The Fireproof Lady"), 79
Gnosticism, 115
gods, in magic, 1–5, 23, 53, 57, 116
gold, tricks with, 26, 53, 97
Golden Bough, The, 2
Gorki, Maxim, 17
gosains, 13
Govindaswamy, 23
"Grand Theatre of the Muses, The," 84
Grant, Ulysses S., 99
"Great Nicola, The," 15
Greenwich Fair, 74
"groat," 66
guillotine trick, 69
guru, 16–17, 19, 23, 25, 29
Guyot, 9
"Gyngells, The," 76
gypsies, 9–11, 61, 65–66, 71, 113–14

H

handkerchiefs, tricks with, 54, 93, 97, 102
Hansen, Steve, 132
Herod, King, 67
Heron, 5
Herrmann, Adelaide, 95
Herrmann, Alexander ("Herrmann the Great"), 95–99
Herrmann, Carl, 95
Herrmann the Great; the Famous Magician's Wonderful Tricks (1897), 87–88
Herrmann, Samuel, 95
Hill, Dr., 110–11
Hinduism, Hindus, xi, 8, 12–33, 37, 64, 97, 115
"Hocus Pocus," xiii, 40, 66, 69–70, 87
Hocus Pocus Junior, or The Anatomie of Legerdemain (1635), 35, 70, 71
Hogarth, William, 74–75
Hokusai, Katsushika, xii, 37–38
Hollar, 81
Holmes, Sherlock, 111
Hopkins, Albert, 68
Houdini, Harry, ix, xiii, 15–16, 23, 91, 99–111, 123
  childhood and family, 102

Chinese Water Torture Cell, 106
death, 112–13
dime museums, 102–3
East Indian needle trick, 103
football escape, 108
handcuff escapes, 106–8
jailbreaks, 106–8
marriage, 103
side show, 104, 110
spiritualism, 110–11, 114
straitjacket escape, 100–6
"The Metamorphosis," 102
Houdini, Wilhelmina Beatrice Rahner (Bess), 103–4, 111
Humphrey, Hubert, 113
Huxley, Aldous, 114
hypnotism, 19, 26, 33, 117

I

Ibn Batuta ("The Traveler"), 17
Iliad, 7
illusionistes, xiii, 88
imps, 2, 54, 56, 66, 69
Inari (fox-god), 40, 42

J

Jacob's rod, 5
"Jacobs" (ventriloquist), 36
jadoo-wallahs, 13, 25–26, 29, 31
Jahangir, Emperor, 25
Jairus, 59
Jajamanekh, 6
James I, King, 57, 70
James, William, 114
jerkin, 60
jesters, 47, 60
Jesus, 5, 59
jewels, tricks with, 6, 26, 32
joglars, 48
John the Baptist, 67
Johnson, Lyndon, 113
Jonas, 84
jongleurs, x, 48
Jonson, Ben, 70
Juggler Street, 48
Juggler, The, 50
jugglers and juggling, ix, 14
  ancient, 6–7

Australia, 120
China, 36
England, xiii, 61
France, 120–21
India, 14, 24–33
Italy, 46
Japan, 38, 41–42
Middle Ages, x, 47–57
United States, 112, 130, 132

K

Keel, John, 17, 23, 29
Kellar, Harry, 18, 28–29
Kennedy, Robert, 113
Khufu (Cheops), 6, 7
Kitsuni-tsukai, 40
knives, tricks with, 2, 13, 16–17, 36, 51, 56–57, 65–66, 69, 79–80, 99, 103, 114, 118, 138–39
kooken'nin, 40, 43
Kreskin, 18, 117–18
Kublai Khan, 35
kybisteter, 7

L

"Lane," 84
Lazarus, 5
lead, tricks with, 78–79
"leaping egg trick," 31
"Learned Goose, The," 82
"Learned Pig, The," 82
Ledru, Nicolas Philippe ("Comus"), 85
LeRoy, Servais, 15
levitation tricks, 15, 18–20, 33
Lewis, Angelo, 9
Lives of the Conjurers, The (1876), 30
London Labour and the London Poor, iv
"long head" trick, 38
Louis IX, King, 48
Louis Philippe of Orléans, King, 91, 93–94
Lucilius, 7
Ludovicus Vives, 7
Lynn, Professor H.S., 28–29, 36, 40

M

McKinnon, Cecil, of the Pickle

Family, 132
Maeterlinck, Maurice, 17
mag, maghdim, 3
Magi, 3–6
magic (def.), xi, 3
"Magic Barrel" trick, 71
magic lantern, 53
magic makers, 1
"Magic Show, The," 116
Magic; Stage Illusions and Scientific Diversions (1898), 68
"Magician" Monthly, "The," 37
magicians (costumes and dress), x–xi, xiii, 6, 16, 49, 52–53, 60–62, 70, 73, 79, 90, 96
Maharaj Ji, 115
Manfre (Manfrède), Blaise, 80–81
Manga, xii, 37–39
mango tree trick, 26, 29–30
Ma'nido, 3
Marchand, Floram (Florian), 80–82
Marco Polo, 13, 35
Marquis of Acapules, 99
Maskelyne, John Nevil, 17
Matthew, Gospel of, 5
May Fair, 74
maya, 14
Mayhew, Henry, iv
mechanical magic, 4, 71, 76, 84–85
medicine and healing arts, 1–2, 49–51, 74, 85, 92, 114
medicine men, xvi, 1–3
mediums, spiritualist, 90, 99, 111, 114–15
Memoirs of Bartholomew Fair (1859), 79
Menominee Indians, 2–3
mentalism, 118
mesmerism, 19, 116
Metamorphosis (Golden Ass), 7
mime, ix, 47, 51, 120, 125, 129, 131
minstrels, 48, 59, 131
miracles, xi, 4–6, 14–15, 35, 53
miracle workers, 3, 95–96
misdirection, 70
Modern Magic, 9
Mogul, 14
Moors, 65
Morley, Henry, 79
Morning Post, 17
"Morocco," 82
Moses, 4

mountebanks, x, 46, 48–49, 51, 53–54, 74, 78, 92
mugh, 3
Mulholland, John, 8–9, 61
mummies, 6, 92
muscades, 8, 11
Muslims, 13
mystics, 111, 113–15
"Mystifying Bag, The," 93

N

naja haje, 4
naja naja, 26
Napoleon, 91
natural magic, 57, 70
necromancers, 51–53, 60
needles, tricks with, 7, 12, 36
New Testament, 5, 67
Niska Indians, 3
Nostradamus, 64, 113, 119

O

occult magic, xi, 3, 6, 60, 64, 110–11, 113, 115, 117, 119, 140
Odoric, Friar, 35
Ojibway Indians, 2
"Okos Bokos," 70
Old Testament, 4
Orbis Sensualium Pietus (1657), 49
Ozanam, 9

P

Panurge, 9
paper tricks, 26, 37, 39, 41–45
Paracelsus, 64, 113
parapsychologists, 115
Parliament, Acts of, 59, 71
"passes," 141
patter, xi, 19, 28–29, 32–33, 41–43, 51–53, 64, 66–67, 70–71, 92–95, 97–99
Pearson, Sir Ralph, 17
pebble swallowers, 79
Petit, Philippe, 112, 119–23, 132
Pharaoh, 4

"Phillippe," 36
Philosopher's Stone, 53
pichodi, 28
pickpocket tricks, 50, 91, 96–97, 120
Pied Piper, 63, 128
"pile," 67
Pinchbeck, Christopher, 76, 84
plate tricks, 56, 64
players, common, 59
Pneumatics, 5
pocket apron *(gibecière),* xiii, 59–61
Poe, Edgar Allen, 114
Pope Innocent, 48
"Powell," 78
Prayanayoga, 25
prestidigitateurs, x, xiii
"prestigiator," 70
priests and priestesses, 1–2, 4, 6, 35–36, 39, 47, 52–53, 60
prophets, xi
psephoi, psephopaiktai, xiii, 7
psychic magic, ix, xi, 18, 87, 91, 99, 111, 115–19, 140–41, 145
psychokinesis, 118–19
Puharich, Andrija, 118
puzzle tricks, 24
pyramids, 6
Pythagoras, 4

R

Rabelais, 9
Rahamin, Fyzee, 23
Ramaswamy, 23
Ramo Samee, 33
reincarnation, 145
Rhine, J.B., 115
ribbon tricks, 26, 44, 63
rice tricks, 35–38
"Richardson," 77–78
Richelieu, Cardinal de, 80
rings, tricks with, 24, 35, 59, 99
Robert-Houdin, Émile, 23, 94
Robert-Houdin, Jean Eugène, 15, 21, 91–95, 99, 102
"rogues," 59–60
Roman Catholic Church, xi, 47, 53, 64, 70, 82
Rooke, Major G.H., 17
rope trick, Indian, 15–18
rope tricks, 35, 48, 103, 132–33

Royer, Jean, 80
"Rue des Jongleurs," 47
"Rue de St. Julian des Ménétriers," 47

S

"Sabre Swallower," 79
sadhus, 13
St. Bernard, 48
St. Callisto Chapel, 5, 6
St. Denis (Fair), 74
St. Germain (Fair), 74
St. Giles (Fair), 74
"Saint Jacques and the Magician Hermogenes," 56
St. James (Fair), 74
St. Martin's Hall, London, 42
salamandering tricks, 77
samp-wallah, 28–29
samurai, 37
sand, tricks with, 26, 33
sarcophagus, 5–6
Satan, 59
sawing a woman in half, 69
Scientific American, 111
Scot, Reginald, 55–56, 59, 64–68
séances, xi, 90, 110–11, 114–15
"second sight," 94
Secrets of Mahatma Land Explained, The, 30
Secrets of a Prestidigitator, The, 91
Seeman, Baron Hartwig, 19–20
Seneca the Younger, 7
"servante," 60
shamans, ix, xvi, 1–3
shell game, 9–10
Sheridan, Jeff, ix, 124–44
Sheshal ("Brahmin of the Air"), xiii, 20
Shessha-Nag, 27
shills, 77
Shinto, 37, 40
Shogun, Fourth, 36
"Sign of the Astronomico-Musical Clock, The," 84
spoon tricks, 118, 145
Simon Magus, 35
Simons, Margaret, 55
slate-writing, xi, 118
"sleeve magic," xii, 37

slack-rope performers, 73
"smoke face" trick, 37–38
snake charmers, 26, 28
snake-handling, 28
snake-kissing, 27
snake-worship, 115
Snefru, 6
soma, 29
soothsayers, 2, 71, 113
Soirées Fantastiques, 91
sorcerers and sorcery, ix, xi, 25, 47, 51–52
Southwark Fair, 74–76
"Spectra," 118–19
spirit-rapping, xi, 90, 111
spirits, 1–3, 25, 40, 47, 52, 111
spiritualism and spiritualists, xi, 111–14, 118–19
"spirit voices," 88, 111
stage magic and magicians, x, 59, 61–63, 85–99, 115, 117, 126
Staple of News, The, 70
Steeves, Dr., 103
Stirling, Edward, 76
Stodare, Colonel, 27
stones, tricks with, xiii, 2, 7, 32
Stourbridge Fair, 74
street magic (def.), ix
street theater, 130–31
suggestion, 117
surrealism, surrealists, 138
suspension tricks, 14, 20–21
swords, tricks with, 14, 17–18, 30, 36, 40, 48, 56, 66, 103
sword swallowing, 2, 7, 24, 37–38, 77, 79–80, 85, 103

T

table-tiltings, 118
Talma, 15
tarocchinini, 65
tarot, 65
Taschenspieler, xi
Tchatcha-em-ankh, 6
telepathy, 117–18
"testor," 66
thaumatopios, 7
thaumaturgists, 5
theater arts, ix–xi, 63, 106
Theatre of Bacchus, 7

Theatre of Istaians, 7
Theodorus, 7
thimble-rigging, 9–10
thread, tricks with, 31–34, 43
Thurston, Howard, 15, 30
tightrope walkers, 17, 49, 112–13, 120–23
tinkers, 61
top-spinning, 41–42
trasgeters, 48
tregetours, 48, 85, 87, 125
troubadours, 48, 57, 61
Tuck Quy, 36
tumblers, 7, 48

U

Uhon Miyako, 36

V

Vadramakrishna, Sadhu, 17
vagabonds, 59
"vanish," 60

vanishing tricks, xii, 60, 141
vases, tricks with, xii, 32, 37
Vaucanson, M. Jacques de, 84
vaudeville, 103, 116, 128
Vedanta Sutra, 17
Vedic philosophies, 13, 145
ventriloquism, 54, 88–90, 111, 114
Vermifuge Balsam, 92
Voodooism, 115

W

Wales, Prince of, 18
wand, 2–3, 6, 33, 65, 90, 102
"War of the Worlds, The," 116
watches, tricks with, 96–7, 119
water, tricks with, 5–7, 19, 25–26, 35, 37, 42–45, 71, 80–82, 99
Weiss (Weisz), Cecilia, Ehrich, Samuel, Theo, 102
Wells, Orson, 116
Westcar Papyrus, 6
white magic, 1, 53
Whole Art of Hocus Pocus: Containing the Most Dexterous Feats of Slight of Hand, The (1812), 72

Whole Art of Legerdemain or Hocus Pocus in Perfection, The (1722), 65
Wilson, Edmund, 102
wine, tricks with, 5, 7, 35, 69, 80, 99
witch doctors, 1
witchcraft and witches, ix, xi, 25, 47, 52, 54–57, 67, 70, 99, 115, 145
Witts Recreation, The (1640), 70
wizards, ix, xi, xvi, 2, 6, 47, 51, 53

X

Xenophon, 7

Y

"Yeates, the Younger," 76
Yeats, William Butler, 114
yoga and yogis, 13, 115

Z

Zodiac, 6

About the Authors

Edward Claflin was born in 1949 and did not see a real live street magician until 1972 when he came to live in New York. Prestidigitators simply didn't come to Stamford, Darien or New Britain, Conn.—or, for that matter, to Cleveland, Ohio—places where the author grew up. Futhermore, he lived *without television* for the first fifteen years of his life and missed seeing the televised magicians pulling rabbits out of their hats. (He also missed seeing 'I love Lucy', 'Gunsmoke', and 'Art Linkletter'.) He had an uncle who performed card tricks occasionally during summer vacations at Cape Cod, on foggy days when everyone was indoors and irritable. It saved the day.

The author had an American high school experience, went to Amherst College and came to New York. One sunny day he was walking through Central Park. He saw a magician beside the Walter Scott statue. He watched three consecutive shows, didn't give any money (he was poor), and realized magic was in the cards. That magician was Jeff Sheridan, and from that encounter came the beginnings of *Street Magic*.

Edward Claflin is also the author of *Ruffian*.

Jeff Sheridan started performing magic when he was ten years old. He joined a club called F.A.M.E., Future American Magical Entertainers, which held weekly meetings in an empty gym in Manhattan, and he did late night gigs at the Seahunt Supper Club in the Bronx. Later Jeff went to work for Al Flosso (formerly known as the 'Coney Island Fakir') at the Hornemann Magic Company on 34th Street. There he was introduced to many of the greats of the conjuring world, learned the secrets of their trade, and started his own collection of books and prints on the history of magic. At eighteen Jeff became a street magician, performing in Central Park, on Fifth Avenue, and at many other locations throughout the City. His unique conjuring acts and card magic have been admired by thousands of New Yorkers and by visitors from all over the world, and he has appeared on local and national TV. Jeff has given indoor performances at Carnegie Recital Hall, the Cubiculo Theatre, the Kitchen, the Library of the Performing Arts at Lincoln Center, and at Reno Sweeney's. In 1975 he received the Street Enhancers Award from the Municipal Arts Society of New York.